Combined
1980-82 Boards
June 1, 1981

Pictured at Same Site,
Peter White Camp
Near Deerton

Rear: Luff, Duerfeldt, Kingsbury, Treloar, Higley, Fairbanks, F. Allen, Fassbender, L. B. Frazier, Ahmad, Weting, Gramenz, Locke, Glenn, W. A. Mudge, Jr. (kneeling), Maitland.
Front: H. E. Wright, Parolini, Vajda, Payan, Beck, A. L. Niemi, Hetrick.

REACHING OUT

FOUNDER

Frank J. Jennison

Ernest L. Pearce

George Shiras, 3rd

IMPRESSARIOS

DISTRICT GOVERNORS

James H. B. Kaye
1920-21

Harlow A. Clark
1926-27

Earl H. Closser
1973-74

REACHING OUT

A History of the Rotary Club of Marquette, Michigan 1916-1981

by
Richard F. O'Dell

Foreword by Stanley E. McCaffrey
President of Rotary International
1981-1982

Partial Editing and Rephotography
by Pryse H. Duerfeldt

The Rotary Club of Marquette
Marquette, Michigan

International Standard Book Number: 0-9609764-0-X

Library of Congress Catalog Card Number 82-60037

Printed in the United States of America

Copies available at

Marquette County Historical Society
213 N. Front St.
and
Marquette Area Chamber of Commerce
501 S. Front St.
Marquette, Michigan 49855

CONTENTS

ROTARY INTERNATIONAL

Service Above Self – He Profits Most Who Serves Best

1600 RIDGE AVENUE · EVANSTON, ILLINOIS 60201, U.S.A.

Tel: 312/328-0100 • Cable: Interotary • Telex: 724-465

STANLEY E. McCAFFREY

PRESIDENT, 1981-82

FOREWORD

Reaching Out is a very readable as well as scholarly history of the Rotary Club of Marquette, Michigan. It is an extraordinarily detailed portrait of the sixty-five year involvement of a Rotary club, its members and their community. And, as indicated in the title for his history, Rotarian author O'Dell works the fascinating detail into a broad design. His perspective takes the reader beyond the city limits of this Northern Michigan community by recording how its Rotarians and their fellow townsmen played their part in their reaction to national and world events.

In his preface, O'Dell speculates that thousands of Rotary clubs have shared the Marquette experience. Remarkable as his book stands as the history of one club, it has greater value in that it probably does reflect the development of thousands of clubs in the country where Rotary was born. It certainly reflects the Rotary ideal of Service above Self.

Stanley E. McCaffrey
President
Rotary International

18 January, 1982

PREFACE

This book began when Robert J. Pearce, then president of the Rotary Club of Marquette, invited me to summarize its history at its fiftieth anniversary dinner in January of 1966. Through the intervening years my mind has turned outward, from the internal affairs of the club to its role and that of its members in the life of the city and, beyond that, to the larger significance of Rotary International.

I have been intrigued particularly by the vision of Paul Harris, from first to last a model Rotarian, in conceiving a world community in which all people might live in neighborly contentment much like those, as he remembered them, in Wallingford, Vermont, where he spent his formative years. However blurred by sentiment his recollections may have been, the wonder is that Harris was able to inspire so many men—and women—to share his distinctively American dream, not just in Rotary but throughout the many service organizations patterned after it.

I have considered, too, that just as Marquette and the local Rotary club have had their George Shiras, 3rd, Maxwell K. Reynolds, and other men—together with an abundance of women—of the mold of Paul and Jean Harris, there must have been, and still must be, many thousands of relatively obscure Rotarians, Rotary Anns, and people not directly influenced by Rotary who, one way or another, have been motivated by its ideals of fellowship and service. Perhaps, with variations only in detail, thousands of Rotary clubs have shared the Marquette experience.

As political leaders the world over appear to be herding the masses of anxious, indeed despairing, mankind toward Armageddon in our time, there are unlimited opportunities for men and women who strive to maintain faith and composure, compassion, and humility in the face of truth, and who, in the words of the prayer—"mindful of the needs of others"—work unobtrusively for a world a little better than it might have been had they not lived in it.

1
INTRODUCTION

The year 1980 marked the seventy-fifth anniversary of Rotary International; 1981, the sixty-fifth of the Rotary Club of Marquette, Michigan. From a barely perceptible cell implanted in the heartland of the United States, Rotary has grown into a societal network extending throughout most of the non-Communist world. By December, 1981, there were upwards of 19,424 clubs and 897,750 Rotarians in 156 countries and regions.

The ideals and objectives of Rotary have evolved over the years through substantive and stylistic changes into concepts still capable of brief official statement:

THE OBJECT OF ROTARY

To encourage and foster the ideal of service as a basis of worthy enterprise and, in particular, to encourage and foster:

First. The development of acquaintance as an opportunity for service;

Second. High ethical standards in business and professions; the recognition of the worthiness of all useful occupations; and the dignifying by each Rotarian of his occupation as an opportunity to serve society;

Third. The application of the ideal of service by every Rotarian to his personal, business, and community life;

Fourth. The advancement of international understanding, goodwill and peace through a world fellowship of business and professional men united in the ideal of service.

MOTTOES

Service Above Self—He Profits Most Who Serves Best

THE FOUR-WAY TEST

1. Is it the TRUTH?
2. Is it FAIR to all concerned?
3. Will it build GOODWILL and BETTER FRIENDSHIPS?
4. Will it be BENEFICIAL to all concerned?

The Rotary Wheel is instantly recognized by everyone with the slightest familiarity with Rotary International. From numerous designs traceable to Montague M. Bear's 1905 wagon wheel, Oscar B. Bjorge, a Duluth, Minnesota, engineer, fashioned the one which in 1919 became and, with the keyway added later, remains the official Rotary emblem. Bjorge in the thirties and forties frequently visited relatives in Marquette, where his grandnephew, Burt E. Parolini, Jr., long has been affiliated with the local club and has been its 1980-81 president.

When the Rotary Club of Marquette received Charter No. 204 in March, 1916, it entered into fellowship with about twenty-three thousand men in 185 like organizations in the United States, ten in Canada, and eight in Great Britain and Ireland. All but seventy-five of these had come into existence during the three years previous. No more than ten had been formed in cities or towns smaller than Marquette. The later growth of Rotary International is evident in the passage of the Marquette club from District 9 (1916-18) through Districts 15 (1918-22), 10 (1922-37), 143 (1937-49), and 208 (1949-57) to District 622 (1957-—).

1977-1979

1916-1975

1979-—

2
BIRTH IN CONFLICT

During the winter of 1915-16 Europe began to realize the full extent of her involvement in the Great War. The British met disaster in the Dardanelles. Germany classified armed merchantmen as warships subject to attack without warning and launched an awesome assault upon Verdun. David Lloyd George, then British minister of munitions, cheerfully predicted that, thanks to the conflict, "This country . . . so far from being impoverished, will be richer in everything that constitutes real and true wealth," but few shared his optimism. For 1915 alone the *New York Times* placed war costs at five million lives and $56.3 billion.[1]

Although separated from Europe by the broad expanse of the Atlantic Ocean, the United States felt itself inexorably drawn toward the hostilities. Horror at the torpedoing of the *Lusitania* was kept vivid by news of later sinkings and further losses of American lives and property. Col. Edward M. House toured Europe, and Henry Ford sent *Oscar II* on ill-fated peace missions. Congress rejected the Gore-McLemore Resolutions to discourage American travel on armed ships of belligerents. On October 9, 1915, James J. O'Neill became the first Marquette war victim when he was killed in Belgium while serving with the Canadian forces.

Meanwhile, the United States was enjoying almost unprecedented material prosperity, much of it due to the war. In 1915 the average automobile sold for $811, and one prediction held that during the next year one American family in eight would own a car.[2] Air travel was still too primitive to permit sending an expedition to verify the fact, but scientists displayed a lively concern about whether intelligent beings had constructed the mysterious "canals" on Mars.

Reflecting popular demand for more equitable distribution of the nation's wealth, the revolutionary Sixteenth (Income Tax) Amendment had been appended to the Constitution early in 1913. Congress immediately had attached a modestly progressive personal income tax provision to the Underwood Tariff enacted in the same year. As that body was pondering further increases, the Supreme Court on January 24, 1916, upheld the constitutionality of a graduated tax.[3] The next day—by coincidence, certainly not in joyous celebration—a delegation of Wisconsin and Minnesota Rotarians came to town to help establish the Rotary Club of Marquette, Michigan.

An Outpost of Rotary

Marquette in 1916 was a small but enterprising city of twelve thousand inhabitants centrally located on the south shore of Lake Superior in the Upper Peninsula of

Michigan. While here to press a libel suit three years before, former President Theodore Roosevelt had described Marquette as "a most out-of-the-way place."[4] Yet it was the "Queen City" of the peninsula—its unofficial capital. It was the principal port and focus for trade in an area rich in timber and iron ore, and it had a foundry and small machine shops which produced tools and equipment for mining and other industrial concerns. Then, as now, it accommodated a branch of the state prison and a small normal school which has evolved into Northern Michigan University.

For years sportsmen from the East and Midwest, fishing the lakes and streams and stalking game in the rugged, heavily forested interior, customarily had spent weeks, indeed months, each year in and around Marquette. Some maintained permanent homes in town along with camps in the wilderness. The natural beauty of the Upper Peninsula, including the harbor and hills of Marquette, made a deep impression upon sojourners especially. Already, sensitive and reflective men of cosmopolitan background were recognizing the need for long-range programs to conserve the timber and game resources of the region.

The principal facts surrounding formation of the Rotary Club of Marquette have been well established. While on a business trip to Ohio in July, 1915, Frank J. Jennison, cashier of the Marquette (Union) National Bank, was invited by William Cook Rogers, president of the Piqua Handle Company (soon to locate a plant in Marquette), to attend a meeting of the Rotary Club of Piqua. Inspired by this experience and by later word that his cousin, William F. Jennison, had been elected president of the Rotary Club of Bay City, Michigan, Frank Jennison resolved to bring Rotary to Marquette.[5]

To this end he corresponded with C. F. Laughlin of Cleveland, Ohio, who was governor of District 7, and with Rotary headquarters in Chicago. The response was friendly. On November 9 the international president of Rotary, Allen D. Albert of Minneapolis, appointed a local organization committee composed of Jennison, Dr. Thomas M. Cunningham, Joseph C. Gannon, George J. Webster, and Alton T. Roberts.

In his letter of appointment President Albert cautioned the Marquette group to select prospective members carefully, to make sure that they were associated with reputable businesses, that they were capable of close friendships, and that they could "express the larger spiritual element" which had accounted for the rise of Rotary. If members were chosen wisely, he noted, attendance at meetings never would be a problem.[6] Keeping in mind Albert's point that quality was more important than numbers, the committee at a meeting on November 24 agreed upon a list of eighteen leading Marquette business and professional men to be enrolled as charter members.

As every Rotarian knows, Rotary had originated in Chicago, where in 1905 a young attorney, Paul P. Harris, had called together a mining engineer, a tailor, and a coal dealer to form the first club. Diverse occupations, Harris reasoned, would be to the mutual business advantage of the members and would provide breadth of view and talent along with a minimum of personal rivalry and friction. The name "Rotary" came from the early practice of meeting in rotation in the members' offices, though weekly luncheon gatherings elsewhere soon proved more feasible.

While vocation was the basis for membership, Rotary proved to be no ordinary trade or business organization. Fellowship and service as well as profit motivated Harris and his associates. Rotary was on the opposite scale from Social Darwinism and economic enterprise for material gain alone. Save for its greater emphasis on fellowship, Rotary's affinity was for the American Gospel of Wealth and the ideals of philanthropy. Rotary's vehicle was voluntary association, which has done so much to refine the characteristically American concept of individual freedom balanced by individual responsibility, and from which has come much social progress and reform.

A National Association of Rotary Clubs was formed around a nucleus of sixteen local units in 1910. Also in that year Rotary first crossed an international boundary, to Winnipeg, Canada. Additional requests for charters in Canada and the British Isles resulted two years later in the organization of an International Association of Rotary Clubs (redesignated Rotary International in 1922). World War I halted the spread of Rotary to the continent of Europe and other parts of the world, but new clubs sprang up in the United States.

During the negotiations leading to establishment of the club in Marquette, someone discovered that instead of bearing a jurisdictional relationship to Ohio and District 7, Marquette and the Upper Peninsula lay in District 9, comprising Wisconsin, Minnesota, and the Dakotas. Consequently it was District Governor W. J. Zimmers of Milwaukee who, with seven Rotarians from Superior, Wisconsin, and two from Duluth, Minnesota, visited Marquette to determine the suitability of the town and the qualifications of its candidates for Rotary. The delegation arrived by train early in the morning of Tuesday, January 25, 1916, and spent the day becoming acquainted with their hosts and the community.

Satisfied by their investigation, the visitors joined fifteen of the eighteen prospective Marquette Rotarians for dinner at the Hotel Marquette. Service, the principal object of Rotary, furnished the theme for the evening. "*In Rotary*," said Zimmers in the main address, "*business is service*, and that word as you have learned here tonight is the *foundation of Rotary*. . . . In Rotary, business means, first—to serve society, and second—to make money." Through friendship, honesty, and a genuine desire to serve, Rotarians aimed to establish higher ethical standards in business and to promote community welfare. As for the mechanics of organization, Zimmers assured his audience that he would report favorably to the Chicago office and that they should adopt a constitution and elect officers.[7]

The Marquette *Mining Journal* gave the January 25 meeting excellent coverage in both the daily and weekly editions. In the latter it added editorially: "At first glance, some of our fellow citizens had the opinion that a Rotary club must, perforce, have some connection with fighting snow on U.P. railroads. If they watch the newspapers they will be fully disillusioned."[8] A decade later charter member Ernest L. Pearce was to write admiringly of the visiting Rotarians: ". . . to think that ten out-

Organization Meeting, January 25, 1916, Hotel Marquette

siders would come from such distances to aid in starting a Rotary Club in Marquette—no organization expenses, no fees or anything of the kind!"[9]

The Marquette group moved quickly to fulfill the remaining requirements. On Saturday, January 29, a majority of the charter members met at the Marquette Club, a social organization to which they all belonged. Here they adopted the standard constitution and bylaws of Rotary, determined a schedule of membership fees and dues, and elected a full slate of officers headed by Jennison. They chose Pearce vice-president, Peter White Phelps secretary, Alfred F. Maynard treasurer, and Arthur F. Jacques sergeant at arms.

On this occasion the members also voted to make the Marquette Club their permanent meeting place and Monday at 12:15 p.m. their regular time. The location has changed—to the Hotel Northland (1930), to the Clifton Hotel (1941), back to the Northland (1965), and on to the Holiday Inn (1976), where the club meets today. Meetings frequently have been held elsewhere. The time has seldom varied.

The Earliest Members

With the issuing of Charter No. 204, dated March 1, 1916, the first Rotary club in the Upper Peninsula officially came into being. On the sixteenth, the board of directors elected as the nineteenth member James H. B. Kaye, president of what at the time was the Northern State Normal School. English-born Kaye, "a gentle, generous and

Marquette Club (right) on East Side of Front Street North of Marquette (Union) National Bank

lovable friend," in 1918 became the club's third president and, in 1920, the first district governor from Marquette.

John M. Longyear

Four days after the election of Kaye, the board conferred its first honorary membership, upon John M. Longyear, who had come to Marquette in 1873 as a landlooker and then had acquired timber and mining interests far beyond the confines of the United States. Longyearbyan, Spitsbergen, was named for him. He had been mayor of Marquette, 1890-91, and a founder and first president, 1892-1922, of the exclusive Huron Mountain Club thirty miles to the west.

With a partner, Longyear had donated the site for Northern State Normal School and singly had given the land for the Peter White Public Library and for St. Luke's Hospital, now Marquette General Hospital. He was the principal founder and first president, 1918-22, of the Marquette County Historical Society, which today houses the John M. Longyear Research Library. Following his death in 1922, he was described as one of the wealthiest men in Michigan.[10]

Longyear's son-in-law, Alton T. Roberts, succeeded him in the presidency of the Union National Bank, renamed the previous year as a result of a reorganization of the Marquette National. Ironically, Frank Jennison lost out in the bank changes of 1921-22 and moved from the city. He left the Marquette Rotary Club as an honorary member and returned for several visits during the twenties. He died in 1935 in New Orleans.

The club's first printed roster, dated October 1, 1916, contained thirty names headed by a list of the original officers, all of whom had been reelected in July to serve consecutive terms totaling eighteen months each.

In choosing their early members the Marquette Rotarians had the pick of the town. The other men's service organizations—Lions, Kiwanis, and Exchange—came later. Generally speaking, the charter group did not consist of ambitious, rising youngsters, but of mature, established community leaders. Of the eighteen Ernest Pearce was the youngest. Already manager of the Lake Shore Engine Works, he was only thirty years old. But jeweler George N. Conklin was sixty-six, and the average age was nearly fifty.

Almost all of the charter members were both personal friends and neighbors. Sixteen of them lived no more than a ten- to fifteen-minute stroll from each other within a residential area bounded by North Front and East Ridge streets, East Hewitt Avenue, and Lake Superior. Every one was within easy walking distance from his home to the main downtown intersection of Washington and Front streets. The men probably had each other's telephone numbers memorized—from Peter Phelps' 4 to James E. Sherman's 938-W, on a party line.

Within this small group family and church ties also were close. Arch Bishop Eldredge's son Ralph married Jean Farrell, daughter of Austin. Six of the men were Episcopalians; three, Presbyterians; three, Roman Catholics. One was a Methodist, another a Lutheran. The religious affiliations of the other four have not been determined. Conklin was a trustee of the First Presbyterian Church for sixty years.

The charter Rotarians dominated the three-hundred-member Marquette Commercial Club, forerunner of the Chamber of Commerce. Officers of this organization as rejuvenated in 1913 were Joseph Gannon, president; Alton Roberts, first vice-president; and Frank Jennison, treasurer. In 1915 John D. Mangum became the first elected secretary. All were Rotary founders.[11]

Gannon owned a wholesale grocery house. He had been a young officer on the U.S.S. *Oregon* when it made its famous voyage from the Pacific Ocean around Cape Horn to join naval operations in the Atlantic during the Spanish-American War, thus dramatizing the need for a canal through Central America. Mangum had been mayor of Marquette, 1900-01, and postmaster, 1902-06. He was chairman of the Republican State Central Committee from 1916 to 1918.

Another charter Rotarian who had served as mayor, in 1897, was James E. Sherman, better known as the "father" of the city's department of light and power than as its chief executive. For a quarter century he was in effect the general manager of the electric utility. In 1916 Pearce and he were members of the city commission. Less political in his interests was chemist Austin Farrell, manager of the Pioneer Iron Company, a subsidiary of the Cleveland-Cliffs Iron Company. After a trip to Germany in 1893, he had introduced into the Upper Peninsula the Otto Hoffman process for making coke. He headed CCI's chemical and blast furnace department and supervised the company's lumbering operations from 1913 until his death in 1925.

Henry R. Harris, manager of the Lake Superior & Ishpeming Railway (later Railroad), unquestionably was the most volatile of the group. It is said that once, in exasperation, he drove a pen into the top of a beautiful board room table in the Union

National Bank. Nevertheless, he seems to have been widely respected as a man "who really knew how to run a railroad."

Besides Jennison three other Marquette Rotary Club founders soon left the organization. Attorney Arch Eldredge, president of the Duluth, South Shore & Atlantic Railway (Railroad after 1949), had headed both the Marquette County Bar Association and, from 1912 to 1914, the Michigan State Bar Association. He died in 1918 and was succeeded in the club by his son, a lawyer like himself.

Dr. Thomas Cunningham and George Webster resigned in 1920 and moved to California. There Cunningham became a principal founder and first president, 1925-27, of the Rotary Club of La Mesa.[12] Marquette Rotarian Matthew C. Bennett, today dean of the local surgeons, visited him in 1931 and remembers him as "a wonderful man."

The First Months

Early in the year 1916, while awaiting word of formal acceptance by Rotary headquarters in Chicago, the Marquette club went ahead with regular weekly meetings. On Monday, January 31, Roger Andrews, a past president of the Los Angeles organization, "gave a most inspiring talk on 'What Is Rotary?' " The next week, President Jennison presented all the members with Rotary neckties, gifts from the Superior club. For some time after, the Marquette group made a similar presentation to each initiate. At the same meeting of February 7, Farrell spoke on the manufacture of pig iron, thereby setting a precedent followed at intervals ever since of having members keep the club informed about recent developments in their occupational fields.

After a series of meetings devoted mostly to recruitment and vocational talks, Farrell on April 10 commented that the club lacked service projects. Looking ahead, he suggested study of the condition of sidewalks, which in his opinion were "a disgrace to the city." President Jennison at once appointed a committee on public affairs consisting of Harris, Edward O. Stafford, and Jacques. (If this project of the Marquette Rotarians now seems to have been too modest, it should be recalled that the first interest of the parent organization was in the installation of public comfort stations in Chicago's city hall—over the decided objections of saloon keepers and department store owners.)

And so the spring passed pleasantly enough. Fred Warner, the popular three-term former governor of Michigan, was a guest at one of the luncheons. Jennison represented the group at the Cincinnati convention of the International Association of Rotary Clubs. (He was also the first Marquette Rotarian to attend a district conference, in 1918 at Minneapolis.) Gannon urged the local members to wire the Michigan senators to vote for the Chamberlain Universal Military Training Bill before Congress. Jennison appointed a committee on stunts, though soon afterward he suggested that each member think of "some good move to take hold of."

The highlight in May was a weekend outing at the Peter White camp near Deerton. With most of the men traveling in a railroad coach provided by their host, Mor-

At Peter White Camp
1916

gan W. Jopling, the Rotarians spent two days hiking, taking pictures, boating, swimming, shooting, playing croquet and indoor games, discussing politics, singing, and indulging in other activities to which the club's records refer obliquely. The big event was a baseball game, at the close of which the umpire "was roughly handled."

George Shiras, 3rd

During the summer of 1916 the Marquette Rotarians became seriously concerned with service. On June 26 guest speaker George Shiras, 3rd, addressed them on the beauties of Marquette and on the need for better hotel accommodations. Shiras had been a part-time resident of Marquette since 1870, when his father, George Shiras, Jr., later an associate justice of the United States Supreme Court, had brought him as a boy from his home in Pittsburgh, Pennsylvania. Like his father, the younger Shiras had studied and practiced law. He had served in the Pennsylvania legislature and in the lower house of Congress. His marriage in 1885 to Frances P. White, daughter of Marquette's almost legendary Peter White, also had given him a connection with the Jopling and other prominent local families.[13]

Shiras's extraordinary love of nature and his sensitivity to it had led him to spend much time at the Peter White camp, which he used as a laboratory for his early experiments in outdoor photography. His automatic tripping devices and his flash-light pictures of deer, particularly, had helped win him an international reputation as the "father" of wildlife photography.

While in Congress (1903-05) Shiras had introduced a Migratory Bird Bill to prohibit spring shooting of wildfowl in flight to their breeding grounds. Enacted into law in 1913, this measure paved the way for the Migratory Bird Treaty of 1916 with Canada and Great Britain, providing closed seasons and other protection for birds migrating between Canada and the United States. In later years Shiras influenced game legislation in Michigan.

One of four Shiras photographs, exhibited by the United States Government, which won the Gold Medal and diploma at the Paris World Exposition of 1900 and another Grand Prize at the 1904 Louisiana Purchase Exposition (World's Fair) in St. Louis, Missouri.

From 1908 to 1940 Shiras was a trustee of the National Geographic Society. It published many of his articles and, in 1935, his *Hunting Wild Life with Camera and Flashlight* (2 vols.) containing nearly a thousand photographs made in various parts of the United States and Canada. This last he prepared largely at the urging of Theodore Roosevelt, his friend of many years–though long after the latter's death. The former President was Shiras's house guest during the 1913 libel suit in Marquette.

Lacking time to discuss his hotel proposal in sufficient detail at the Rotary meeting in June, Shiras invited the entire membership to dinner on Monday evening, July 3. At this time he persuaded the Rotarians to establish two committees—one on building costs, the other on the choice of a site. After John R. Van Evera, chairman of the first committee, submitted an estimate of one thousand dollars per room, Jennison expressed doubt that Marquette alone possessed enough money, talent, and experience to engage in so ambitious an enterprise. Nevertheless, Shiras clung to the belief that the local prospects should be canvassed thoroughly before funds were sought elsewhere. In fact, he announced that he would subscribe fifty thousand dollars if two other sources he had in mind would do the same.

Nothing came of the hotel project at the time. The club promptly elected Shiras to membership, but soon turned its attention to other matters. Late in July the Rotarians decided to support the Boy Scout movement in Marquette. In September, Dr. Raymond W. Boyer began a series of talks on the importance of compulsory den-

International President
Arch O. Klumph

tal examinations for school children. These presentations, which continued over several years, have been credited with leading to the employment of a health worker for the Marquette public schools.

On August 28 Shiras reported that he himself had been surveying sites for swimming and bathing. He had inquired into the cost of excavating at the Picnic Rocks or at the neck of Presque Isle so that the public might enjoy a bathing beach and children could learn to swim in water warmer than Lake Superior. If the club was interested and would assume responsibility for construction, he would honor a draft for five thousand dollars. The members accepted gratefully, and promptly referred the project to the committee on public affairs. The money ultimately went to the city with the understanding that it be used only for the purposes envisaged by Shiras—at Presque Isle Park.

During the fall of 1916 the international president of Rotary, Arch O. Klumph, visited Marquette and left expressing satisfaction at the club's progress. Toward the end of the year Secretary Phelps observed that the organization "is too young to have many achievements behind it, but in taking advantage of opportunities for service the Club has established a certain reputation which makes its moral support in most enterprises eagerly sought."

War Related Activities

Early in 1917 the imminence of American entry into the war in Europe drastically redirected the thoughts and involvements of Marquette Rotarians. A few days after the German government ordered unrestricted submarine warfare and President Woodrow Wilson severed diplomatic relations with Germany, the local Rotarians committed themselves as a club to support compulsory universal military training and service laws. After the official war declaration in April, at least three members—Morgan Jopling, Alton Roberts, and Dr. Roscoe C. Main—went into uniform. In the postwar era several other Marquette veterans joined the club.

Throughout the conflict Marquette Rotarians vigorously promoted the American Red Cross. At one Rotary meeting every man present enrolled as a member of the organization. Each later pledged himself to raise one hundred dollars for it. Phelps assumed special responsibility for its work in the initial stages. Rotarians, notably Ernest Pearce, from time to time chaired the Marquette County chapter over a nearly twenty-five-year period.

The Rotary club also helped organize the Marquette County War Relief Association, sold Liberty Bonds, gave prize money to boys and girls who proved most successful in growing foodstuffs, and approved curtailing the manufacture of liquor as a means of insuring the food supply of the United States and the Allies. Philip B. Spear was the Marquette County food administrator.

Nor did the Marquette Rotarians hesitate to let the national government know their feelings on the emotional issues of the day. They informed Michigan's senators that the club favored expulsion of Robert LaFollette from the Senate for his antiwar statements, and they joined other Rotary clubs in seeking a constitutional amendment subjecting congressmen and all other federal, state, and local officeholders to the same income tax levies as everyone else. When the end of the war was in sight, the club on October 14, 1918, wired President Wilson urging him to accept nothing less than the unconditional surrender of Germany.

The Influenza Epidemic, 1918-1919

At about the same time, the great epidemic (pandemic) of the popularly designated Spanish influenza, which caused more than twenty million deaths worldwide and 500,000 in the United States alone, came to Marquette by way of Newberry and soon spread particularly among boat and railroad men and their families, also in nearby lumber camps. Within a week the mayor and commissioners, on the advice of Dr. Charles P. Drury, city health officer; Rotarian physicians Thomas Cunningham and Arthur K. Bennett (father of Matthew C.); and the rest of the local medical fraternity, prohibited all public gatherings, including those in churches and theaters, and agreed to closing of the schools.[14] Rotary did not convene again until January 2, 1919, shortly after the bans were lifted.

The disease attacked Marquette in three waves, afflicting 1,759 persons and causing fifty-one resident and sixteen non-resident deaths before subsiding finally in May of 1919. Emergency hospital facilities were quickly provided. Peter White Phelps, chairman of the Marquette County chapter of the American Red Cross, and Dr. Bennett were instrumental in procurement of enough serum to inoculate twenty-five hundred persons in the city by mid-January, when Dr. F. MacD. Harkin concluded from a survey of his colleagues that no one who had been vaccinated had died from the pneumonia which so frequently killed victims previously weakened by influenza.[15]

Foresight, vigor, and constant scrutiny by the Marquette physicians, not least among them Cunningham, whose talk to his fellow Rotarians on February 17 led to an "animated discussion of ways and various methods of combatting" the flu, must be given great credit for the relatively few fatalities from the disease. Many elements in the situation, however, were beyond the doctors' control. Immediately after each of the Armistice, Thanksgiving, Christmas and New Year celebrations, also the Upper Peninsula basketball tournament in the spring, the incidence of influenza cases rose rapidly. Moreover, movement of people into and out of town was unavoidable.

Resurgence of the flu in January could not persuade the mayor and city commission to reimpose the outright bans of the preceding months. Further school closings would have made a shambles of the academic year, and it was feared that the economy could not stand a return to severe restrictions on physical movement and congregation. During the early part of 1919, reliance continued to be placed on the other limitations such as quarantine, school inspections, and requests that people wear gauze masks in public, that but one person do the family shopping, that merchants control admissions to their stores, and that church and theater attendance be held to half of capacity.[16]

Analysis of Marquette's vital statistics for the years before and during the influenza epidemic leads to one extremely interesting conclusion which Drury (who joined Rotary in 1921) noted in his 1919 report as health officer. Despite the twenty deaths due to the flu in 1918 and the thirty-one attributable to the same cause the following year, overall mortality in the city remained remarkably stable: 156 resident deaths in 1916, 149 in 1917, 156 in 1918, and 144 in 1919. In fact, the Marquette death rates of 12.5 and 12.26 for each of the last two years were *lower* than those for all but five of the other sixteen from 1903 through 1920.[17]

The layman may wonder whether, had influenza never struck during the war period, most of the Marquette residents who succumbed to it would have died of something else anyhow!

Postwar Concerns

In the aftermath of World War I, the Rotarians devoted many meetings to problems growing out of the struggle and to prospects for economic recovery and expansion. They relived vicariously the wartime experiences of returning doughboys, sailors, and aviators, and entertained thirty-five veterans in a body on June 2, 1919. They were alert to the spread of Bolshevism and weighed the advantages and disadvantages of maintaining universal military training in the postwar world of continuing political instability. They listened with intense interest to Morgan Jopling's account of his months in Russia.

After hearing Rev. Bates G. Burt speak on the task of Herbert Hoover and the American Relief Administration, the local Rotarians on December 27, 1920, individually pledged $1,055 to alleviate suffering in Europe. In a happier mood, they enjoyed Col. Alton Roberts's account of his work when head of the national American Legion committee which arranged Marshal Ferdinand Foch's 1921 victory tour of the United States.[18]

Of all the troublesome postwar issues, the League of Nations disturbed the Marquette Rotarians most. In response to a request from international headquarters, they gave several meetings in 1919 to the question of United States adherence to the League. On March 12, 1917, Dr. Arthur Bennett had imparted an international flavor

Marshal Ferdinand Foch, Commander of Allied Forces in France during World War I, Flanked by Franklin D'Olier, Past Commander of the American Legion (left); Hanford MacNider, Commander of the American Legion; and Alton T. Roberts (right) on the Rim of the Grand Canyon, 1921.
According to Roberts, Foch on this occasion remarked, "What a wonderful boundary line this would make between France and Germany!"

to the first Marquette Rotary Ladies Night by sharing with the local men and their wives some of his experiences as a medical missionary in Mesopotamia. Two years later the Rotarians elaborated on the world theme by choosing Ladies Night as the occasion for inaugurating their discussions of the League.

On the evening of March 17, 1919, James Kaye and John Van Evera presented the topic in a manner which was "instructive and much enjoyed." The Rotarians devoted parts or all of four of their next six regular meetings to the League and maintained an active interest in it until the Senate in 1920 finally rejected the Treaty of Versailles and the League Covenant.

It has been said that in the summer of 1914 not one responsible statesman in Europe wanted war but many wanted something just a little more than they wanted peace. Five years later, when the continent lay prostrate and a generation of potential political leadership had been almost wiped out, the old generals and statesmen, who had survived intact, shared the common feeling of sadness and revulsion. But no more than a handful, if any, were prepared to attribute the greatest crime of the early twentieth century to other than God's will or the nature of things. As men in wartime had gone into battle hopeful that death was reserved for some other fellow, so they and their leaders reverted to peace persuaded that the guilt lay with someone else.

3
CIVIC IMPROVEMENT

At the conclusion of hostilities abroad the people of Marquette and the Upper Peninsula sang, laughed, played, and joined most other Americans in the chase after dollars. But they did not share extensively in the national economic boom of the variously designated "Roaring Twenties," "Jazz Age," and "Coolidge Prosperity" years. The federal census showed that while the population of the United States and of Michigan as a whole was climbing rapidly, that of the peninsula actually slipped, from 332,556 in 1920 to 318,675 a decade later.

Lumbering in the region continued a long decline. Price drops and lower production costs in the American West reduced average employment in the Copper Country mines from 12,235 in 1919 to 7,834 in 1929. During the same interval iron ore production remained high and stable, but the mean number of iron miners dropped from 16,160 to 8,894.[1] A population rise in the city of Marquette from 12,718 in 1920 to 14,789 ten years later did not compensate for the general downward drift in Marquette County from 45,786 to 44,076 during the same period. Agriculture took up some of the slack, but young people gravitated to the cities of southern Michigan and Wisconsin. The well-to-do relied largely on investments to maintain and enhance their wealth.

The temperate economic clime and the physical remoteness and quiet of the Upper Peninsula kept Marquette Rotarians relatively conservative, sober, and reflective by the standards of the day. They personally encouraged and materially assisted the unfortunate. They broadened their understanding of the great political and social changes going on in the world. And they did their part in spreading the influence of Rotary as a responsible service arm of business, industry, and the professions. It took the Great Depression to reveal that private philanthropy was not enough.

The Power Center

The local Rotarians as a body were never more influential in public affairs than from 1921 through 1923, when they constituted both the real and "shadow" government of the town. During these three years Rotary President Harlow A. Clark was mayor; Rotarians Pearce, Sherman, Gurn S. Webb, and Edward J. Hudson occupied all but one of the commission seats. Another club member, Charles Retallic, was superintendent of the department of light and power.

Mayor Harlow Clark and City Commission, 1919 (Rotarians designated R) *Left to right*: E. L. Pearce (R), J. E. Sherman (R), E. J. Sink, Clark (R), J. P. Werner.

"Old" St. Luke's Hospital 1915

Michigan State House of Corrections and Branch Prison

The St. Luke's Hospital board of trustees was solidly Rotarian. Every one of the eighteen men appointed to it between 1911 and 1952 was a Rotarian or Rotarian-to-be. James Kaye was still president of Northern. Willard M. Whitman was the new public school superintendent, and Henry A. St. John, Alton Roberts, and Edward S. Bice comprised a majority of the board of education. Bice, executive vice-president of the First National Bank, was president of the Michigan Bankers Association in 1921. Daniel Powell and Arthur Jacques served on the Peter White Public Library board. Theodore B. Catlin was warden of the Michigan Branch Prison from November, 1920, until his death early in 1922. His predecessor, Rotarian James Russell, had held the post for eighteen years before him. The listing is only partial.

John W. Stone

In 1920 four distinguished citizens, including George Shiras, joined John M. Longyear as honorary members of the Rotary Club. John W. Stone had come to Marquette in 1890 as circuit court judge. He had been elected an associate justice of the Michigan supreme court in 1908 and was in his second term when he died in 1922. Throughout the entire time, he maintained his local residence in a house still standing at 524 Spruce Street.

The first clergymen to join the club were Rt. Rev. Robert L. Harris, bishop of the Episcopal Diocese of Marquette (now Northern Michigan), and Rev. Fr., later Rt. Rev. Msgr., Henry A. Buchholtz, pastor of St. Peter's Cathedral parish. They were elected active members in the spring of 1918 and were given honorary classification two years later. When Msgr. Buchholtz died in 1945, long after having left the club, he was extolled as the "most widely known priest in the Upper Peninsula." The city hall, all schools public and private, and many businesses closed during his funeral.

The early Marquette Rotarians were masters, not servants, of the clock despite their strict observance of the time limitations for meetings. No one knows how much business was—and still is—transacted personally before, after, or even during the Monday luncheons. The men were able to make on-the-spot decisions which could have quick and marked effect in the community. (Rotarian Albert J. Pearce *did*, on August 8, 1921, recite from memory the telephone numbers of all forty-five members present.)

Most of the club's own business, certainly, was conducted at the regular weekly meetings. Initially the group was so small that until the summer of 1919 the board of directors met only once a year, to elect officers. For the next six months it sat sporadically. It convened five times in December, to deal with such matters as membership eligibility and raising the annual dues from ten to fifteen dollars. During 1920 the directors gradually settled into the present schedule of regular monthly meetings, with special sessions as needed.

Expanding Influence

Long before the world returned to an interval of peace, the Marquette Rotary Club in November of 1917 had appointed an extension committee to help organize clubs in neighboring cities. On January 24, 1918, the parent group played host at a Marquette "round-up" of fifteen key men, prospective Rotarians from different parts of the Upper Peninsula. Small though the meeting was, the presence of International President E. Leslie Pidgeon of Winnepeg suggests its unusual importance. This was the second and apparently the last time an international head has visited Marquette while in office.

International President
E. Leslie Pidgeon

The Marquette organization sponsored its first club in February, 1918, when it sent Ernest Pearce, acting deputy district governor for the occasion, and eleven other Marquette Rotarians to Menominee. Thereafter, with Pearce and William S. Wright as its most active emissaries, the Marquette Rotary Club sponsored in rapid succession new units at Sault Ste. Marie (1918); at Escanaba and Houghton (1920); at Hancock, Iron Mountain, Crystal Falls, and Kenosha, Wisconsin (1921); and, over a longer period, at Manistique (1923), Munising (1926), and Ishpeming (1937).

Between 1921 and 1932, Marquette men assisted unofficially in the formation of clubs at Gladstone, Ironwood, Bessemer, Wakefield, and Ontonagon. James Kaye took special pride in the fact that so much of the extension work was done during his term as district governor (1920-21). By January, 1923, there were ten Upper Peninsula clubs with a total membership of 372, including fifty-two in Marquette.

As they had during the first three years of their association, the Marquette Rotarians continued to hold outings—at the Peter White camp, at the Spear camp at Michigamme, and at Ives Lake. Throughout the twenties they met with the other Upper Peninsula clubs in annual family roundups at Grand Island near Munising. They joined with the Marquette and Ishpeming Lions clubs in social events and service projects.

The early practice of chartering special railroad cars for excursions helped enormously in promoting good fellowship among the Marquette Rotarians. In April, 1920, thirteen of them went by rail together to the Wausau, Wisconsin, district conference, at which Kaye was elected governor. The following year, twenty-five traveled similarly to the conference at Fargo, North Dakota. So during the rest of the decade they went—to Duluth, Minnesota; to Milwaukee, Appleton, Madison, and Green Bay, Wisconsin; and to Houghton and Menominee in Michigan's northern peninsula. Chosen head of District 10 at Green Bay in May, 1926, Harlow A. Clark became the second of the three governors from Marquette to date.

By 1929 the greater freedom afforded by the automobile was becoming more

Playing Softball on Grand Island

Joint Rotary-Lions Club Meeting at Lake Shore Engine Works, 1920

highly prized than social solidarity; when visiting Wausau for the second time, some members chose one mode of transportation, some the other. Over the next few years all became converts to the automobile.

For journeys to international conventions of Rotary, the railroad and steamship remained indispensable. Members of the local club traveled coast-to-coast for meetings in this country. In the early days five Marquette men represented the club at conventions outside the United States: Kaye at Edinburgh (1921), August Syverson at Toronto (1924), Clark at Ostend (1927), James Cloyd Bowman at Havana (1940), and Martin Johnston at Toronto (1942). The board awarded Bowman one hundred dollars "to cover expenses" of his trip. Marquette Rotarians have always enjoyed the intangible as well as material benefits of club and personal association with business and professional men abroad.

During the early twenties the Rotarians were attracted to that most ambitious proposal for concrete economic and political cooperation between the United States and Canada—the St. Lawrence Deep Waterway, as it then was called. A centuries-old concept which in the 1890s had become widely regarded as both possible and feasible, it was for obvious geographical reasons of great interest to the people of Marquette.

The local Rotary club formally endorsed the project in May, 1919, and was especially gratified by the appointment of a Marquette Rotarian, John A. Doelle, to a state commission promoting it. Displaying the optimism so essential to his success as secretary-manager of the Upper Peninsula Development Bureau, Doelle predicted in February, 1920, that work would probably begin about March 1 of the following year and that the waterway would open in the spring of 1922. A Detroit conference and tour of inspection later, Doelle abandoned his prophecy as to time of completion, but clung bravely to the idea that opposition in the northeastern United States was diminishing. He estimated the cost of the undertaking to be about $252,000,000. This was in July, 1921, shortly after he was elected president of the club.

Community Projects

Plans for the economic and cultural development of Marquette itself were, of course, more limited. George Shiras in the fall of 1920 offered five hundred dollars annually for the use of a Rotary committee on outdoor improvement, urging that one of the three members be a golfer. The next spring, the club voted to award cash prizes to the five Marquette householders who kept the best lawns.

Meanwhile, during the summer and fall of 1919 Shiras and his friends had revived the hotel project, with the prospect of having it managed by Fred Pantlind, a well-known Grand Rapids hosteler. Still estimating the cost at one thousand dollars per room, they contemplated a stock subscription of from $250,000 to $300,000 in five or six units of fifty thousand dollars each. Shiras regarded three of these as "assured," one "practically" so, and a fifth "hopeful." His dream was a decade away from realization.

Although temporarily thwarted in this endeavor, Shiras did see another reach a most satisfying fruition. Between Sunday noon and Monday evening, July 3 and 4, 1921, more than three thousand residents of Marquette and vicinity took "their initial plunge into Marquette's new bathing lagoon at Presque Isle." On the afternoon of the Fourth, nearly two thousand people, ranging in age from fifteen months to seventy-seven years, crowded at one time into the new Shiras Pool, so named by the city commission.[2]

Twenty-five thousand dollars had gone into construction of the facility, which when fully developed was expected to include three lagoons, a children's play area, tennis courts, a football and a baseball field, parking lot, and streetcar loop.[3] Shiras and the city, with some aid from the Rotary Club, put thousands of dollars into landscaping and other improvements over the next ten years.

Two more ventures of the early twenties, one commercial, the other civic, deserve notice. On December 20, 1920, the Marquette Rotary and Lions clubs met jointly to

Aerial View and Close-up of Shiras Pool

consider forming a corporation to buy out the Portage (Wisconsin) Knitting Company, maker of "full-fashioned" underwear. After a long discussion, the men present subscribed twenty-one thousand dollars for the purpose. Late in August, 1921, the *Daily Mining Journal* announced that the Marquette Knitting Mills plant would soon employ about thirty persons in the Bureau block on South Third Street.

Engaged in the manufacture of "made to measure union suits," the new company would use various grades of material ranging from cotton and wool to imported Italian silk, so that its "Knitofitu" products would range from eight to forty-eight dollars in price. Speculation was that "by the time winter sets in, Marquette will surpass almost any city its size in the country as a 'silk underwear' town."[4] The Marquette Knitting Mills plant did not survive to the next issue of the telephone directory.

The civic project grew out of the feeling that Marquette should have a memorial, in the form of a community center or house, to the soldiers and sailors of World War I. In July, 1919, the local Rotarians endorsed a municipal bond issue and soon became interested, with other citizens, in the purchase and removal to the city of a building already in existence—the Palestra at Laurium. By April of the next year, it appeared that the Palestra could be bought and relocated at an estimated cost of thirty thousand dollars, a prospect which delighted Marquette businessmen.[5]

The interested parties secured an option on the structure, only to see the Marquette taxpayers reject a proposal for the city to purchase and remove it. The referendum was held on July 28, 1920, one day before the option was to expire. At this critical moment the sponsors hurriedly organized a People's Development Company and bought the Palestra for approximately fifteen thousand dollars. They later reorganized as the Palestra Company and opened their stock subscription to the public. In September, 1921, having secured pledges of thirty-one thousand dollars, they signed articles of incorporation and elected officers and directors. Rotarians Arthur E. Miller, Nathan G. DeHaas, and Albert Pearce became president, vice-president, and treasurer, respectively. Club affiliates among the directors and stockholders numbered at least twenty. One was John M. Longyear, Jr., a Rotarian from 1919 to 1922, who subscribed to stock along with his father.

If the Palestra was to be ready for use in the winter of 1921-22, no time could be lost in relocating it in Marquette. For this work the new company engaged Edward Ulseth, a Calumet contractor. Ulseth and seventy-five workmen needed just fifty-five days to dismantle the building, load it on railroad cars, and unload and reconstruct it on a site at the north end of Third Street leased from the Pioneer Iron Company, subsidiary of the Cleveland-Cliffs Iron Company and forerunner of the Cliffs Dow Chemical Company. The only task which had to be jobbed out was that of taking the steel framework apart and transporting it by water.

With the authorization of William G. Mather, president of CCI, Marquette Rotarian Edward J. Hudson, manager of Pioneer Iron, appears to have negotiated the agreement whereby the Palestra Company leased the land for twenty-five dollars a year while Pioneer Iron continued to pay the taxes. When the city acquired the Palestra many years later, local Rotarians who were executives of Cliffs Dow also transferred the land for one dollar.

Although removal of the Palestra was accomplished with great speed and skill, its readiness for skating was, ironically, delayed by mild weather. At last, on December 26, 1921, the reassembled structure was opened formally, and over two thousand paying customers swarmed through the gates. On the twenty-eighth, two U.S. Amateur Hockey Association teams from Eveleth, Minnesota, and Sault Ste. Marie, Michigan, introduced the town to superior hockey. Rotarian Ralph Eldredge was a member of the first Marquette team to use the arena.[6]

Despite its barnlike appearance, the Palestra was to prove its worth many times over, as a skating rink, demonstration hall, and general recreation center. In 1925 it was the scene of a prizefight in which world middleweight champion Harry Greb knocked out Jimmy Nuss of Newberry in the fourth round.[7] The gate return of seventeen thousand dollars stood for many years as the largest on record for a single

The Palestra Outside
. . . and In

Upper Peninsula sporting event. In later years, while owned by the city, the Palestra was the home of the professional Marquette Iron Rangers, a United States Hockey League team.

Shiras's "18-point" Program

Always alert to indications of civic pride among the people of Marquette, George Shiras in the summer of 1921 decided to capitalize on the enthusiasm created by completion of the new swimming pool, by successful conclusion of the "Better Yards Contest," and by prospects for new industry and for relocation of the Palestra. In cooperation with the other honorary members of the Rotary Club, who had charge of the program for August 29, he devoted his share of it to presentation of an "18-point" plan for community improvement. He accompanied it with the suggestion that the club divide into eighteen committees of three members each for study and implementation.

Twelve of Shiras's points related to "General City Improvements." As modified during the next week or two, these included beautification of Marquette through the planting of trees along selected streets; removal of abandoned structures and unsightly waste materials; the landscaping of municipal, hospital, and church grounds; and park and cemetery improvements. Under the same classification came proposals for an option on a golf course site, acquisition of a building for the collections and displays of the Marquette County Historical Society, new bathhouse facilities on the lake shore south of Standard Oil Company property, securing of the shoreline property from the lighthouse to the Picnic Rocks "by interests that will preserve it in its natural state," "reopening of Lake Shore Boulevard from Picnic Rocks to furnace with adequate sea-wall protection," and provision for tourist campgrounds for 1922.

The other six suggestions pertained to "Presque Isle Improvements"—to provision for shrubbery and ornamental rocks, observation platforms, parking facilities, a memorial arch, expansion and improvement of the zoo, and organization of an aquatic sports association.

As they invariably did whenever Shiras spoke, the Marquette Rotarians listened closely while he described his proposals, sounding "as though he could produce eighteen more when we have finished those."

So enthusiastic was Shiras that Judge Stone, program chairman for the day, delayed adjournment to allow John M. Longyear to tell about his part in developing the Spitsbergen coal fields. This was the last appearance for both Stone and Longyear before the club.

The *Daily Mining Journal* for August 30 (p. 3) greeted the Shiras projects with benevolent reserve: "At first thought most of them would seem to be of comparatively small importance, but the program, taken as a whole, opens up an avenue through which the club can accomplish many things that would be greatly appreciated by Marquette citizens."

By September 15 the Rotarians had endorsed Shiras's proposals, had reconstituted themselves into the requisite number of committees, and had set aside $250 for planning money. Having designated Shiras their "Official Whip" and Ernest Pearce his "Assistant," they set their sights on January 1, 1922, as the deadline for reports and for completion of the lesser tasks. They also printed a four-page pamphlet entitled *A Public Service Program*.

In the latter part of October the committees presented a round of reports. These so gratified George Conklin that he composed a commemorative song of seven stanzas, set to the tune of "John Brown's Body." The first of these established the tone for the rest:

Our Public Service program is working us right hard;
We're tack-el-ing Dead River and the Lake Shore Boulevard,
Coralling all wild animals from Marquette to the Soo
To enlarge our Presque Isle zoo.

Chorus (repeated three times, then adapted to the vagaries of the last three verses):

Glory, glory to our Public Service plan,
We will beautify our city in every way we can,
So hurrah! for Rotary.

Enthusiasm was not enough. The committees did not submit their final recommendations until late in the summer of 1922. Even then there was dissent as, for example, when Edward Macdonald proposed, unsuccessfully, to substitute a polar bear for a skunk at the Island zoo. Work on the projects was not completed until 1936 when Mrs. Carroll Paul, daughter of John M. Longyear, donated a building to the Marquette County Historical Society. By that time the only remaining point of importance was a memorial arch (to Peter White or to the veterans of World War I) at the entrance to Presque Isle Park. This has never been constructed.

A Lake Superior Riviera

Throughout the 1920s Shiras's favorite schemes for city beautification, a golf course, and, above all, a new hotel continued to occupy his mind. The improvement of Marquette was only one, though a key, part of a much more ambitious plan to transform into a Lake Superior Riviera the 150 miles of coastline from the Munising Pictured Rocks to the Keweenaw Peninsula. On September 14, 1925, in the best remembered of several "booster" talks to the Marquette Rotary Club, Shiras spoke on "What's the Matter with Lake Superior?"[8] Pointing out that during many years of travel he had visited the leading European resorts and all but two states in the Union, he asserted his competence to compare tourist prospects anywhere in the developed world with those of the Upper Peninsula, in which he had lived much of the past fifty-five years.

A half century earlier, he recalled, thousands of tourists were coming to the north country on passenger steamers from Buffalo and Chicago. Why had they stopped? Because there was only one summer hotel on all of Lake Superior. For lack of suitable overnight accommodations, no steamship or railroad line could advertise the area, nor tourists make the trip by automobile. Lake Superior was widely known as the largest body of fresh water on the planet, but few people had ever actually seen it.

Shiras believed that Florida offered a particularly interesting basis for comparison. Except for its congenial winter climate, he insisted, it had few natural attractions. He noted that John James Audubon had once said that the state was "forever doomed to be the natural home of the mosquito and the alligator and civilized men would give it a wide berth." Yet Florida was drawing winter visitors from all over the Northeast and Middle West, as far as forty-five to fifty-five hours in travel time from Miami. (Shiras's own winter home was at Ormond Beach.) More than eighteen million summer prospects resided within twenty-four hours of Marquette.

Because Upper Peninsula lumbering and mining were in decline, it was imperative, reasoned Shiras, that the area start cultivating the tourist trade. Fortunately, Lake Superior's summer climate was "unparalleled on the American continent in the same latitude or altitude," and "in climate and scenery there is no comparison" between upper Michigan and points east. But a successful tourist promotion would require a string of new hotels at Sault Ste. Marie, Grand Island, Marquette, and in the Keweenaw Peninsula.

Moreover, and he was speaking now with the authority of a trustee of the National Parks Association, if Isle Royale were made into a national park, as he believed it should be, it would be the only one east of the Mississippi. Good hotels and golf courses could make Grand Island the foremost recreational attraction in the Middle West. The Pictured Rocks should be embraced in a state park; game refuges and public shooting grounds should be created; the state and federal governments should carry on extensive reforestation programs; and the rivers and lakes of northern Michigan should be liberally stocked with game fish, particularly with whitefish in Lake Superior.

Shiras concluded his talk with another bid for completion of his earlier projects, emphasizing again the hotel needs of Marquette. He announced formation of a Lake Superior Development Company, capitalized at about one hundred thousand dollars, to promote community enterprises. This company already had purchased two hundred acres of land in South Marquette for a golf course, had bought a strip of beach near the Picnic Rocks, and had secured an option on the "Bosworth property" at the northwest corner of Ridge and Front streets with the idea of converting it into a clubhouse for the Marquette Federated Women's Clubs. (In 1926 Shiras deeded this property to the women "on most generous terms.") To expedite the work he had outlined, Shiras urged the establishment of an advisory committee representing all the municipal and civic agencies in town.

Shiras ranked a first-rate golf course next in importance to the projected hotel. An old "Horatio Seymour" course had in fact existed for a decade after 1896 or '97 in an area roughly bounded by Crescent Street and Fair Avenue near Lake Superior, and in 1901 the first Upper Peninsula golf tournament had been played on it.[9] In the early twenties the Rotary Club periodically re-examined the possibilities for a new layout. In the fall of 1924 the members spent an entire Saturday evening discussing the matter at Shiras's home.

Shiras's purchase of land in South Marquette quickened the interest of local golfers, but his tract was too hilly and its topsoil too thin. At last Rotarians Elmer W. Jones, Ralph Eldredge, and Edward Macdonald joined with non-Rotarians on a committee which in 1926 secured an option on more than four hundred acres of dairy land from the Longyear estate. Located west and north of the Shiras tract, the old Longyear (Emblagaard) property in November, 1926, became the site of the present Marquette Golf and Country Club.

4
COMMITMENT TO YOUTH AND OPTIMISM

Warm though its interest was in civic betterment, the Marquette Rotary Club's deepest and most lasting concern was to be for the welfare of youth. This took the form of direct involvement in public school administration through the election of Rotarians to the local board of education, through Rotary support for improved educational facilities and higher salaries for teachers in the public schools and in "the Normal," and through loans to students, wider vocational and social opportunities for Marquette's young people, and aid to the physically handicapped children of the city and surrounding area. Fr. Buchholtz on August 9, 1920, explained the position of his church on religious education in what Secretary Ralph Eldredge appraised as "one of the most interesting and scholarly addresses ever given before the Club."

After one lamentable probe of school textbooks and curricula to weed out favorable references to Germany during World War I, the members have refrained from trespass upon the academic domain. To the contrary, their record has been one of positive support. Rotarians and their wives have participated individually in a variety of fund-raising drives for the schools, public and parochial. Occasionally the club as such has lent a hand in the achievement of specific educational goals. In December, 1928, the Rotarians engaged O. H. Ennis, a speech correctionist from Los Angeles, to alleviate stammering in upwards of twenty children and adults in a series of classes spanning ten days in Marquette.

On September 29, 1923, in his maiden speech before Rotary, John M. Munson, Kaye's successor as president of Northern State Normal and a newcomer to the club, told the members to raise twelve hundred dollars to advertise Northern "and be quick about it." Ernest Pearce further admonished, "Do it now and here." While it is reported that the Rotarians actually donated fifteen hundred, the pressure may have induced several resignations.

The Student Aid Program Inaugurated

One of the club's major financial commitments has been to its student loan and scholarship program. Impetus for this came on December 23, 1921, when the board of directors recommended the awarding of "a scholarship of $250 for one year for a graduate of the Marquette Senior High School." The members consented on June 26,

1922, and on September 21 payment was made to a young man entering the University of Michigan.

This turned out to be an interest-bearing loan, as was true of three more grants to the same student for a total of one thousand dollars during his four years as an undergraduate. It took the borrower eighteen years to retire the debt; he made the last payment, representing two hundred dollars in interest, in April of 1945. By that time he was a dentist and a Rotarian in southern Michigan. The club made no further loans before the Great Depression, nor any outright gifts until after World War II, but it had made a start.

Boys' Welfare

Interest in the young males of Marquette led the Rotary Club into several other projects remotely or not at all academic. In February, 1918, President Arch Eldredge had appointed a committee "to look after boys' welfare work." Known from then on as the boys' work committee, this agency gave vocational advice and helped boys obtain gainful employment, sent some to summer camp, sponsored father and son banquets, and promoted picnics and luncheons at which fatherless youngsters were the guests of "big brothers" in Rotary. The club as a whole aided needy children and families at Christmas.

In the early days the boys' work committee also had charge of Boy Scout activities and participated in community drives for their financial support. Perhaps because this was a period when numerous sons of Rotarians were Scouts, the club from 1923 to 1948 specifically sponsored local Troop 307. Nevertheless, genuine enthusiasm was difficult to generate among the membership at large. When writing about a Rotary meeting at which Scouts had presented a program of knot-tying, lifesaving, first aid, and band and drum corps music, Secretary Willard Whitman (who also was the school superintendent, it will be recalled) noted:

> The disappointing feature . . . was not the excellence of the Scouts' program but the lack of interest shown by the Rotarians in this work. Of the thirty-seven Rotarians that were present, about twenty-two remained to give their support by their presence. . . . This query kept running through the mind of the Secretary during the evening—"What do we mean when we say that as Rotarians we back the Boy Scout movement?"

The Marquette Rotarians did become much involved in other youth activities. The climax of their May, 1922, Boys' Week must have left an indelible impression upon almost every lad in town. On the afternoon of Friday the nineteenth, club members took eight hundred youngsters in over one hundred automobiles for "joy rides" to Negaunee and Ishpeming. Some of the youths never had been in an "auto" before. All present had previously heard an outside speaker estimate that there "is not an alarming amount of juvenile delinquency in Marquette" and that the town's fifteen hundred boys were worth at least six million dollars to the community (an astronomical sum when adjusted to today's inflation).[1]

The next morning, a thousand boys paraded through town, took in a free movie, and spent the rest of the day in track and field events, baseball games, and soccer. On Sunday they attended church—with such Rotarians as were still ambulatory.

Occasionally the Marquette Rotary Club paid the expenses of delegates to Older Boys' Conferences sponsored by the Young Men's Christian Association. Rotarians helped make arrangements for a seven-hundred-member conference held in February, 1926, in Marquette. Again there were speeches, parades, and athletic contests. Highlights were a basketball game between Northern and the Michigan College of Mines, and two addresses by the University of Michigan's famed football coach, Fielding H. "Hurry-up" Yost. At Christmas of that year the Rotary Club purchased skates for children whose parents could not afford them, and presented pocket knives to all the members of Boy Scout Troop 307.

Care of Handicapped Youngsters—The Northern Michigan Children's Clinic

During the twenties and thirties the Marquette Rotarians generated an almost crusading spirit for the treatment of physically handicapped children. Between 1917 and 1920 the club had investigated the difficulties of three young people, paying for an operation on one boy and for artificial legs for him and for a girl. This was about the time that Rotary clubs generally were starting to help impaired youngsters.

On January 31, 1921, Miss Alberta Chase, Rotarian nurse for District 9, addressed the Marquette club on her work with children downstate and suggested that the local Rotarians cooperate with those in her area. She returned the next year to explain the operation of orthopedic clinics in southern Michigan whereupon a committee headed by Peter Phelps began to study the possibilities for holding annual clinics of this type in Marquette. In April, 1923, the committee reported opposition from local physicians and, although favoring a clinic supported by the United Charity organizations of the city, advised against Rotary sponsorship.

At this point the nurse's brother, Marquette Rotarian Lew Allen Chase, a professor of history at Northern, determined that the club should move.[2] Chase, a crusty, strong-willed man who had suffered from seriously defective vision all his life, in 1924 accompanied club President William Wright to a meeting in Detroit of the Rotary-sponsored Michigan Society for Crippled Children. Soon afterward Chase became chairman of the local committee and spurred it into action.

The group first took an informal census of handicapped children in the area, then assigned Rotarians to visit prospective patients in their homes prior to holding a clinic in May in the Marquette city hall. Chase appointed a reception committee of his own, and Clyde T. DeHaas obtained cars and drivers to transport the children. On Saturday, May 31, Dr. W. E. Blodgett of Detroit, assisted by Miss Chase and by members of the staffs of St. Luke's and St. Mary's hospitals, examined seventy-six children, prescribing treatment as best he could for so many in one day.[3]

This was but an encouraging start. The Marquette Rotary Club now began making financial contributions to the Michigan Society for Crippled Children and loaned one young man enough money, without interest or a deadline for repayment, for an operation by Dr. Blodgett. For months to come each Rotarian followed the progress of a patient assigned to him. In the summer of 1925 Chase sent a questionnaire to the previously treated children and their families, and summarized the returns in a comprehensive report to the club.

The Chase findings indicated that of the patients examined in 1924, twenty-four had shown improvement and that Rotarians were continuing work with an equal number. After hearing the report, the club voted overwhelmingly to support another clinic.

Although almost three years were to elapse before it was held, Chase and his associates persisted in their help to the handicapped. Early in 1926 the Marquette Rotary board of directors elected Chase to the advisory council of the Michigan Society for Crippled Children. That spring, while a visiting professor at the University of Michigan, he acquainted himself with developments downstate and relayed information to Marquette.

During Chase's absence and after his return home, Rotarians continued to obtain hospital and outpatient care for the handicapped children of the peninsula. To the neediest they gave money for surgery and artificial limbs. They also joined a statewide movement to secure special legislation to facilitate treatment. One important objective was realized when the legislature established a Michigan Crippled Children's Commission in July, 1927.

After much preparation the Rotary Club, Marquette County Red Cross, Marquette District Nurses' Association, Marquette-Alger Medical Association, and the Michigan Crippled Children's Commission arranged a two-day clinic in Marquette. On July 20 and 21, 1928, as they had done before, local Rotarians brought children by automobile, this time from as far as forty miles away. A total of eighty-two patients were examined. Each morning a line of them, many on crutches or with other types of support, hobbled slowly and often painfully like so many Tiny Tims up the steps of the city hall.[4]

A Rotary committee headed by Dr. Samuel H. Buck, a veterinarian and milk dealer, had food for the visitors. Another, chaired by Buck's good friend, past President August Syverson, superintendent (eventually president) of the Lake Superior & Ishpeming Railway, supplied entertainment. Stories, accordion solos, motion pictures, and games, all helped relieve the tedium of long waits. For some children an emotional lift was badly needed; it was on this occasion that Dr. Blodgett commented on the increasing number of mental problems he had been encountering lately. These he attributed to "speeding too hard, living too carelessly, and ruthlessly burning ourselves out."[5]

By the late 1920s civic leaders throughout the northern peninsula had become convinced that occasional traveling clinics were inadequate. Appeals for outside assistance culminated in an announcement in May, 1930, that the Michigan Children's Fund, created several years earlier by Detroit philanthropist and U.S. Senator

James A. Couzens, would establish and maintain a permanent children's clinic adjacent to St. Luke's Hospital in Marquette. The fund would appropriate seventy-five thousand dollars for a building and fifty thousand annually for its operation.

Ground for the resulting Northern Michigan Children's Clinic was broken on October 27, 1930. Miss Elba L. Morse, Upper Peninsula director and nursing representative of the Michigan Children's Fund, and Rotarian Phelps, president of the St. Luke's Hospital board of trustees, participated in the ceremonies. After completion at a cost somewhat larger than the original figure, the clinic building was dedicated on June 11, 1931. Five hundred Upper Peninsula citizens attended a concluding banquet addressed by Michigan Governor Wilber M. Brucker and by Alexander G. Ruthven, president of the University of Michigan. Rotarian Ernest Pearce was toastmaster.[6]

Dr. M. C. Cooperstock became the first medical director of the new Children's Clinic and was elected to Rotary in October, 1931. Miss Morse, continuing as the field representative of the Children's Fund, became the clinic's administrative head.

Private Assistance

Outside the direct purview of the Rotary Club, individual members and their wives in great numbers have been active, at first primarily through their churches, in all phases of child and family welfare. Following several years of service on the board of trustees of the Michigan Children's Home Society, Harlow Clark and Frank A. Bell of Negaunee, who was not a Rotarian, were joined by Marquette club members Edward Bice and Dr. Charles P. Drury in establishing an Upper Peninsula branch of that agency. Two years later the name of the parent body was changed to Michigan Children's Aid Society. Clark was to be president of the northern peninsula arm for

Northern Michigan Children's Clinic

twenty-seven years; Bice, a board member for thirty-eight. From the beginning, foster home care and problems of unwed parents were paramount.

Donations from private sources soon were supplemented by contributions from county boards of supervisors and from the region's Community Chests. During the twenties, also, the activities of the Upper Peninsula branch of the Michigan Children's Aid Society became interwoven with those of the Michigan State Department of Social Services, the Catholic Social Services of the Upper Peninsula, and the Lutheran Social Services of Wisconsin and Upper Michigan, as all worked closely with school administrators, juvenile courts, and county welfare boards.

After its founding in 1929 the Marquette Family Welfare Agency became a vital member of the complex of local and regional social agencies. Its purpose was to provide counseling and financial assistance, including that for medical and dental care, to needy or troubled families. Ernest Pearce was the first chairman of the new group, whose board of directors initially included Rotarians Whitman, Syverson, Hudson, Maxwell K. Reynolds, and James E. Jopling.

Conduct of Meetings

Indispensable to the continuity and success of service efforts have been the weekly Rotary luncheon meetings where, in an atmosphere of relaxed congeniality, programs and discussions on a great variety of topics have given members a common knowledge useful in achieving unity of purpose. From June 20, 1921, through April 10, 1922, the club divided itself into groups of four or five men in rotating responsibility for programs. A printed list of group members and of meeting schedules appeared quarterly during this period. Attendance for forty-three meetings averaged eighty percent.

Music always has played an important part in putting the Rotarians in a good mood for the serious portions of their programs. Especially in the early days, when their number was small and there was horseplay, banter, and some practical joking, even untalented members performed vocally and instrumentally, sometimes, like Conklin, making up their own lyrics.

The first evidence that music was being incorporated into the weekly club "ritual" appears in the minutes for May 2, 1921, which announced President Doelle's appointment of Whitman and Chase as song leader and pianist. Later in the month the directors authorized "the song committee" to compile and prepare for printing in one book all of the selections used by the club.

When Conway Peters, a music professor at Northern, joined Rotary in December of 1923, he seems quite early to have accepted the assignment of song leader, though perhaps with the expectation of occasional relief from Eldredge, Boyer, Whitman, and others. After Peters resigned from the club in January, 1933, Martin M. Johnston, who had been identified at least two years before as a man with a "beautiful tenor voice," was recruited immediately to replace him. Johnston, a faculty member at the

Graveraet High School, was director of its band and orchestra, and also supervisor of instrumental music in the public schools.

In the summer of 1926 the Rotary board voted to engage a pianist at the rate of one dollar per week plus the meal. On October 4 Miss Myrtle Nyquist ("our own Myrtle"), a student at Northern, began an association which was to last four years. She was succeeded in August, 1930, by another college student, Miss Genevieve Sedlock ("our own Genevieve"), who delighted the Rotarians with her solos as well as her accompaniments. Having rented a piano for many years, the club purchased one in the spring of 1929, but sold it a year later to the public schools.

Another practice begun in the twenties was that of issuing a supplement to the minutes for distribution among the members. Secretary Whitman produced the first of these, a mimeographed "Weekly Letter," on November 4, 1922. For a time—from May 19, 1923, until the end of March, 1924, certainly—it was designated "Bulletin" and, later, "Occasional Bulletin." In 1926 the sheet was headed only "Marquette Rotary Club." The next year, it began appearing as "SPARKS from Marquette's Rotary Wheel." Charles Retallic, who was secretary from 1929 to 1936 and editor of the publication most or all of that time, probably holds the record for the number of issues edited by one man.

Club Programs

Each year throughout its history, the Rotary Club has devoted several programs annually, one of them invariably at the time of the district governor's visit, to the ideals and meaning of Rotary. During the 1920s by far the largest number of the rest dealt with topics of local and regional interest: agriculture and the extractive industries; conservation; roads; gas and electric utilities; transportation in all its forms; communication, particularly telephone, radio, and newspaper; money, banking, and insurance; retailing; tourism; sports; crime and penology; health, medicine, and drugs; postal service; state and local government; social welfare, including the work of the YMCA (although there was no local facility), Marquette Family Service Society, Red Cross, and Salvation Army, and financing through the Community Chest (now the United Way); industrial relations; schools and education; the Peter White Library; the geology, geography, and history of the Upper Peninsula; science and technology; ethics and morals; religion and philosophy.

The Rotarians also did justice to national and foreign affairs. Lew Chase kept the club abreast of political developments at home and abroad, and even made an excursion into Egyptology. Patriotism (most frequently in the observance of national holidays); the Constitution, law, and civil rights; veterans' problems and programs; immigration; railroad rates and regulation; the federal farm loan program; the Federal Reserve System; prohibition; calendar reform (in 1929 the Marquette Rotarians declared in favor of thirteen months of twenty-eight days each); international understanding and world peace—all these and more were scrutinized by the club.

Sometime in 1926, apparently, George Shiras published a pamphlet entitled *An*

Marquette Rotary Club. Bulletin No. 11.

Oct. 22, 1923.

"WE WERE ROLLING ALONG"
The Secretary has confidence in the Janitor of the Guild Hall.
"How beautiful upon the mountains are the FEET of them that Preach"
SEARS ROEBUCK
Dr. Bennett read a long list of Dry Goods.
Mrs. Dr. D
"Any woman caught going home with her own husband will be fined five dollars."

A ladies' night was held on Tuesday last. A Good time was had by almost all.

American Plan for the Promotion and Maintenance of International Peace; Summary and Revision of an Address Before the Rotary Club of Marquette, Michigan, August 10, 1924 . . . Supplementary Statement—January 10, 1926. No record exists of Shiras's having discussed such a topic on or about August 10, which was a Sunday. However, on August 25 he did give "a most interesting talk, or rather a series of talks, taking as his subjects 'Weather Conditions'; Game Reserve; Male [Mule?] deer in [the] vicinity of Grand Canyon; League of Nations; and Lake Superior from Keweenaw Point to Grand Marais as a Summer Resort for the Middle West."

In his publication Shiras urged withdrawal of all American countries from the League of Nations and their banding with the United States to create an American League corresponding to that which would remain for Europe. The Pan-American Union might be the matrix for the American organization. The final step would be for the two Leagues to form an Inter-League Union which would be firmly based on a codified international law. This body would have jurisdiction over the Atlantic Ocean and adjoining seas, including the air above and the island areas. An Inter-League Court would adjudicate disputes between members of the two Leagues. The Union would be financed by license fees paid for the use of international waters.

Aside from its novelty, the plan at least had the merit of encouraging official United States participation in world affairs at a time when people in this country were drifting further and further into an isolationist attitude, one with which Shiras himself could sympathize.

Programs with the greatest personal involvement naturally were the most appealing. Members reported enthusiastically about their participation in international conventions and visits to foreign clubs, and both local Rotarians and guest speakers gave accounts of trips to virtually all parts of the globe. Oral presentations often were augmented by lantern slides.

Shiras recalled his association with Theodore Roosevelt, including a private conversation at Oyster Bay, and another member read several letters the former President had written Shiras. Prof. C. C. Spooner of Northern reflected on his college days at Amherst, where he was a classmate of Calvin Coolidge. At a Lincoln's Birthday meeting in 1924, five Marquette Civil War veterans shared with the club their experiences of sixty years before.

Joseph Schnitzler, a former president of the Rotary Club of Mount Pleasant, Michigan, talked about handicapped children. He had lost both legs and one arm, yet had managed to obtain a university education and become a lawyer. A Presbyterian missionary, Rev. George A. Thomas of Point Hope, Alaska, discussed his adventures "on the trail" and among the Eskimos. The club's bylaws were waived to permit a collection to advance his work.

What for the Upper Peninsula were the two most tragic events of the decade, both in 1926—an iron mine disaster at Ironwood which claimed forty-three lives, and another at the Barnes-Hecker mine near Ishpeming where fifty-one died—caused the Marquette Rotary Club to suspend other business at two meetings so that it might adopt resolutions of condolence.

Maj. Gen. Charles P. Summerall

On May 17, 1928, Maj. Gen. Charles P. Summerall, U.S. Army chief of staff, spoke to the Rotarians and Lions on the way the Great War had united the country, also his role in the capture of Cantigny. The occasion of his visit was the thirtieth anniversary of the departure of local volunteers for the Spanish-American War, in which Summerall, too, had participated. Later in the day he addressed a full house at the Delft Theater on "Preparedness."

Noting woeful unreadiness at the outbreak of all previous wars, particularly that of 1898, Summerall pointed out that the latter nevertheless had taught the country how to transport troops across expanses of ocean and that it, together with the war of 1917-18, had shown how to utilize the railroads effectively. In partial summation he said:

> Today the thinking American citizen has lost all illusions as to his immunity from unforeseen conflict. The man on the street and on the farm realizes . . . that the entire manpower of the nation, as marshaled by a selective service act, is our only dependence for security. We have learned also the necessity of co-ordinating our industries so as to enable them to meet the strain of national defense without the dislocation of their peace-time functions.[7]

On The Lighter Side

Four months after the Summerall appearance, John Philip Sousa on September 11, prior to two band performances at the Delft, "dropped in" on the Rotarians and Lions, regaling them with some of the memorable events of his career.[8]

This was but one of many programs the local Rotarians gave to entertainment during the 1920s. Both the Normal and the Marquette public high school periodically provided music. On January 17, 1927, Conway Peters brought his Northern colleague, Miss Ruth Craig, and thirteen normal school students to present a variety program by vocal soloists, a male quartet, a string quartet, and a small orchestra. Secretary L. Roy Walker observed in the minutes, "This was undoubtedly the best musical program ever given to the club."

Rotary personnel and guests on other occasions read poetry and dramatic selec-

John Philip Sousa

tions, and displayed and explained art works. Two or more programs featured the "orthophonic" phonograph. In October, 1929, soon after the introduction of "talkies," a representative of the Delft Theater chain (controlled by Marquette Rotarians Morgan W. and Alfred O. Jopling and Hugh S. Gallup) predicted that baseball fans soon would see an entire World Series at their local movie houses.

Among the local Rotarians none surpassed Willard Whitman in wit nor, as secretary, left more delightful minutes.[9] Whitman was a portly man, urbane, light on his feet, and skilled in dramatics. He recorded that one day in June, 1933, when Vice-President Eldredge, another man of size, was in the chair, "Ralph dispensed with the music because he was very hot and somewhat fat. This was decided after consulting the secretary, who was also very hot." Another time, Whitman grudgingly admired an introduction of a speaker which had the effect of "exciting great jealousy in the breast of the Secretary."

The levity which persisted most of the year was softened by sentiment at Thanksgiving and Christmas. Beginning in December, 1924, with Henry van Dyke's *The Mansion*, Whitman annually until 1942 presented programs of readings or dramatic sketches appropriate to the holiday season. Aside from selections from van Dyke, he favored Kate Douglas Wiggin's *The Birds' Christmas Carol.* Once two high school students joined him in a Christmas playlet.

Social Highlights

In addition to roundups and other outings, the gala affairs were those held in the evening with the Rotary Anns. One such was a banquet celebrating the tenth anniversary of Marquette Rotary, on January 18, 1926, at the Marquette Club. Almost all of the fifty-four active and six honorary members, together with their wives, attended. President August Syverson was toastmaster. Ernest Pearce and Ralph Eldredge reviewed the club's history. The governor of District 10, Lee C. Rasey of Appleton, Wisconsin, spoke on "The Fundamentals of Rotary," and past District Governor Kaye admonished the group to "Carry On." The Normal orchestra furnished music.

The official Ladies Nights were usually if not invariably held in the Guild Hall of St. Paul's Episcopal Church. Three were especially memorable. The mood of the first, in 1921, when Clarence B. Randall,[10] Phelps's son-in-law, came from Ishpeming to speak movingly of his recent visit as a Legionnaire to France and Belgium, contrasted sharply with the other two. These lightly graced the winter of 1926-27, making it far and away the most splendid social season of the decade, as the Rotarians viewed it.

"Giving Thanks for Marquette's 'Home Talent' " was the theme for November 29. J. Cloyd Bowman, a professor of English at Northern, stressed the need to preserve the cultural heritage of the Upper Peninsula through literature. Mrs. A. L. Swinton, second vice-president of the Michigan Federation of Music Clubs, told how dull life would be without music. Miss Emilie Van Brocklin, vice-president of the Marquette Federation of Women's Clubs, praised the energy and foresight of the local club-women and called attention to the uniqueness of a city the size of Marquette in having both a Federation and a clubhouse for women. Rotary President Arthur Jacques described the role of the club in the community. Violin and vocal solos provided a suitable musical background.

The climax of the evening came when the men of Rotary presented Booth Tarkington's skit, *Station YYYY.* In the living room of the Winstead family, "Mama" Winstead (Willard Whitman), possibly like Molly Goldberg of later radio fame, dealt with the problems of her daughters Anita (Earle Parker) and Caroline (Ralph Eldredge) and her son Herbert (Ray Johns). Harry D. Lee was "Pa" Winstead, a "radio bug." The parts of Anita's suitor, Roger Colby, and the chauffeur, Charles, were played by Elmer Jones and Rev. Charles Boyd. Mrs. Manthei Howe, society editor of the *Mining Journal*, reported the affair in her own inimitable, spritely style: Ray Johns was "corking"; indeed, "all the cast was the spiffiest aggregation imaginable." The whole evening was "a topping success."[11]

The Rotarians' November, 1926, triumph prompted them to stage another major social event on February 21 of the following year. This took the form of a simulated ocean cruise on a luxury liner, with the members of the Marquette Business and Professional Women's Club as guests along with the Rotary Anns. When Rotarians and ladies entered the Guild Hall, they received tickets for Pullman "Airways Cabin" seats and were assigned tables with names corresponding to those on their cabin coupons—"Oriole," "Hiawatha," "Mariposa"—thirteen in all. Each table or "cabin" had decorations suitable to its name and color. The "Peacock" was adorned by "a gorgeous big bird . . . with flowers in blending shades"; the "Galleon," by "a lovely boat with sails flying." Favors were "gorgeously colored booklets of various cruises." Mrs. Howe's was "a splendiferous one put out by the Canadian Pacific. Mm!" The passengers were served exotic fare from menus resembling those aboard ship.

Group singing and short speeches introduced the program. Then tour director Pearce took over "and the fun was on." Messenger boys, "elaborately uniformed," dashed back and forth trying to keep up with wireless messages and phone calls from all over the world—delivered to the accompaniment of songs and stereopticon views from the countries of their origin. Martin Flanigan heard from Dublin, "where he used to play marbles as a boy." William Wright received a cablegram from the president of Rotary in Vienna. It came collect for $16.30, "and the messenger wouldn't take an I.O.U. for it, either." A Chinese girl (Miss Claire Jacques) brought greetings from a Rotary president in her native land. The program concluded with the singing of "America the Beautiful." Mrs. Howe assured her readers that "everybody had a perfectly spiffy time."[12]

The Northland—A Rotary Hotel

The general expansiveness of the twenties, of which the Ladies Nights were indicative, and a feeling that the modest prosperity which had come to the northern peninsula would never end at last persuaded the Marquette Rotarians to give their full backing to George Shiras's proposals for a new hotel. By 1929, their lingering doubts removed, they were busily engaged in planning for a spacious Kawbawgam Hotel on North Front Street. They had formed a company by that name. Shiras was president; Maxwell Reynolds, vice-president; and Philip Spear, secretary-treasurer. These men together with Frank J. Russell, Arthur Jacques, and E. J. Hudson constituted the board of directors. All were Rotarians. In May, 1929, Shiras presented the Marquette Rotary Club with five thousand dollars worth of Kawbawgam Hotel Company stock.

At a cost of about $350,000, the company built a six-story, fire-resistant structure containing one hundred guest rooms and nine apartments. Its name changed to the Hotel Northland, it was leased to the Roberts-Deglman Company of Winona, Minnesota, for operation. Rotarians and guests were allowed a preview after the regular

A Rotary Hotel

meeting on December 30 at the Marquette Club. The hotel opened for business the first week in January of 1930.[13]

On the twentieth of the same month, the Marquette Rotary Club met for the first time in the Northland. The speaker was Rev. Herbert J. Bryce, Rotarian. His topic, "High Lights of 1929," was a sequel to a similar talk he had given the year previous. Even though this one ran over the allotted time, the members, "by unanimous consent, remained to the end, and universally agreed that it was one of the 'high light speeches' of the year." It had reviewed "the progress made in aviation, golf, radio, and various other activities. . . ." Bryce's 1929 and 1930 presentations set a precedent followed to this day.

Ironically, the Hotel Northland, the Rotarian's crowning physical achievement of the decade, began serving the public within three months after the stock market crash of October, 1929. Few Americans anticipated that the ensuing depression would be of such severity and duration as to alter drastically the course of American history.

Until 1930 most Marquette Rotarians, habitually respected for their vocational and professional competence and community leadership, could enjoy the feeling that the reins of political and economic power and of social influence in the city were firmly—and rightfully—in their hands. Whatever injustice and suffering existed beyond their evident ability or inclination to redress or alleviate were outside their sphere of responsibility. But with the onset of the Great Depression they could not escape the common bewilderment and anxiety inflicted by an increasingly complex, hostile, perhaps unmanageable, world. The doors of the Hotel Northland opened just as those to a secure past were closing.

5
THE GREAT DEPRESSION

Marquette and the Upper Peninsula did not so much plunge as slide into economic depression following the Panic of 1929. Because the region had not reached the heights of prosperity, it did not have so far to fall, and the conservatism of bankers and the public furnished a cushion for the decline when it did, belatedly, occur. There was belt-tightening, to be sure, and no little personal hardship, including near starvation for some. But business failures and home and farm mortgage foreclosures were fewer here than downstate. The official exemption of the peninsula's banks from the Michigan bank holiday of 1933 testifies to the essential soundness of the economy.

While between 1930 and 1940 the population growth rate for the entire state slowed to one-fourth that of the previous decade, the trend in the northern peninsula temporarily reversed itself as many of the young men and women who had gone to the cities now returned to wrest a living, however difficult, from the soil of the north country. By 1940 the number of people in Marquette County and in the city of Marquette had increased to a record 47,144 and 15,928 respectively.

Marquette's First District Conference

For whatever it was worth, the local Rotarians found diversion from stock market losses in contemplation of the Hotel Northland and of its role as headquarters for the 1930 conference for District 10. This was the first time the event had come to Marquette, and the club members looked forward to celebrating their building achievement. They would have the opportunity, too, to display their almost parental pride in the organization of nearly one-third of the forty-two clubs in the District.

President Willard Whitman served with District Governor G. Ray Empson of Gladstone as an official host for the conference. Ernest Pearce was general chairman of committees; past District Governor Harlow Clark had charge of the program. Rotary Anns prepared the Women's Clubhouse to receive visiting wives, for whom luncheons, games, and automobile tours were scheduled. Uniformed Boy Scouts were engaged to act as guides, and the high school band and the Northern band and glee clubs to furnish music at the several sessions.

Beginning Sunday afternoon, May 18, Marquette braced itself for a traffic jam of three hundred out-of-town automobiles. Starting early the next morning at the Northland, registration ultimately exceeded 650, including wives, with every club in the district represented. The first session opened at nine o'clock in the Louis G. Kaufman Auditorium of the high school. Empson, Whitman, and D. M. Wright, a director of Rotary International from Stratford, Ontario, delivered brief welcoming addresses which stressed the growth of Rotary and the importance of service. Finally, Grove H. Patterson, distinguished editor of the *Toledo Blade*, took the rostrum to speak on "The Challenge of the Times."[1]

Noting the enormous productive mechanism of the United States in relation to the social and economic ills of the nation and the world, Patterson warned: "The grave question is whether we can guide this great machine with its marvelous capacity; whether we can prevent it from getting beyond our control so that it falls upon and crushes us." Although America led all nations in industrial production, he added, it also led in murder and robbery, and "there are 25,000,000 children in this country who cannot go through high school. . . ."

Patterson cited three turning points of civilization inspired by the advent of religion, science, and democracy. A fourth, he believed, would come with the birth of a new aristocracy created by "the fellowship of those who care; those who want to accept the individual responsibilities which are theirs, to carry the burden."

The Toledo editor doubted that all men are in fact created equal. Progress comes

TOLEDO BLADE

TOLEDO, OHIO, MONDAY, MAY 19, 1930

TWENTY-SIX PAGES

TO WED FOOTBALL STAR

TARIFF BILL'S FATE RESTS WITH SENATE

DEBENTURE PLAN STUMBLING BLOCK

Upper House Must Agree to Compromise or 16 Months of Effort Will Be Wasted.

ZEPPELIN BATTLES ST ON WAY TO SEVILL

Enjoyable Trip Aboard Zep Is Recounted by Lady Hay

Giant German D by High Wind Goal on Fir

Greater Cleveland Grows to 1,197,8

Headlines, May 19, 1930

Grove H. Patterson

Pvt. Harold R. Peat

from the few "who have shouldered the burdens and accepted their responsibilities." In addition, the times required perspective, "the ability to discriminate between the important and unimportant things of life"; imagination, "the illumination of the soul"; and individual expression, "the power and ability to turn our impulses into action." Patterson observed that Rotary was well equipped to promote a sense of individual responsibility and should do so.

While the women enjoyed their own repast, the men divided into three luncheon groups to consider the topics of community service, club service, and Rotary ideals in business. All reassembled in the afternoon for an address by the famous Canadian World War I veteran, Pvt. Harold R. Peat, on "The Inexcusable Lie."

"If I were going to sculpture a monument to war," began Peat, "I'd tell the truth. I'd take as my model a raving maniac I saw in the trenches." There other men found the most adequate defenses against insanity to be drinking, swearing, and the ability to laugh at absurdity. They did not pray readily, "for prayer calls for tenderness [and] humbleness, and war is not the thing that brings out those feelings. They did not want to kill but they had to kill and they spoke in the language of killers." To Peat, war meant a "spiritual crash, spiritual disintegration." He confessed that he had no particular plan for peace. He doubted that there was a shortcut to it except as the world learned the facts about war. The important thing was "to evaluate peace differently, to reward constructive effort"—in other words, "make peace heroic."

Though perhaps in press before Peat spoke, the *Mining Journal* editorialized without reference to him, "Men who have known each other across the Rotary board will find it hard hereafter to cultivate the hate which is the first essential of war."[2]

After so much heavy fare from Patterson and Peat, the Rotarians in the late afternoon welcomed a light, Whitman-directed play, *A Servant in the House*, about a woman who was overly ambitious for her husband. Still more agreeable, no doubt, was the address which followed the conference banquet that evening. The speaker was Edward James Cattell of Philadelphia, a man who enjoyed great popularity in Rotary circles. The local paper described him as "a rosy-faced man with white hair, white imperial and side whiskers, the cheeriest, happiest kind of man."

Cattell was obviously influenced by the recently deceased French psychotherapist, Emile Coué, whose almost proverbial "Day by day, and in every way, I am becoming better and better" he restated as "Life is getting better and sweeter all the time." Cattell attributed people's troubles to "a sour outlook." Said he, ". . . if you can't get what you want, like what you have got" and nurture "kindly feelings." He continued mostly in this vein:

> The strides we are making in this day bring all the world closer together and nearer to God. You can't visualize unless you vitalize. I believe the greatest danger

> to the country is the intellect that is divorced from the soul . . . these pessimistic articles about the country going to the dogs and the dogs going to the devil are written by men educated beyond their intelligence.

Because in his travels of some eighty thousand miles and appearances before many clubs he had found "a certain nervousness and apprehensiveness among folk that seemed to him un-American," he had made courage the theme of some of his talks. Concluding on the note of service, Cattell observed that the world "is crowded with opportunities to help some one who is struggling along. . . . Rotary is drawing men nearer together all over the world and nearer to God."[3]

At the end of Cattell's speech, the Rotarians and their ladies adjourned to the Brookton ballroom for the Governor's Ball. Thereafter, it may be surmised, many delegates who might have experienced a restless night had the proceedings ended at 3:30 in the afternoon went to bed and slept soundly.

Early Tuesday the officers breakfasted together, then went into a business session with the delegates. Later in the morning Edwin Robinson of Sheffield, England, a member of Rotary International's finance committee, addressed the conference on "Are We International?" Stressing the need to reorganize Rotary "along truly international lines," he insisted that the clubs of each country must be allowed to follow their own inclinations rather than remain under Anglo-Saxon domination.

During the conference, delegates had shown a good deal of interest in the Northern Michigan Children's Clinic, which at that time was still in the planning stage. The success of the Marquette Rotary youth activities, together with the emphasis of Rotary International on work with young people, made the closing address especially suitable. This was delivered by Charles A. Nyman, assistant vice-president of the First National Company of Detroit, who spoke on the topic, "What a Man Can Do for a Boy." Nyman called upon the Rotarians to help youths cultivate tolerance, good will, honesty and prudence—and to teach them to diversify their investments!

Toward the end of the session Fred J. Jordan of Rice Lake, Wisconsin, who had been elected by acclamation to succeed Empson, was presented to the delegates. At noon they broke up into final luncheon groups, after which the District 10 conference adjourned.[4]

The momentum of good feeling created by this regional gathering carried through the rest of the year and was expressed through several meetings of Marquette Rotarians and various local and peninsula groups. Much discussion attended plans for the summer roundup, which had been held at Grand Island every year since 1920. This time Blaney Park entered a bid, but was ruled out because it could not seat enough people for the usual banquet. So, early in July, the Rotarians met once again at Grand Island. Not until 1933 did Blaney Park secure the roundup, and then for only that year and the next.

As it had at times in years past, the Marquette Rotary Club met in July, 1930, with the local Lions, at the Lake Shore Engine Works. Members of the Town Club of Ishpeming also attended. In October, Rotarians from the Munising and from the Canadian and American Sault Ste. Marie clubs visited Marquette. With them came a large Rotary Wheel which had "rolled" into about sixty cities on similar expeditions.

Retrenchment

The deepening Depression forced the Marquette Rotarians to economize. Total club membership hovered between fifty-five and sixty, but the turnover increased as some of the men fell behind in their dues and had to resign. The indebtedness of individual members reached a peak of almost fourteen hundred dollars in fiscal year 1933-34. Commensurately, the club's charitable donations, which had averaged about five hundred dollars annually in the late 1920s, fell abruptly to less than $150 in 1929-30, then wavered back to their former level toward the end of the decade. So severe was the stringency in 1933 that "SPARKS From Marquette's Rotary Wheel" was issued but once a month that year.

In the face of hard times, the principal monetary contributions of the Rotary Club shrank to those for the annual kickoff luncheons and suppers of Community Chest workers, for handicapped children's expenses, and for youth activities, including small sums for the Boy Scouts. In September, 1930, the directors agreed to pay "as usual" two-thirds of the cost of the Chest supper, and in December they allotted the customary fifteen dollars for the children's Christmas party given by the Michigan Children's Aid Society.

On December 23, 1931, the Rotarians joined members of other Marquette agencies as ticket takers and ushers at the Delft Theater. The purpose was a benefit performance to which townspeople gained admission with donations of food and other gifts for the poor. The next April the club established a fifty-dollar emergency food relief fund, to be drawn upon by teachers in the public and parochial schools "when and where a child is known to be suffering from lack of food and there is no other immediate way of providing such relief." The following year the club spent eighty dollars for children's lunches in the North Marquette School.

During the early thirties the Rotarians also drew closer to their own sons and daughters and to the Boy Scouts, whether related or not, in Troop 307. The club sent lads from that unit to the 1931 Older Boys' Conference in Iron Mountain, and the next summer was entertained by the Marquette Scouts at their Pickerel Lake camp. In June, 1933, the Rotarians celebrated a father and son day with both sons and unrelated Scouts. The real novelty of the summer was a father and daughter banquet, at which the girls literally sang for their suppers.

Straitened circumstances of Marquette college students, combined with a modest increase in money available for the purpose, caused the local Rotarians to alter their policy on student loans. They reactivated their ambiguously labeled "Scholarship Loan Fund" by distributing smaller amounts among several youths instead of granting a large sum to but one as in the twenties. Aided by modest dividends from the Kawbawgam Hotel Company stock, which had been earmarked for the fund, the Rotarians between 1932 and 1934 advanced up to one hundred dollars to each of six young men.

By June, 1936, when total assets stood at $1,486.88, eight students owed $920. By the end of 1941 the club had granted twenty-six loans amounting to thirty-three hundred dollars to fifteen males. By 1945 all debts were cleared although not in every case with interest. On June 30 of that year the amount in the fund was $4,094.32.

The Bay Cliff Health Camp—Paul Harris's Visit

When the Northern Michigan Children's Clinic opened in the spring of 1931, the Rotarians of Marquette and the Upper Peninsula gave a collective sigh of relief and satisfaction. They expected that the new agency, generously endowed by Couzens money, would meet most of the needs of handicapped children in the region. However, before many months had passed, it became evident that still more facilities and services were required. Consequently, Rotarians and Lions together supported the Marquette Chamber of Commerce in its sponsorship of the first Upper Peninsula conference of the Michigan Society for Crippled Children, held on October 6 and 7, 1933, in Marquette.[5]

Dr. Raymond Boyer, chairman of the Marquette Rotary Club's crippled children's committee, opened the conference and with Lew Chase welcomed delegates and visitors. On Friday afternoon members and guests toured the city by automobile, visiting the prison, Presque Isle, and the Northern Michigan Children's Clinic.

ADMINISTRATION AND EMERGENCY FUND

This is the cost of clerical help and postage, and the collection expense for pledges. An emergency fund is maintained for increased demands during the 12 month period.

MISS AGNES BRALL,
Secretary, Community Chest Office.

Administration	$ 750.00
Emergency Fund	2,000.00

Budget, $2,750.00

Total Chest Budget

$18,875

The Community Chest is responsible to:

COMMUNITY—
in the sense that it purposes to furnish the community with adequate social services, adequately operated.

TO THE GIVERS—
those persons who furnish funds for social services, an economical administration.

TO THE AGENCIES—
whose funds are entrusted, that the funds are expended to render service compatible with the expenses.

All three of the responsibilities are carefully carried out by the officers of Community Chest:

—1931-'32—

President:
MRS. D. M. BEGOLE, Visiting Nurse Association.

Vice-President:
MR. P. G. TEEPLE, Rotary Club.

Secretary:
MISS CATHERINE WILLIAMS, Family Welfare Society.

Treasurer:
MR. CHARLES RETALLIC.

Directors:
MR. HARLOW A. CLARK, Michigan Children's Aid Society.
MR. M. K. REYNOLDS, Salvation Army.
MR. E. L. PEARCE, Red Cross.
MR. L. W. BIEGLER, Boy Scouts.
MRS. F. B. SPEAR, Girl Scouts.
MRS. G. A. CARLSON, Marquette Woman's Club.
MISS SUSAN BATES, Business and Professional Woman's Club.
BISHOP H. S. ABLEWHITE, Lions Club.
MRS. H. A. WILSEY, W. C. T. U.
MRS. S. BOUCHER, Woman's Relief Corps.

Every budget is carefully examined both for expenditures and service rendered—and this year the amount is

$18,875

GIVE ONCE---
BUT FOR ALL

Campers Spell BAY CLIFF

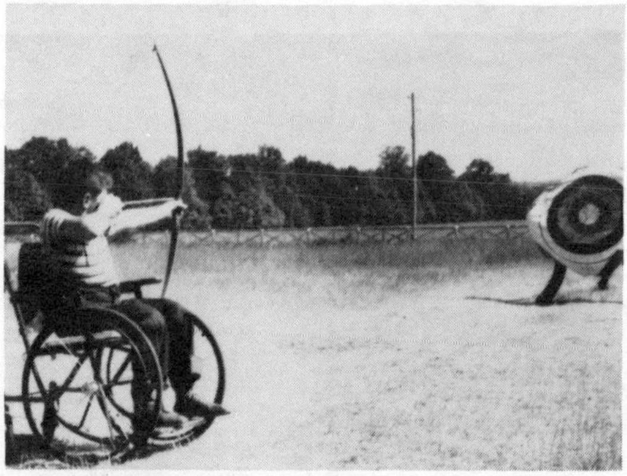

Marquette Rotarian E. L. Pearce and Ishpeming Rotarian Walter F. Gries present check to Miss Elba Morse, 1961.

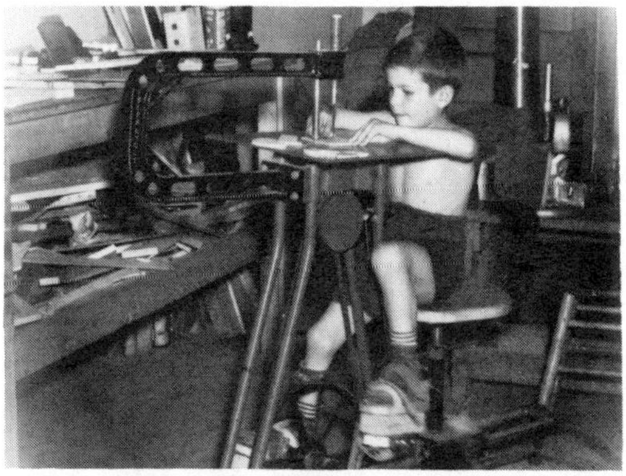

The presence of Paul Harris, who with Mrs. Harris was on a seven-week journey through the northeastern states, made the gathering one of truly historic importance for the Marquette and Upper Peninsula Rotarians. The Harrises were chauffeured by Dr. and Mrs. Samuel Buck. At the Friday evening dinner, with Harlow Clark presiding and Walter Gries of Ishpeming performing as toastmaster, Harris gave the principal address, on "Rotary's Interest in the Movement." He praised Edgar F. Allen of Elyria, Ohio, for having started the organized Rotary effort to help handicapped children many years earlier.

The conference disclosed that the peninsula had 1,110 active cases of physically impaired children, of whom 682 were being sent outside the region for treatment, at considerable cost for transportation. As of June 30, 1933, Marquette County alone had a file of 136 handicapped youngsters. At the Saturday morning breakfast meeting the conference members endorsed a proposal to engage a resident orthopedic surgeon. When in 1934 Dr. E. R. Elzinga was appointed to serve in that capacity in Marquette, he was promptly inducted into the Rotary Club.

From the quiet, sustained efforts of many Rotarians and other persons also came the establishment, in 1934, of the Bay Cliff Health Camp at Big Bay, thirty miles northwest of Marquette. Made possible through financial contributions from Horace H. and Mary A. Rackham of Detroit and from the Couzens Children's Fund, the camp was headed first by Dr. Goldie Corneliuson and Miss Elba Morse.

The Bay Cliff Health Camp's first object was to combat undernourishment among the children of the Upper Peninsula. In 1938 it began treating diabetes; in 1940, poliomyelitis. Four years later it undertook speech therapy and alleviation of hearing problems. It since has come to embrace all physical difficulties during the summer season when the camp is in operation. By 1968, when it broke precedent by establishing a kindergarten for the preschool handicapped, the camp was reported to have served a total of five thousand children, all from the peninsula. By 1981 the number had reached about seven thousand.[6]

Harlow Clark and Ernest Pearce were among the early leaders in the movement to establish and sustain the Bay Cliff camp. The latter became, and for many years remained, its treasurer. The Marquette Rotary Club furnished fireworks for July Fourth celebrations, even as it provided toys for tubercular children at Morgan Heights Sanatorium and clothing at Christmas for patients at the Children's Clinic. After the Rotary Club of Ishpeming was formed in 1937, Samuel H. Cohodas and fellow members of that organization assumed prime responsibility for the camp although as it expanded it continued to rely for financial and material assistance upon the Marquette Rotary Club and other service groups in the peninsula.

Depression Issues

Prolonged business stagnation caused the weekly programs of the Marquette Rotary Club to reflect and contribute to the members' deepening awareness not only of its local effects, but also of its national and worldwide impact. When Rev. Herbert Bryce became program chairman, he invited Lew Chase to follow his example in presenting the news "Highlights" of the preceding year. Chase's talks of January 12 and 19,

1931, were so well received that they were continued annually, in two segments, until his retirement from Northern in 1944 and subsequent departure from the city.

In the early thirties Ernest Pearce's contributions, always informative, took on particular significance. From his experience as one of the state's foremost banking authorities (he was president of the Michigan Bankers Association in 1935-36), Pearce spoke on such topics as "Around the Corner" and "The Three T's: Troubles, Technology, and Taxes"; also the need to continue the club's city beautification program. In 1935 he addressed the members on "The National Debt," describing the probable effects of dollar devaluation.

Outside speakers further analyzed the nation's problems. David B. Reed, U.S. senator from Pennsylvania, in August of 1931 ranged over such diverse topics as bonus payments to war veterans, the Federal Farm Relief Board, and the proposed St. Lawrence Seaway. He returned four years later with suggestions for stimulating business.

For Marquette and perhaps most of the Upper Peninsula, the depths of the Depression were reached in 1932-33, as club programs for those years testify. On May 16, 1932, the guest speaker was S. R. Elliot, manager of mines for the Cleveland-Cliffs Iron Company. Reminiscent of Detroit Mayor Hazen S. Pingree's promotion of his "potato patch" plan in the 1890s, Elliot suggested that the mayor of Marquette appoint a committee to secure and prepare unused land for garden plots for the unemployed. Elliot's talk was interrupted by delivery of a telegram from Cleveland instructing him to close all CCI mines in the county from June 1 to November 1. The club immediately adopted a resolution supporting his garden plan, and Fred Archambeau urged members to consider getting an industry which would employ women and girls.

During the same year of 1932 Miss Adda Eldredge, sister and law partner of Ralph, reported on the work of the Family Welfare Agency, and Thomas Clancey of Ishpeming talked on "The Tendency of Our Youth Towards Communism." As winter drew near, Capt. Sherman Deskin of the Salvation Army outlined his program for feeding transients. He was able, he said, to provide two meals a day per person for a limit of three days at a stretch.

In February, 1933, L. Roy Walker, the county agricultural agent, spoke on "The Farm Today," noting the surplus of farmers and the downward trend of farm prices during the previous decade. Dr. E. H. Campbell, superintendent of the Michigan State Hospital at Newberry, added another measure of conditions and need in the peninsula. In October he informed the club that all twelve hundred beds at Newberry were occupied, at a total cost of fifty-six cents a day per patient.

The inauguration of President Franklin D. Roosevelt and institution of the New Deal made national government assistance available to Marquette and the Upper Peninsula. The Civil Works and Public Works Administrations undertook road repair and construction, the Civilian Conservation Corps set about reforestation, and other federal agencies came in to help restore the area to economic health. But a frontier region which prided itself on its independent spirit and on its ability to solve its own economic and social problems was deeply suspicious of outside aid. Marquette Rotarians listened with attentive skepticism to explanations of federal programs. City officials sought and secured no new public facilities beyond a post office building. On the other hand, when improvements elsewhere threatened the immediate interests of Marquette, the local Rotarians were quick to join in expressions of jealous concern.

With respect to transportation they relied heavily upon the judgment and advice of K. I. Sawyer, the county road superintendent, who spoke to the club a half dozen times in the twenties and thirties. On March 14, 1932, he informed the members of his efforts to relieve unemployment among his seventy-five men by having them work on a staggered system of three days a week.

In April, 1935, representatives of chambers of commerce, city commissions, road commissions, and county boards of supervisors from the central portion of the Upper Peninsula met at Escanaba and unanimously adopted a resolution requesting early completion of U.S. highways 2 and 41. A few days later the Marquette Rotary Club urged priority for U.S. 41. This was to link Escanaba and Marquette north and south, whereas U.S. 2 was being run east and west through Escanaba along a route whose closest point was fifty miles from the Queen City.

During 1933 the question of state financial support for the public schools of Michigan became a critical issue. The advantage of a new three percent state retail sales tax was offset by a recently adopted constitutional limitation of fifteen mills on real estate tax assessments and by abandonment of the state's claim to revenue from that source and from personal property taxes. At midyear, friends of education started a drive for special legislative appropriations for the schools.

On July 31 Paul C. Voelker, state superintendent of public instruction; Frank Cody, superintendent of the Detroit public schools; Dwight B. Waldo, first president of Northern, then head of Western State Teachers College at Kalamazoo; and Allan Freeland, president of the state board of education, all appeared before the Marquette Rotary Club to urge support for an additional fifteen million dollars in state aid.

Speaking for the visitors, Voelker noted that without the supplemental appropriation only ten percent of the state's schools could get through all nine months of the coming school year and another ten percent could remain open for but a month. For the sake of increased efficiency, Voelker also recommended creation of centralized county school boards and one central state board of education for all of the public colleges and universities in Michigan.[7]

As the prospects for school aid became still bleaker, the board of directors of the Marquette Rotary Club on November 9 sent a resolution to the governor requesting "immediate measures to assure adequate educational facilities for all children of school age in the state of Michigan." Fortunately, the legislature did appropriate enough money to enable most schools to maintain at least basic programs until the following June.

Although during the thirties talks on depression topics and on special government and private efforts to combat economic ills were prominent among the local Rotary programs, presentations on routine business and professional topics remained essential fare. Continued, too, were inspection trips—to the ore docks, Northern State Teachers College (as "the Normal" was named from 1928 to 1941), the Lake Shore Engine Works, and, within a few weeks' time in 1935, to the agricultural experiment station at Chatham, the *Mining Journal* building, Marquette radio station WBEO, and the Children's Clinic.

Rotarians and non-Rotarians, including a surprisingly large number of presumably impecunious teachers, reported on trips to foreign lands—to Japan, China, Palestine, Iran, England, Spain and other parts of continental Europe, Mexico, Central and South America, and even Russia—also to the Chicago World's Fair: "A Century of Progress" of 1933 and 1934. And, as they often did, Marquette Rotarians filled speaking engagements elsewhere. Webster H. Pearce, president of Northern, addressed the district conference at Appleton in 1934; Harlow Clark, the one at Rhinelander, Wisconsin, in 1936.

Entertainment During Austerity

Less serious club programs featured music, drama, readings, debates, magic, and ropeskipping. On November 23, 1931, the Marquette Saturday Music Club, in the first of many appearances over several decades, presented a playlet with a Thanksgiving theme. The rest of its programs were musical. Conway Peters continued to display the talents of Northern music students. Miss Craig on three or four occasions directed the girls' glee club of the college.

Prof. Forest A. Roberts (no relation to Alton), who had charge of speech, drama, and debate at Northern, was joined on October 10, 1930, by his wife Esther and a student, Eileen Richards, in a skit, *Finders-Keepers.* A few weeks later he read excerpts from J. M. Barrie's play, *The Will.* When president of the Marquette Summer Theater Players during three of their four years in existence, 1937-40, Roberts discussed drama with the club. Following a year of special graduate training, he gave talks on speech correction during and after World War II at Rotary and before similar groups.

Mrs. Abby Beecher Roberts, daughter of John M. Longyear and first wife of Alton Roberts, was the principal sponsor of the Summer Theater Players, who staged their productions in the Players' Dell on the grounds of her home at Deertrack, also in the Kaufman Auditorium. More than half of the sixty-six individual patrons in 1937 were Rotarians and/or Rotary Anns. Willard Whitman served one term as vice-president and another as treasurer. Outside professionals and local amateurs comprised the acting troupe.

Gunther Meyland, a colleague of Roberts in Northern's English department, was another popular speaker at Rotary, equally at home with such topics as human personality and mushrooms. On George Washington's bicentennial birthday in 1932, the two men brought debate teams to the club to argue the question of whether Washington or Lincoln was the greater man. No decision was announced.

Women guests at Rotary were among the most entertaining—and entertained. At a meeting in July, 1933, Miss Elba Morse demonstrated first aid techniques. She first stretched Gust Syverson out on the floor and gave him artificial respiration, then carried Roscoe Young across the room on her back, remarking that when she found a man to her liking she just might make off with him.

Three years later the colorful, enterprising Manthei Howe not only described her duties at the *Mining Journal*, but turned the tables on her hosts by using them for her own purposes. In a long follow-up article, she gave her impressions of the meeting at which she had appeared, and of some of the members. She concluded, "All of them give you the feeling of being men of accomplishment and ability, of conservative sense and sagacity, but drat 'em some of them are terribly heavy sitters . . . a bit lacking in resiliency of mood, if you know what I mean. . . ."[8]

On February 21, 1936, the Marquette Rotarians and Rotary Anns celebrated the twentieth anniversary of the club. Following dinner at the Northland (at one dollar per plate), past Presidents J. Cloyd Bowman and Ernest Pearce reviewed the history of the organization, some of the members' daughters sang and danced, and several newcomers were inducted with appropriate ceremony. After the program all adjourned to the Delft Theater for a late performance of Shirley Temple in *The Littlest Rebel.* James Beckman headed the club that year.

Particularly after the recession of 1937-38 wore off, renewed confidence in the nation's economy was revealed locally in more active fellowship within the Rotary Club and between it and other groups. In August, 1940, the Munising, Escanaba, and Marquette clubs met at Pearce's and other camps at Middle Island Point. A year later the Marquette Kiwanians, Lions, and Rotarians held a joint meeting in town. In October, 1941, Dr. Charles P. Drury entertained his fellow Rotarians at his camp on Conway Lake.

By the time of the twenty-fifth anniversary of the Marquette Rotary Club, it was possible, despite the world's turbulent condition, for the seventy-five members and their Rotary Anns to recapture briefly the gaiety of the twenties. Meeting on the night of May 12, 1941, in the Sidney Adams Gymnasium of the high school, most of them enjoyed an evening of pure delight, complete with doormen, turkey dinner, and "penthouse trim." As he did so often during his many years of membership in Rotary, florist Arnold C. Lutey provided flowers for the occasion. Don Young's nine-piece orchestra and a vocal trio, the "Melo-Dears," furnished music for both dancing and listening.

Remarks by District Governor Alexander B. Hill of Wisconsin Rapids and historical highlights by Ernest Pearce were followed by a variety program of vocal and instrumental numbers, toe and tap dancing, pantomine, and a Topsy and Eva act featuring Mrs. Margaret Roberts and Mrs. Ellen Graff. The men were intrigued by a boxing match involving four boys from the Holy Name Orphanage.[9]

Club officers during the anniversary year were John D. Morrison, president; Drury, vice-president; Munro L. Tibbitts, secretary; and Philip B. Spear, Jr., treasurer. All four were to live through the golden anniversary, and all but Spear remained members to that time.

Private Philanthropy

Considering the comparatively small amounts of money appropriated for student loans and charitable purposes during the thirties, it may seem that the Marquette Rotarians dissipated their energies in discussion, debate, and diversion instead of dealing squarely and vigorously with the city's economic and social ills. To conclude that is not quite fair. Club records do not take into account the private contributions of individual Rotarians to churches, hospitals, schools, and relief agencies. Common report has it that for several years some of the town's well-to-do citizens, including Rotarians, assumed personal, primary responsibility for the support of numerous less fortunate persons and families unrelated to them.

Moreover, in 1936 and 1939, Rotarian Simon A. Williams, owner of a large laundry, with Mrs. Williams donated to the city several lots on the south side and eight more on the north side of Ohio between Pine and Spruce streets for development into a recreational area. This was named Williams Park in their honor. About ten years before his death in 1939, Williams had given a large pipe organ to the First Methodist Church.[10]

The best publicized and one of the largest donations of money ever given to the people of Marquette came from George Shiras and his wife. In September, 1937, Mr. and Mrs. Shiras announced the formation of a non-profit corporation to promote "recreational, beautification, and cultural activities" in Marquette, and endowed the new agency with over one hundred thousand dollars in cash and securities.[11] For this action the Rotary Club's board of directors commended Shiras "as the one who has done most for the City of Marquette."

On at least one occasion a Marquette Rotarian, through his ingenuity and resourcefulness, was able to bestow upon the people of the town and the Upper Peninsula a benefit beyond monetary measure. In 1940 a poliomyelitis epidemic swept through the region, overwhelming St. Luke's Hospital with ninety stricken children brought in by train and airplane, as well as by automobile, within a week's time. No fewer than twelve of these patients required a respirator, whereas the hospital had but one.

In this emergency Maxwell K. Reynolds, a hospital trustee, drew upon his general engineering experience and skill to design makeshift devices using oil drums, vacuum cleaners, and simple wooden boxes. Machinists and cabinetmakers in his employ were able to assemble respirators from these materials at the rate of four hours each.

Seeking no profit from his invention, Reynolds made a parts list, detailed written instructions, and photographs available to the many people who inquired about it. The Council on Physical Therapy of the American Medical Association printed a pamphlet containing this information.[12]

Williams Park

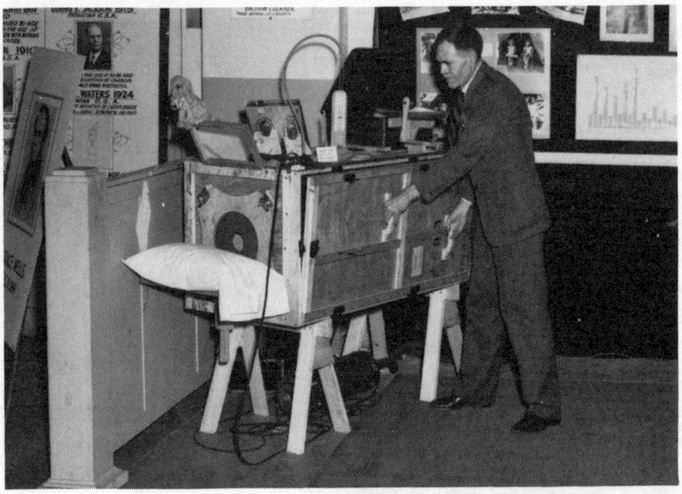

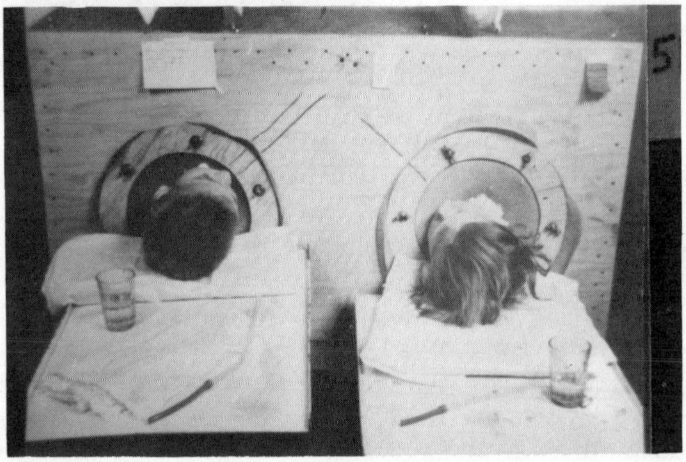

Maxwell K. Reynolds and His Respirator on Display and in Use

The increase of international tension and the outbreak of war in Asia and Europe intensified American interest in the all-absorbing problem of the Depression years, that of a fairer distribution of wealth and income at home and abroad. Locally the concern was well expressed when on the evening of June 19, 1941, Marquette Rotarians and Rotary Anns were among the more than 450 persons who attended a dinner meeting of the annual convention of Michigan State Nurses held in St. Peter's Cathedral Hall. The principal speaker was William J. Norton, executive vice-president and secretary of the Michigan Children's Fund.

Norton's address was memorable for at least two statements: that the social sciences had failed completely "in affording equitable distribution of . . . products of [natural] science to all people" and that "the have nots arose to challenge the haves; because the haves haven't had the wisdom or ethical courage to cease thinking entirely of themselves. . . ."[13]

The 1940s were to see no lessening of pressure on Rotarians everywhere to realize more fully their ideal of service.

6
WORLD WAR II

The Marquette Rotary Club entered its second quarter century as it had its first—against a setting of international turmoil and war. Japan's encroachments in Manchuria and China, the Italo-Ethiopian and Spanish Civil wars, Germany's seizure of Austria, the Czechoslovakian crisis and Munich Pact, and, finally, engagement of most of the world's powers in full-fledged hostilities forced upon the Rotarians a bleak, thorough awareness of global problems.

Starting about 1937, the weekly luncheons became serious and subdued as charming travelogues yielded to grim firsthand accounts of human suffering in strife-torn areas. Guest missionaries, religious and medical, reported on political and social conditions in and outside war zones—in Kuwait, Persia, India, China, and many parts of Europe.

French Salvation Army Maj. Irene Peyron recounted her experiences as the only white woman ever allowed in the penal colony at Devil's Island. A. E. Rosholt, for seven years an Associated Press correspondent in the Orient, shared his memories of the siege of Shanghai. World traveler Sherwood Eddy and Loyalist army veteran Ellsworth Bisson vividly described the Spanish conflict as they had witnessed and participated in it.

In April, 1939, Mrs H. J. Seddon (née Mary Lytle of Marquette), who as the wife of an Englishman was living in London, portrayed life in her adopted country while facing the imminence of massive air attack. Four months later her husband, in proud defense of free political institutions, spoke on "Parliamentary and Local Government in England."

Recognition of the strong possibility if not probability of another American military involvement abroad made Marquette Rotarians particularly sensitive to defense needs and plans. Club members listened attentively to fellow Rotarian L. N. Jones, who reported on his Reserve officer training at Fort Knox, Kentucky; to Col. Hayes Kroner, commander of Fort Brady at Sault Ste. Marie, who spoke on "The Responsibility of the Citizen and the Soldier"; and to Mrs. Catherine Prickett, a resident on the outskirts of London, whom they questioned about English air defense.

In August, 1941, the Rotarians joined the Kiwanians and Lions for addresses by U.S. Navy and Marine Corps officers about the work of Navy flying units and of the Marines. At its October 7 meeting the famous Arctic explorer Vilhjalmur Stefansson was a guest of the club. He had lectured that morning at the recently renamed

Vilhjalmur Stefansson

Northern Michigan College of Education to an audience of students, faculty, and townspeople, including Rotarians, on the importance of Iceland and Greenland to the security of the Western Hemisphere.

Having just returned from a two-month survey of flight conditions in the Arctic region, Stefansson was apprehensive that although eighty thousand Canadian troops were said to be in Iceland, the Germans, who now controlled Denmark, might move against that nation's huge island possession, Greenland. On November 17 Rotarian Sidney Smith, chaplain and sociologist at the Marquette branch prison, gave his views on the Sino-Japanese situation. Two Army Air Corps captains discussed the future of aviation on December 1.

Pearl Harbor and Beyond

Thus alerted to danger in a general way, the Marquette Rotarians, though greatly shocked by the choice of target and by the suddenness of the strike, were not altogether surprised by the Japanese attack on Pearl Harbor on December 7, 1941. At the club's regular meeting the next day, Willard Whitman read President Roosevelt's war message to Congress, and Lew Chase considered various aspects of hostilities with Japan.

Reminiscent of 1917-18, the club concentrated in thought and deed on the war effort. Except for the annual Christmas celebration, which this time included a father and son luncheon on December 22, the next several programs set the tone for years to come. Rotarian Henry A. Tape, president of Northern, spoke on "Interdependence"; a Marine colonel, on "Join the Marines"; and Police Chief Donald McCormick, on "Civilian Defense." In May, 1942, Rt. Rev. Msgr. Joseph L. Zryd "gave a very patriotic talk pertaining to the religious side of the war."

When the United States joined in the hostilities, the machinery for inducting men—and women—into military service already was in motion, and there was little difficulty in reviving and augmenting agencies for channeling national energy toward the one goal of Allied victory. By 1943 nine local Rotarians were in uniform.[1] A World War I veteran, charter member Morgan W. Jopling, had died in a boating accident the year before during voluntary patrol duty on Long Island Sound. Uncounted Rotarians' sons, a number of whom joined the club after the war, served throughout.

The regular Rotary meetings during and for several years after the conflict were studded with battle accounts by servicemen on leave or returning as discharged veterans. Toward the end of 1942 Lt. Stanley Long of Marquette described his downing of a Japanese bomber and a Zero fighter over the Aleutian Islands, and Ens. Douglas Syverson of the *Sea Wolf* followed with an account of American submarine operations, as did Lt. David H. McClintock the next March. Meanwhile, Rev. Henry Swan, pastor of the Grace Methodist Church, reviewed the anxieties and inconveniences attending blackouts, also the perpetual danger of being torpedoed while on a ship bound from Bombay, India, to the United States.

During 1943 reports from war zones were especially numerous. Lt. Erro Wiitala of Marquette, a transport pilot in the Army Air Corps, deplored the lack of railroads in Africa and expressed disappointment in most of its cities, "finding them unkept and the standard of living lower than he had expected." Capt. Henry Chisholm, from the same branch of service, recounted the decisive battles of Midway and Guadalcanal. Lt. Dean Tippett, a graduate of Graveraet High School and of Northern, detailed his participation in sixty-six Army bombing missions in ten months over China and nearby territory.

Lt. Warren Lutey, son of Rotarian Arnold J. Lutey, told of his strikes at airfields and shipping in the Guadalcanal area while he was attached to a dive-bomber squadron of the Navy Air Corps. Ens. Norman "Boots" Kukuk, also a Navy pilot, drew upon his experience of several months in and around the Solomon Islands and the New Hebrides. After having been shot down during one raid, he had been rescued from the Pacific Ocean by an American destroyer. Kukuk had high praise for the Marine commandos, whom he described as "the toughest fighters on earth—taking no prisoners." (It appears that Marines credited little of their success to their diet, for Kukuk remarked that one contingent cheered upon learning that enemy bombs had obliterated a depot containing their supply of a well-known brand of canned meat.)

In the summer of 1944 Col. E. L. Miller, commander of the three prisoner-of-war camps in the Upper Peninsula—at Sidnaw, AuTrain, and Evelyn—traced the history of the Geneva Convention and related it to his responsibilities. On June 19 of the same year, Capt. Clifford A. Swanson, who as personal physician to Secretary of the Navy Frank Knox was present at the Teheran Conference in December, 1943, shared some of his wartime recollections with his fellow townsmen.

Over the years many recruiters from the various branches of service were guests of the club. These included representatives of the WAAC (WAC), WAVES, and Marine Corps Women's Reserve. A Marquette Rotarian once expressed the common male belief that the WAVES must be the superior organization because "their uniforms have more class."

The Home Front

In and out of club meetings the Rotarians vigorously promoted civilian activities conducive to victory. They salvaged materials for war purposes, administered the draft, extended hospitality to area youths inducted through Marquette, supported the Red Cross, joined neighborhood war clubs, encouraged other civil defense projects, implemented rationing controls, and collected clothing for needy European refugees.

Simon R. Anderson chaired the club's war service committee and was secretary of the Marquette County rationing board. In 1942 twenty-eight Rotarians volunteered to sell war bonds and stamps in a door-to-door campaign; on August 10 the board of directors voted to put two thousand dollars from the student loan fund into government bonds. The club responded to several more financial appeals as the war progressed. In August, 1943, a club questionnaire disclosed that eighty-seven percent of the members were employed in an aggregate of 312 individual efforts pertaining to the conflict.

Interspersed among the many narratives of military, naval, and diplomatic events at the weekly luncheons were discussions of national and local civilian problems. Throughout the war Ernest Pearce addressed the Rotarians and other groups on such topics as "Finances and the War," the Red Cross, and the significance of Rotary. Other members and guests dealt with food production, wood processing, new chemical products, rationing (particularly of sugar and gasoline), scrap salvage, censorship, patriotism, National Guard training, contributions of the schools to the war effort, the Boy Scouts, manpower allocation, hospital needs and plans, medical progress, comprehensive federal (including medical) insurance, the training of chaplains, meteorology, the railroads, and iron ore and steel production. Rotarian Ralph E. Benson, warden of the prison, arranged for an unusually large number of club programs outlining the problems connected with his work.

The Rotarians' preoccupation with the war lessened their interest in young people of pre-service age. Although the men invited high school and college youths to give talks, present musical programs, and attend meetings as guests, they reduced their financial contributions to child care groups, indeed to almost all social welfare agencies. Perhaps because wartime prosperity had reduced need, they loaned money to but one student.

In July, 1943, Regional Administrator Birkett L. Williams of the Office of Price Administration, who also was the immediate past president of the Rotary Club of Cleveland, Ohio, visited Marquette to determine its suitability as a location for the Upper Michigan office of the OPA, situated at that time in Iron Mountain.

While in Marquette, Williams addressed a joint meeting of the Rotary, Lions, and Kiwanis clubs and the directors of the Chamber of Commerce. After describing the federal rationing and price control system, the speaker frankly stated his opinion that the OPA had done "only a fair job." He said he had been brought up to regard government subsidies as "an instrument of the devil," but in present circumstances he could conceive of no feasible alternative. Prices could not be allowed to rise without limit. To freeze them at fixed levels would bankrupt too many businessmen. To freeze and then adjust them upward would be inflationary. All that could be done was to "roll back prices and pay the producer to continue production of his goods without loss. . . ." The trouble was that a $20 billion inflationary gap already existed between savings and the meager stock of consumer goods on the market.[2]

The advantages of a removal of the OPA office to Marquette were well appreciated by Secretary C. Morgan Beckman, who noted in the club minutes: "The payroll of this Upper Peninsula office, plus personnel, involving rentals, etc., runs into considerable revenue and would, therefore, be a real asset to our community." However, the Marquette bid failed.

Internal Changes

The war years brought marked changes within the Rotary Club itself. In April, 1941, weekly meetings were shifted from the Northland to the Clifton Hotel while the former underwent extensive remodeling. When this was finished, the members had the choice of a new basement, artificially lighted, L-shaped dining room in the Northland or of the principal dining room off the lobby on the main floor of the Clifton. They voted to make their temporary quarters permanent despite the lack of a full-time catering staff. They had to contract with no fewer than three women's groups before they found one which served good food at a price they deemed satisfactory.

Two personnel changes also affected the routine of the club. When non-Rotarian Harold Kellan, who for about nine years had played the piano, was called into service in 1942, he was succeeded by Rotarian Alex P. Hamby. Similarly, when Martin Johnston moved from the city in July of 1943, he was replaced as song leader by another Rotarian, Rev. Arthur C. De Vries.[3] In his tribute to the departing Johnston, President Emery E. Jacques said "it would be difficult to fill his shoes," whereupon Lew Chase remarked that the club was not interested in his shoes, just his voice.

After a lapse of several years, the local Rotarians on July 3, 1944, resumed publication of their weekly bulletin. Nameless at first, it was headed The ROTATER beginning with the July 17 issue. Since the start of the second volume the corrected spelling of ROTATOR has been used.[4] From mid-1945 to the summer of 1946 or on into 1947, the bulletin was a monthly four-page leaflet printed on enamel paper. It then reverted to a single 8½-by-11-inch mimeographed sheet issued weekly as before the war. For eight or ten years before November of 1968 it was on the same size paper folded once, then it again appeared unfolded. Beginning in early 1974 it has been produced on legal size sheets. Over the decades it has been prepared by a committee, the club secretary, the vice-president, and by dedicated individuals outside the main line of club administration.

Space not taken up by attendance information, listings of guests, announcements, abstracts of regular and directors' meetings, personal notes, and, periodically, by a roster of members, officers, directors, and committeemen has been filled with jokes of uneven merit. That these have lacked the spice of the knee-slappers exchanged at directors' meetings held in the relaxed atmosphere of an out-of-the-way camp once was acknowledged by the compiler who wrote:

> The guy who thinks our jokes are rough
> Would quickly change his views
> If he'd compare the jokes we print
> With those we're scared to use.

Transition

The most significant internal changes occurred with the acquisition of new members and the passing or retirement of those with long Rotary affiliations. During World War II three honorary members were lost through death in little over a year.

George Shiras died in the early summer of 1942 after an extended illness. Classical scholar Earle M. Parker, whose own membership in the club dated from 1919, prepared its memorial:

> George Shiras lived and worked with us through his greatest days, and we knew him . . . as an ideal Rotarian. We saw him in sorrow and misfortune, in loss and trouble, in affliction and misery, but never in such distress that he forgot the other man. . . .
>
> We loved George Shiras. There was about him a dignity that approached austerity, but beneath that exterior there was a soft appreciative feeling for nature, God's creatures and mankind that made him loved by all who knew him. A fern, a bit of moss, a doe with her young, a moose, a man in need, were each a tremendous thing to him, and the value he found in each of these . . . made him an everlasting value to us who have lost his presence. . . .

Within a month charter member Peter White Phelps, too, was gone. For a half century he had been associated as a member and then as sole owner with the insurance firm founded by the man for whom he had been named. He had become a

St. Luke's Hospital trustee in 1911 and was president of its board from 1922 until his death. He was a staunch friend of the Marquette County chapter of the American Red Cross from its inception. He was also a trustee of the Shiras Institute from its beginning.

When Dr. Raymond W. Boyer retired from his profession a few months before his passing in October, 1943, he was known as the oldest practicing dentist in the Upper Peninsula. During a career of fifty-two years he had served the inmates at the prison for forty-five.

J. Cloyd Bowman left teaching for writing in 1939 and, upon departing the city two years later, was elected to honorary membership in the club. After withdrawing from Spear and Sons and from the presidency of its subsidiary, the Marquette Dock Company, past President Frank B. Spear, Jr., in January of 1944 was chosen the first senior active member in the club's history.

Lew Chase retired from Northern a few months later and resigned from the club in 1945. His last personal appearance was on June 18 of that year, when he predicted that Franklin D. Roosevelt would be remembered as "a very great man" and that, although military preparedness would be essential still, there was not much danger of war with Russia because that country "has always been friendly to us." During his twenty-five-year affiliation, Chase had provided or had been a major contributor to more than fifty club programs.

At a luncheon meeting broadcast over Marquette radio station WDMJ on February 19, 1945, to mark the fortieth anniversary of Rotary International, club President W. J. "Bill" Weber briefly explained the Rotary ideal of service and noted that the Marquette organization with ninety-eight members was the largest in the 143rd District, comprising the western Upper Peninsula and northern Wisconsin. With Willard Whitman, Secretary Arthur G. Callahan, and two of the three charter members still in the club, Ernest Pearce and Arthur Jacques (George Conklin was absent), Weber traced the history of Rotary, with emphasis on the wartime activities of the Marquette group.

Of the three other original members then living, Joseph Gannon was present that day as a guest; Alton Roberts and Edward Stafford had moved from the city long ago. Before the year was out Conklin, who had owned his jewelry and music store in Marquette from 1870 to 1929, and Jacques, who had just been elected president of the Union National Bank after having been a director since 1928, died at the ages of ninety-five and seventy-one respectively.

Jacques had been an executive of James Pickands and Company, of the Marquette Dock Company, and of the Kawbawgam Hotel Company. He had served the city of Marquette as mayor, 1934-39, the Peter White Library as a trustee, 1914-24, and the Rotary Club as president, 1926-27. Pearce succeeded him in the bank presidency.

Deaths, resignations, and loss of members to military service prompted President Emery Jacques, son of Arthur, to promote a recruiting drive which brought seventeen new members into the club during his term of office, 1943-44.

In the earliest days the president customarily had welcomed the novitiates with a few well-chosen words, and they, in turn, had expressed their pleasure at being admitted.[5] They had an opportunity to talk to the group about their vocations or professions later in the ordinary course of events.

Toward the end of the thirties the practice had evolved of having three or four new members as a group give brief vocational talks at the same meeting. On March 31, 1938, four men who had joined the club within the past year—Frank Shaw, Thomas Kelly, Roy Clumpner, and Lincoln B. Frazier—were allotted ten minutes each for this purpose. By October 28, 1940, when Ben E. Knauss and the younger Jacques were scheduled, there had been a shift from vocation to autobiography.

Perhaps this gradual structuring of initiate responses persuaded Emery Jacques as president to give, on November 8, 1943, "a very fine induction talk" to six newly elected members. The next month, Ernest Pearce welcomed two more with a most impressive, comprehensive speech on the history of the club and on the meaning of Rotary.

Since then, formal induction talks and autobiographical sketches by new members, in groups or singly, have virtually been standard procedure—all in good time. Although Earl H. Closser was elected to membership in April, 1942, he did not present his autobiography until December, 1943. In other instances the time lapse may have been even greater.

So interested were the Rotarians in Max Nunemaker's life in his native Switzerland that they gave him the entire February 14, 1944, meeting for an account of his career down to his association as vice-president with the Munising Wood Products Company. Nunemaker suggested that Switzerland had been able to maintain its neutrality during the war because its government had threatened to blow up the tunnels through which Germany was supplying Italy with men and munitions unless its integrity was respected.

Preparing for Peace

Surprisingly early in World War II the Marquette Rotary Club began looking forward to the end of hostilities and to the problems of peace and postwar readjustment. Six months after Pearl Harbor, Rev. Arthur F. Runkel, pastor of the First Methodist Church, spoke on "Making Up Our Minds," in reference to peace. In January, 1944, Runkel, by that time a Rotarian, again addressed the members, on "The Church in the Postwar World."

In mid-1943 Prof. Werner S. Landeker of the University of Michigan suggested that upon its defeat Germany be converted to an agricultural nation and that its surplus population be encouraged to emigrate voluntarily to other countries "of their choice." His opinions were in accord with the Morgenthau Plan then being considered by the Roosevelt Administration.

A few weeks later Congressman John Bennett advised the Rotarians and Kiwanians that since the United States would emerge from the war with a national debt of about $300 billion, much of it due to Lend-Lease, this country should insist on a major role in the peace settlement. He was not sanguine about relations with Russia, particularly as she would be pressing for territory in Europe and for increased political influence in Germany and France through their Communist parties.

Domestic postwar problems came under club scrutiny beginning with the visit of District Governor John P. Adler on October 18, 1943. He reported on a meeting of district governor candidates in St. Louis, Missouri, at which the responsibilities of Rotarians for economic planning, youth projects, and the employment and, as necessary, rehabilitation of returning servicemen had been emphasized. The local Rotarians assured Adler that several luncheon programs along the lines suggested already had been scheduled starting the next week.

On October 25 President Jacques announced the appointment of a postwar planning committee, and Northern's President Tape introduced a series of related talks with one on "Education and Its Importance in the Postwar World." W. D. Cochrane, head of the Cochrane Freight Lines based in Iron Mountain, on November 1 urged the Lions and Rotarians to engage at once in careful, imaginative planning throughout the Upper Peninsula, where wood, copper, and iron would soon encounter stiff competition from aluminum and synthetics in the manufacturing processes. He warned that at least fifty-four million Americans would have to be accommodated in the national labor market after hostilities ended.

The next week Ernest Pearce, counseling preparation for peace in time of war, called attention to efforts already under way by the federal government, municipalities, Rotary International, and other associations to insure a healthy economy and a minimum of unemployment. As Secretary Morgan Beckman paraphrased the speaker's words:

> . . . there must be a fifth freedom, the freedom of individual initiative and the political conception of private enterprise, namely, the American Way of Life. Initiative and freedom from dictatorship have enabled American industry to outproduce our enemies and if allowed to continue along that line American industry and business in general will solve the post war problems.

Pearce cautioned, however, that there must be "thrift *now* by individuals, corporations and by our government," implying that saving instead of feverish wartime competition for scarce commodities would both help combat inflation and provide purchasing power to satisfy the public's pent-up demand for an array of new articles and to keep employment high. Postwar prosperity would reduce the need for government welfare programs and for continued high taxes.

This cycle of programs on planning concluded with discussions by Miss Alice Snyder, superintendent of nurses at St. Luke's Hospital, of proposals for hospital expansion and for an increase in the number of graduate nurses, and by Victor Hurst, city recreational director and a physical education professor at Northern, of the necessity for new recreational facilities and improvement of the Palestra.

During the next two years Michigan's Governor Harry F. Kelly addressed a joint meeting of the Ishpeming, Munising, and Marquette Rotary clubs on the state's role in postwar planning, as did George Bishop, secretary-manager of the Upper Peninsula Development Bureau, before the Marquette group alone. Bishop reminded his audience that tourism was Michigan's second largest business. Soon after the end of hostilities a round table of eighteen panelists from the club and of two from outside it agreed that industrial reconversion posed no special problems for Marquette.

Early in 1945 the question of how to give the United Nations a permanent legal structure began to occupy the Rotarians. On January 15 Richard Current, Chase's replacement in Northern's history department, reasoned that peace in the world required populations that were "well fed, working, and fairly prosperous" and that "some uniting of nations" would be indispensable to that end. In July, Congressman Bennett, who had attended the San Francisco Conference at which the United Nations Charter had been adopted, discussed ratification. Toward the close of the year Rotarian Albert H. Burrows, professor of sociology and economics at Northern, perceiving a similarity between the fourth object of Rotary and the purposes of the Charter, urged the club to support it.

Meanwhile, Rotarian Edward L. Pearce, in banking with his father Ernest, explained on December 11, 1944, the extensive GI benefits which were becoming available. The club quickly realized that these could be of substantial aid to the people of Marquette at large. Although the city lost its bid for the Upper Peninsula Veterans' Administration Hospital, federal funds for the education of men and women returning from military duty were channeled through Northern in significant amounts. Secretary Callahan kept matters in perspective with his observation in the club minutes that while veterans "are entitled to every bit of help they may receive, it is a tragedy that all of it is necessary."

War Reminiscences

Having paid no official heed to such momentous events as D or V-J days or the atomic bombings of Hiroshima and Nagasaki, and having but hesitantly celebrated victory in Europe a day ahead of time, the Marquette Rotary Club nevertheless retained great interest in reports from returning warriors. By the end of 1945 three of the nine enlistees from the club had told of their experiences: Lt. L. W. "Ike" Brumm, who had been with the Seabees in the South Pacific; Cpl. Joe Hill, with Army ordinance; and Dr. Warren T. Lambert, Bronze Star winner, who, having had forty-one months of Marine Corps service, twenty-five of them abroad, talked about the lives and customs of the Japanese and responded to questions about the Iwo Jima campaign, in which he had been wounded. The secretary's account of Lambert's speech, given on December 31, contains the first reference to the atomic bomb.

Another speaker with a service background was Air Force Lt. Ralph Roberts of Marquette, who participated in many B-29 bomber missions in the Orient and told of bailing out twice over China. Navy Lt. Stanley E. Susan, also of this city, described the stringing of nets among the Gilbert and Mariana Islands to prevent enemy torpedoes from reaching their destinations, and his entertainment of natives and Navy personnel with magic shows. Willard M. Whitman, Jr., for four years a college teacher in Istanbul, Turkey, just before the war and an RAF flying instructor in Africa during it, recalled living conditions in the two areas and, particularly, the Turkish struggle to remain neutral. Several guests discussed their work in wartime intelligence.

The two grimmest narratives ever unfolded before the Marquette Rotary Club also came early in the postwar period. Dr. William C. Birch, an Army Medical Corps officer from Sault Ste. Marie, appeared on November 5, 1945. He had been stationed for six weeks at Buchenwald immediately after it was taken by the Allies. At that time it held eighty-one thousand prisoners of twenty-three nationalities and more than ten thousand unburied corpses. Records indicated that over one million persons had died there during its thirteen years in operation. Birch believed the German people well knew what was happening in the camp and after the war were sad about it, though not contrite.

Of an excruciatingly personal nature was the October 21, 1946, account by Rev. J. Carel Hamel, a Presbyterian missionary to the Orient, who with his wife had been interned by the Japanese. He held the members "spellbound while he related events we had all heard about but never expected to hear repeated firsthand."

The Marquette natives who emerged from the war with the most obvious distinction were Maj. Gen. Ralph Royce and Rear Adm. Clifford A. Swanson. Royce, a West Point graduate, addressed a combined meeting of the Rotary, Lions, and Kiwanis clubs on August 23, 1948. He talked mainly about his current employment as director of the Michigan Department of Economic Development and but briefly about his responsibilities as commander of thirteen bombers which made long-distance raids on Japanese bases in the Philippines during 1942.

Unlike Royce, who had spent much of his early life in Houghton, Swanson attended the Marquette public schools and was salutatorian of his high school class of 1918. He earned a bachelor's degree at Northern, was graduated from the University of Michigan medical school, and in 1925 was commissioned a lieutenant (jg.) in the

Maj. Gen. Ralph Royce

Rear Adm. Clifford A. Swanson

Navy Medical Corps. The Navy sent him to Harvard and the University of Pennsylvania for postgraduate training, and encouraged him to publish many professional articles.

By the outbreak of World War II, Swanson had become a noted bronchoscopist. His research on color and night vision and the effects of barometric pressure on the eye was a significant contribution to deep-sea diving and to the treatment of glaucoma. By the time of his first appearance before the Marquette Rotary Club in 1944 he had served on the battleship *Iowa* prior to becoming Secretary Knox's personal physician.[6] Through the years he had maintained his legal residence at 320 Harrison Street in Marquette.

On November 27, 1946, President Harry S. Truman named Swanson surgeon-general and chief of the Bureau of Medicine and Surgery in the Navy with the rank of rear admiral, succeeding Vice-Adm. Ross T. McIntyre. It was in this capacity that Swanson returned to speak at the annual dinner of the Marquette Chamber of Commerce on May 15, 1947. Marquette Mayor and Rotary past President James Beckman was toastmaster.

In his address Admiral Swanson discussed the future of the Navy against the setting of the recent war, emphasizing the importance of the Medical Corps in achieving victory. He noted that, by contrast, the medical failures of the Japanese had "militated catastrophically against them." Swanson revealed his breadth of concern in his remark that during the past year thirty thousand babies had been born in naval hospitals and, especially in his concluding passage, in which he conceived it his task

> to realize and maintain the highest standards of medical care attainable for the personnel of the Navy and to keep the Navy's medical corps in the keenest possible state of efficiency. Not with the primary or all-absorbing thought that the medical corps will be concerned solely with the long-heralded and somewhat provincial and cold-blooded functions of keeping as many men at as many guns as many days as possible, but that it may participate in the fullest measure among those agencies whose far more noble mission it is to make growth more perfect, decay less rapid, life more vigorous and death more remote.[7]

On November 29, 1948, the Marquette Rotary Club's board of directors elected Swanson to honorary membership. On June 20 of the next year, during a visit home, he spoke at a regular luncheon meeting on the Navy's contributions to medicine and on a trip he had made recently through the Pacific bases, Japan, the Aleutians, and over the North Pole. He affirmed his faith in democracy and in the ability of the Germans and Japanese to respond favorably to it.

A few weeks earlier, on May 23, 1949, Rotarian James Wright, pastor of the First Methodist Church, provided the club's epitaph for World War II when, according to the minutes, he "gave a wonderful address on the theme of Memorial Day." The essence of his message was that "we must all change our method [mode?] of living and moral standards if we are to have everlasting peace . . . [so] that those who lost their lives in the last war did not die in vain."

7
ANXIETY AND HOPE

The moral revolution which Wright and so many other Americans hoped the Atomic Age would inspire did not, perhaps could not, materialize. Although the first years of the postwar period lacked the boisterous innocence of the 1920s, the more than century-old faith in science and technology survived the shocking thought that for the first time in recorded history mankind might soon be able to obliterate itself.

That morbid idea already had been sublimated to the continuing beliefs that science and invention were, on balance, beneficent, and that man's best hope for universal peace and brotherhood lay in heightened material prosperity for everyone. Had not the same war which had facilitated development of The Bomb also hastened the marketing of new antibiotics, sulfa drugs, electronic devices, petrochemicals, and plastics, along with synthetic rubber and fibers? The peaceful applications of nuclear energy were conceived to be limitless.

Looking Ahead

The Marquette Rotary Club's traditional interest in material progress was reflected in its programs almost before the guns of the late war were silenced. On November 12, 1945, at a joint meeting of Rotarians and Kiwanians, Ben R. Marsh, a Michigan Bell Telephone Company official from Detroit, reviewed his firm's operations in the state and announced the investment of eight hundred thousand dollars over the next five years in a new building and dial phone system for Marquette. The next month a horticulturist presented facts about DDT and a new weed control chemical.

Then came a succession of programs on the improved treatment of polio, the distribution of motion picture films, continuing Red Cross needs, artificial insemination of livestock, job training for veterans, and air and rail transportation. In April of 1946 a speaker from Milwaukee described imminent improvements in home appliances, such as refrigerators and laundry equipment. He predicted that in the next year a quarter of all radio listeners would own television sets.

The approach of summer brought seasonal concern for tourism and highway safety. In July, Prof. Luther S. West of Northern, who had served in the Army as an entomologist, discussed tropical diseases and the future of the Army Medical Corps. The following January, Edward Bentzen of the Lake Shore Engineering Company, who was a member of a six-man committee to make an international study of labor-management relations, outlined some of the conflicting grievances. The next month, Michigan's Governor Kim Sigler discussed the essential unity of the two peninsulas of the state and the opportunities for much greater trade within it.

However, Marquette Rotarians did not become so absorbed in economic development and physical comfort that they neglected the broad spectrum of world affairs. Peacetime conscription became a live issue. Northern Prof. Harry B. Ebersole early in 1946 gave "a splendid talk on foreign relations" upon his return from seven weeks in Washington, where he was one of a hundred teachers from thirty states studying and listening to Congressmen and diplomats.

In June, 1947, the Rotary Club financed a two-day visit by Cedric Foster, a Boston journalist and Mutual Radio Network commentator. On Wednesday, the eighteenth, after having made his regular noon broadcast from WDMJ over four hundred stations nationally, he appeared at a specially adjourned meeting of the Rotarians. Denouncing communism as an ideological force sowing confusion and chaos wherever possible, he singled out education as the best means of combatting it. He stressed that teachers "can make your children loyal, devoted, patriotic citizens—or the opposite." He also warned that "labor and capital must find a common ground if we are to survive" as a free society.

That evening Foster addressed nearly fourteen hundred persons in Northern's Kaye Auditorium on "Communism in America." Contrasting "godless communism and the capitalistic system," he repeated much of what he had said in the afternoon, urged perpetuation of wartime unity among the Western powers and support of the United Nations with or without Russia, and lamented the decline of American military strength in Europe. He cautioned that Americans "are just as safe and secure with the atom bomb as the French were with the Maginot Line" and that, quoting Gen. Douglas MacArthur, in another great war "the white race will destroy itself, and the fragments will be picked up by the yellow, the black and the brown."

In his second noon broadcast the next day, Foster identified Marquette County as "one of the greatest iron producing centers of the world" and followed with a concise historical and statistical summary of its contributions. He noted that although the vast deposits of iron would be exhausted someday, new ways of processing low grade ore could delay the unhappy end. After a Marquette Chamber of Commerce luncheon, Foster concluded his stay with tours of the Cleveland-Cliffs Iron Company's underground Mather B mine in Negaunee and of several industrial plants in Marquette.[1]

Late in 1948 Senator-elect Karl Mundt of South Dakota also talked to the local Rotarians on foreign affairs. The next spring, Lt. Col. Ronald MacDonald of the Michigan Adjutant General's Department discussed the role of the National Guard and unification of the armed forces within the new federal Department of Defense.

Renewed Sociability

The austerity of the war years had kept recreational pursuits of the Marquette Rotarians at a minimum. In September, 1940, the directors had decided to permit some

Cedric Foster

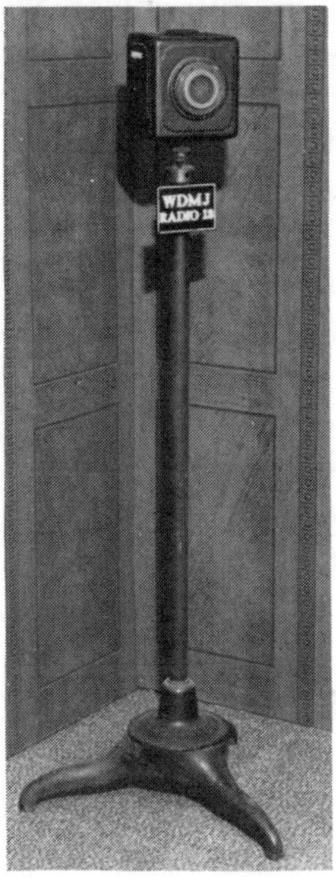

of them "to form a bowling team and bowl under the Rotarian name." This they did for the rest of the decade, briefly with two teams. Aside from a program of instrumental music given by Northern students, a Labor Day picnic in 1943, and two intercity meetings with the Ishpeming and Munising Rotary clubs in 1942 in Ishpeming and the next year in Munising, the only other significant relief from wartime cares came at Christmas.

In 1942 and 1943 Earl Closser presented several appropriate readings, then in 1944 read for the first time passages from Dickens' *Christmas Carol.* Three years later, as had Willard Whitman long before, he pleased the members with Henry van Dyke's *The Story of the Other Wise Man.* The rest of the decade's Christmas programs were musical. When president of the club, Closser in 1946 participated with thirteen other members of the Saturday Music Club in a rendition of the cantata *Child Jesus*, narrated by Arthur De Vries. The same organization provided another program two years later. In 1949 students from Graveraet High School performed under the direction of faculty member Joseph Patterson.

Toward the end of the war the Marquette Rotarians held their first Ladies Night since the club's twenty-fifth anniversary. Including the members of the Ishpeming Rotary Club and their Rotary Anns as guests, 220 persons attended a dinner party on June 25, 1945, in the Masonic Temple.

A simulated Rotary Wheel hub, the standard for an American flag, stood in the center of the room; tables decorated with blue candles and small flags extended outward as spokes. Upon entering, each Rotary Ann received a rose. A women's instrumental trio played during the meal. The two club presidents, W. J. Weber of Marquette and Wilbert H. "Waba" Treloar of Ishpeming, made the introductions, which included that of Samuel Cohodas. The latter was president-elect of the Ishpeming organization and was, like Treloar, a charter member of it.

After the amenities, jovial Ishpeming Rotarian Walter F. Gries, superintendent of the Cleveland-Cliffs welfare department and probably the Upper Peninsula's most popular and humorous after-dinner speaker at that time, shared his wisdom about "Women." What he had to say on this topic of unflagging male interest was not, unfortunately, recorded.

In a now thoroughly relaxed atmosphere, Weber introduced District Governor Robert A. Burns, and Harlow Clark presented William E. Wagener, a past district governor from Sturgeon Bay, Wisconsin, who addressed the group on "Symbols." "It is the spirit that counts," said Wagener. The essence of Rotary lay in "what the . . . spirit of Rotary does for the 'man inside himself.' " It was the superior moral, democratic strength of Americans which was enabling them to triumph militarily over the Germans, Italians, and Japanese.

Rotarians and Rotary Anns gave the rest of the evening to dancing or cards. Between dance numbers, according to the *Mining Journal*, "there were hilariously diverting hillbilly songs sung by Mrs. Munro L. Tibbets [*sic*], who played a concertina, and was accompanied by Horace Roberts, guitarist, and Glen Wilson, pianist, who also did some novelty piano numbers."[2]

Just nine days after the surrender of Japan the Ishpeming Rotary Club, reciprocating the hospitality of the Munising and Marquette Rotarians, invited them to a tri-city meeting on August 23, 1945, at the Wawonowin Country Club. Fifty-six men from Marquette joined the members from Munising and the host organization, as did representatives from the Escanaba, Iron Mountain, and Crystal Falls clubs. Samuel Fraser of Rochester, New York, secretary of the International Apple Association and a onetime teacher in Scotland, spoke on Washington and world affairs.

The three Rotary clubs of Marquette and Alger counties did not meet together again until January, 1947, when they dined in the St. Paul's Guild Hall in Marquette, witnessed a Marquette-Canadian Soo hockey game at the Palestra, and returned to the Guild Hall for hot chili and coffee.

The village of Big Bay on Monday, November 18, 1946, was the site of the first annual "deer hunters' roundup," held by the Marquette club to solve its attendance problem at the first meeting after the opening of hunting season. In 1947 women of Big Bay served a ham dinner in the recreation room of the school, whose faculty and students afterwards provided a variety program. The next year, meeting in a restaurant, the Rotarians had to eliminate their entertainment because the place was too crowded with other guests.

Giving

The Rotary Club's financial contributions had continued evenly throughout the war. During the fiscal year 1943-44 donations totaled $427 distributed among ten agencies; in 1945-46, $662 among fourteen. The largest sums, $150 each year, went to the Community Chest. The club sponsored a junior baseball team during the summer of 1946 only. Except in 1947, the Rotarians have contributed since 1938 to the expenses of local delegates to Wolverine Boys' State, a convention of high school youths which meets annually in a mock-up of Michigan's government.

In 1947-48 the Rotarians made a special grant to the Palestra's artificial ice rink fund, also another extraordinary gift of one thousand dollars to the Rotary Foundation in memory of Paul Harris. Through the decade the club paid annually for from five to eighteen subscriptions of *Revista Rotaria*, the Spanish language version of *The Rotarian.*

When the Marquette Rotarians, Kiwanians, and Lions hosted campaign workers for a Community Chest kick-off luncheon on October 22, 1945, at the Guild Hall, they resumed an annual practice which had been discontinued from 1942 through 1944. These meetings continued without interruption for the rest of the decade, there and at St. John's Catholic Church. In February, 1946, Ernest Pearce and Miss Mary Skeoch, superintendent of St. Luke's Hospital, successfully solicited a donation from the Rotarians during a special Red Cross drive to raise twenty-five thousand dollars in Marquette County.

For the first time since the establishment of the Ishpeming Rotary Club, the Marquette group in July of 1945 renewed financial support of the Bay Cliff Health Camp with a gift of one hundred dollars, which was to be repeated each of the next ten years. After their regular luncheon meeting on the thirtieth, most of the men drove to Big Bay for a tour of the Ford Motor Company plant and a visit to the children's facility to present the check. This was one of many calls made at the camp over the years.

The Uthrotar Movement

In the middle and late 1940s the club became more determined to interest high school boys in Rotary. Beginning with its meeting on September 18, 1944, it invited some to its weekly luncheons. From one to three at a time came at irregular intervals until the end of December, when the practice stopped. The year 1945 was notable in youth relations mostly for the appearance of the entire basketball squad and a Little German band of five students from Graveraet High School at two meetings in March.

On February 11, 1946, however, Carroll C. Rushton, Marquette County judge of probate and a member of the club's youth guidance committee, described a plan already approved by the board of directors to invite sixteen senior boys from Bishop Baraga, Graveraet, and John D. Pierce high schools, each lad to attend four of the next sixteen meetings. Between February 18 and June 3 seventeen boys made a total of thirty-seven appearances at fourteen sessions. The spring program reached its climax on June 17, when three student commencement speakers from Graveraet repeated their addresses on the theme—"Youth Looks at Peace"—before the Rotarians.

The local youth movement merged logically and easily with Uthrotar, a district-wide junior Rotary program begun in 1936 by Robert Burns with a nucleus of eight boys in Wakefield. When visiting Marquette in October, 1943, Governor Adler had urged the club to examine its possibilities. Now, in the summer of 1946, the Marquette Rotary Club sent two local boys as its official delegates to a Uthrotar summer camp at Clear Lake. One of them, Kenneth Nielsen, returned home as district governor of the organization.

On September 9 the two came before the club with founder Burns, who gave a brief history of the movement and expressed the hope that it would expand into a national and international project. Young Nielsen stated that Uthrotar's purpose was "to provide youth with opportunities for training in leadership, service and fellowship," then explained its operation and ways the club could support it.

Max P. Allen, a professor of history at Northern, became chairman of the club's youth service committee in October. On November 4 he notified the general membership that six Marquette Uthrotars would attend the luncheon meetings through the next May. They would sit together at the first and last of these, but would be scattered among the men the rest of the time. The boys would hold special evening meetings of their own at least once a month at the home of a Rotarian or another adult to hear vocational talks. On December 2 the board granted Uthrotar membership automatically to all sons of Rotarians who approved.

Through the spring of 1947 Uthrotar attendance at club meetings was surprisingly good. In January the Rotarians sent Governor Nielsen to a conference of his peers at Escanaba and in May paid his expenses and those of three other Marquette boys to the Uthrotar meeting held simultaneously with the district conference of Rotarians at Wausau, Wisconsin. Nor was there any lessening of enthusiasm during the next school year.

Looking ahead to the district conference and its Uthrotar adjunct soon to be held in Marquette, the local Rotarians gave their March 15, 1948, luncheon program to the boys' activities. Three out-of-town Rotary speakers, including Robert Burns, discussed the philosophy, organization, and functions of Uthrotar, also how other clubs were assisting it. Allyn Roberts, who had attended the Wisconsin meeting as a student from Marquette, offered "Impressions and Suggestions from a Uthrotar." During the eighteen months ending in June of 1948, thirty-two local boys paid 140 visits to forty-five Rotary luncheon meetings.

While the Rotarians and Rotary Anns assembled downtown for the annual conference for District 143 on June 13 and 14, 1948, seventy-six Uthrotars from twenty-four clubs registered at Northern Michigan College of Education. The boys then toured the campus and the Cliffs Dow Chemical Company plant and visited the Marquette branch prison before joining their sponsors for a fish dinner and a band and male choral concert at Presque Isle.

In general session the next morning, with their District Governor Kent Herath of Wausau in the chair, the Uthrotars were welcomed by Northern's President Tape and by Robert Burns prior to dividing into sectional meetings to view films and to participate in discussions led by Rotary faculty members. Rotarian C. V. "Red" Money, athletic director at Northern, spoke at the noon luncheon.

Former Governor Nielsen conducted the afternoon session, for which "The Future of Uthrotar" was the theme. There the delegates defined their aims: "to acquaint Rotary with youth and youth with Rotary" and to offer their membership vocational guidance. Norman Thomas of Marquette was chosen secretary for the coming year. In the evening the Uthrotars attended the Rotary district banquet at the Clifton Hotel, then enjoyed their own dance in the college gymnasium.[3]

Marquette's Second District Conference

As in 1930, the Rotarians registered at their headquarters in the Hotel Northland, where they were greeted by General Conference Chairman W. J. Weber, president of the Marquette-Alger County Credit Bureau; by club President E. J. "Pat" LaFreniere, who was president of the Marquette Board of Education and, as he had been for many years, a partner in the Morrison Audit Company; and by a gigantic reception committee chaired by Mrs. Carroll Rushton. Two hundred ninety-three Rotarians and 225 Rotary Anns, including 106 (a record high) of each from Marquette, represented forty-four clubs at the conference. Counting the Uthrotars, total attendance amounted to 594.[4]

After separate President's and Secretary's breakfasts at the Chalet and El Rancho restaurants early Monday morning, District Governor Paul T. Tobey of Wausau opened the conference at 9:30 in the Kaufman Auditorium. In the first of three major addresses during the day, Tobey established the theme for all: greater understanding "regardless of race, creed, color or station in life" as an important step toward world peace. He commented on each of the four aspects of service in Rotary, then observed:

> With the greatest telescopes man has perfected and with which he has mapped stars and planets millions of light years away, we still cannot reach the outer rim of space nor learn from whence we came nor where we are going.
>
> Why then is man so unduly puffed up that he spends the brief moment he has on earth in coveting his neighbors' riches and waging wars to acquire by conquest those things which will impoverish his fellowmen, yet those things which he cannot take with him when his time here is spent?[5]

Underscoring Tobey's remarks, Richard Vernor, treasurer of Rotary International, noted in the principal speech of the morning that through Rotary, "We have set up a chain of understanding." The *Mining Journal* paraphrased some of his remarks as follows:

> The greatest field before Rotary . . . is in human relations . . . management and labor will be closer together when industry understands that a job is a way of life, in addition to being a way of making a living.

The next paragraph quoted Vernor directly:

> We must remove class hatreds before we can achieve steadiness in industry, and this steadiness is needed if we are to prevent economic depressions. In turn we need economic stability as one of the strongest factors for peace.[6]

Vernor urged Rotarians individually to strive more earnestly for fulfillment of Rotary's principles.

Before adjournment Governor-elect Larry D. Randall of Iron Mountain was presented to the delegates. Thereafter they divided into four groups, each symbolizing one of the four aspects of Rotary service and, accordingly, lunched in three local churches and the Guild Hall.

Gregor Ziemer

In the afternoon foreign correspondent and radio commentator Gregor Ziemer addressed the Rotarians on "America Leads, Like It or Not." Ziemer began by identifying some of the many areas in which the United States was leading the world: living standards; education; freedom of religion and of the press; health; and physical power. This being true,

> Why don't we act as leaders? Why do we have that peculiar feeling of fright hanging over us, why do we act as if we are afraid, why do we waste so much thought—so many hours of fruitless effort—on things that are selfish and the opposite of the Rotary emblem of service?

The speaker called for a demonstration of Rotary leadership through promotion of international exchanges of teachers and students, praised Rotary's success in helping to solve domestic problems, and concluded:

> Perhaps Rotary and its members can become leaders again in helping to create in our country a new spirit. What a grand thing it would be if tomorrow morning every American would wake up with just a fraction more realization of what it means to be an American. . . . For, like it or not—America leads.[7]

The Rotary delegates held their business session late in the afternoon and in the evening attended their conference dinner at the Masonic Temple with the Rotary Anns and Uthrotars. Bergen Evans, professor of English at Northwestern University, identified the basic ingredients of humor in his address "On Being Funny." Following that, all moved to the Kaufman Auditorium for a stage show of psychic reading, sleight of hand, and general comedy. Then the Rotarians and their wives parted from the Uthrotars and congregated in the Adams Gymnasium for the closing Governor's ball.[8]

Aftermath

Perhaps both the Rotary district conference and an extremely successful mock political convention at Northern earlier in the spring contributed to a most unusual and refreshing burst of idealism and exuberance among some of the high school and college youths in and around Marquette. Whatever the reasons, three Marquette Rotary Club meetings in the late summer featured accounts of the vacation travels and accomplishments of several young people.

On August 30 Uthrotar James Leskee, whom the American Legion had sent to Wolverine Boys' State, related his experiences not only in Lansing, where he had been elected governor, but in Washington, D.C., to which he had traveled with the rare distinction of having been chosen one of Michigan's two boy senators as well. The club minutes referred to this as "one of the best programs we have had . . . this year."

Previously, at the July 19 meeting, Northern students George Liephart[9] and Donald Pangborn, both of Munising, told of hitchhiking to Philadelphia, where they had served as page boys at the Republican national nominating convention. Finally, recent high school graduates Jeannette Smith and Rita Underhill on September 20 described their eighty-five-hundred-mile trip by bicycle, train, and boat under the auspices of the American Youth Hostel. They had traveled from New England through Canada to the west coast, down into California, and back to their starting point.

By this time the Marquette Rotarians had reason to believe that their youth programs, directly or indirectly, were inspiring young people to accomplishment and were assisting in their character development. This impression should have been reinforced by the knowledge that Rotarians in other parts of the nation also were vigorously and successfully establishing close ties with the younger generation.

J. Cloyd Bowman had become affiliated in retirement with the St. Petersburg, Florida, Rotary Club, which through its boys' work committee had established in 1926 the first of thirteen service clubs for fifth and sixth grade boys in that city's grammar schools. Bowman described this "Four Square Club" movement in considerable detail in the December, 1948, issue of *The Rotarian*. He noted that after twenty-two years of gratifying operation, three of the boys had become members of the local Rotary club, none had ever been in trouble with the law, and the St. Petersburg example was being followed in other Florida communities.[10]

Why, then, did the Uthrotar movement in Marquette abruptly drop from sight following the 1948 district conference? It had engaged the interest of some excellent young men. Two of them were to become members of the local Rotary club—past President L. Wallace Bruce, a stockbroker, and Donald R. Elzinga, an orthopedic surgeon—though primarily because of parental ties to Rotary. Allyn Roberts, son of

Forest and Esther and today a clinical psychologist in Madison, Wisconsin, still fondly recalls his association with Uthrotar:

> I felt most honored, and the experience gave me a feeling of respect and friendship with some of the Marquette business leaders who previously had seemed remote and "on high." It was valuable for me to get a sense of how a service organization works. I believe our inclusion in the weekly noon meetings was of major significance for most of the boys who participated.[11]

Norman Thomas, a professor of political science at the University of Cincinnati, feels much the same: "I think my most positive experiences were getting to know better some of the leading business people in town. There were also pleasant acquaintances struck up with students at the two other high schools."[12]

No one now recalls precisely why the program so suddenly collapsed. One explanation is that Max Allen's increased duties as Northern's new director of instruction caused him to withdraw from active leadership and no one else from the club stepped forward to replace him. Thomas also suggests that after the 1948 conference there were no "creative or service projects to keep us going."

No boys attended the local Rotary meetings during the school year 1948-49, and the club records for that period contain only two references to Uthrotar—one suggesting that its future would be discussed with the district governor in February, the other stating that the club would send no Uthrotar delegates to the annual district conference in May.

Most puzzling is the fact that when Governor Randall addressed the local Rotarians, he spoke mainly about the general principles of Rotary, then "added his own ideas on the subject of delinquent children and the effect that so-called comic books, crime movies and crime stories on the radio are having on the children today." Apparently not a word about the positive, counteracting influence of programs like Uthrotar.

Marquette's Centennial Celebration

Another abortive club effort related to general community development. On January 27, 1947, Ernest Pearce, chairman of the civic improvement committee, distributed mimeographed copies of George Shiras's "18-point" plan of 1921 and conducted a panel discussion on a possible sequel to it. With Pearce, three other Rotarians comprised the panel—Marquette Mayor James Beckman; Gerald Bush, president of the Chamber of Commerce; and Frank J. Russell, Jr., grandson of Shiras, president of the Shiras Institute, and publisher of the *Mining Journal*.

Satisfied that the new program would not overlap or conflict with the work of the city's new planning board or the Chamber of Commerce, also that it would be received favorably by the public and, perhaps, by the Institute, the civic improvement committee recommended establishment of six subcommittees—city functional, city healthful, city hospitable, city cultural, city recreational, and city beautiful—each composed of five Rotarians and all to report to the club within six months.

Possibly for lack of provision in the 1947-48 budget, Pearce emphasized that a project "must not be one requiring a large expenditure of money" and advised that the members should "follow the policy of moving quietly in each endeavor, without making a lot of publicity over it." The club accepted the civic improvement committee's report and three weeks later extended the life of the subcommittees to June, 1948.

According to Rotarian R. Wesley Jenner,[13] both Pearce and Bush were motivated, in view of Marquette's sluggush economy and high unemployment, by a desire to have as many Rotarians as possible think about ways in which the city could be made a more attractive place in which to live and work.

The city beautiful subcommittee circulated a questionnaire asking club members to check on a list of twenty-seven proposals the five they regarded as most important. On March 24, 1947, W. J. Weber, chairman of that group, reported the preferences: 1) a comprehensive campaign to educate the whole citizenry on its responsibility for "making and maintaining . . . a beautiful community"; 2) "a program of protest against unsightly billboards at the approaches to the city"; 3) improvement of Shiras Park which would "rid it of the nuisances and increase its usefulness"; 4) improvement of the city's Dead River properties; and 5) "a paintup-cleanup program for the entire community through . . . publicity and prizes."[14]

Albert Burrows, chairman of the city functional subcommittee, on April 21 reported a combination outline-questionnaire of sixteen possibilities and, following newly established precedent, asked his fellow Rotarians to designate the five to which they wished to give highest priority. Included in this two-page document were proposals for an industrial survey and establishment of an industrial district; social, cultural, and leisure activities; publication of a brochure to advertise Marquette; establishment of an international relations institute; "a Dads' Citizenship Panel for children in need of a mature friend and counsellor"; erection of historical markers; construction of a World War II memorial community building, and study of the municipal assessment and tax structure.

The results of the survey are unrecorded as, indeed, are any activities in which the four remaining subcommittees engaged. When in July, 1947, the Shiras Institute contributed $130 toward payment of a bill for $143.60 incurred by the club for City Beautiful buttons, the Rotarians may have felt that they had been sent a message along with the check. Although a full complement of subcommitteemen was appointed through fiscal 1949-50, they may have concluded long before, particularly because of the two limitations Pearce had imposed on them in the first place, that they had been "had."

On the other hand, beginning in February of 1947, six of the nine men who were to serve on a new Marquette planning board during the four years necessary to produce its first major document were Rotarians: Jenner, Richard J. Barry, Norman Dobson, Lynn Halverson, Max Nunemaker, and George Smedman. Halverson succeeded Nunemaker as chairman after the latter declined reappointment.

The talented young city planning engineer, Harvard-educated George N. Skrubb,

Marquette Planning Board
Clockwise from lower left: R. W. Jenner (R),
M. W. Nunemaker (R), N. J. Dobson (R), R. J. Barry (R),
L. H. Halverson (R), G. N. Skrubb, G. J. Smedman (R).

working under the direction of the board, on October 20 gave the Rotary Club a progress report on the "master plan." Calling it "a blueprint of the Marquette of the future," he indicated that it would incorporate recommendations for five areas of operation, also a set of maps illustrating the city's needs for a decade to come. He appealed to the club, prominent among the 131 civic, religious, patriotic, service, and educational organizations in Marquette, for help in fashioning the document and implementing its recommendations.

The Marquette Centennial in July, 1949, helped to put the public in good humor for long-range community planning. Mayor L. W. Brumm was a Rotarian, as were City Commissioners William H. Schneider and Leo W. Bruce. Months in advance, club members joined most other men in a beard-growing contest and in selling season tickets for the main events.

Twelve to fifteen thousand people, many in nineteenth-century costume, on Friday, June 24, crowded into the downtown section for a pre-Centennial Promenade past gaily decorated store windows featuring artifacts dating from fifty to one hundred years before: photographs, plumbing fixtures, guns, pharmaceutical remnants, Gramophones, wearing apparel, business equipment including typewriters, and household utensils and furnishings. At the Rotarians' June 27 luncheon meeting, W. Kenyon Boyer,[15] son of the late Dr. Raymond Boyer, reviewed the history of Marquette and some of its business firms.

On the afternoon of Friday, July 1, the coast guard cutter *Mackinaw* came into the lower harbor, and a few hours later a crack Boy Scout drum and bugle corps arrived from Racine, Wisconsin. The Rotarians and Rotary Anns dined in Northern's Carey Hall, then adjourned to the Lee Hall ballroom where, under Rotary auspices, a Centennial Grand Costume Ball headed the schedule of events for the next three days.

At nine o'clock the next morning a mock aerial bombardment and the blowing of whistles and ringing of church bells constituted an "opening salute." "Keystone Cops" from the Junior Chamber of Commerce brought beardless men to "justice" before a kangaroo court. From then until 10:30 Monday night, crowds aggregating fifteen thousand daily participated in or witnessed a wide range of events: baseball games, a pistol shoot at the prison, a children's treasure hunt at Presque Isle, vaudeville shows throughout most of each day, a junior costume ball sponsored by the Lions Club at the Palestra, religious observances (Sunday was designated Bishop Frederic Baraga Day in memory of the saintly nineteenth-century Catholic missionary), boat races, an aquatic exhibition, a scenic trip to Big Bay, the judging of beards and costumes, band and drum and bugle corps concerts, the Centennial Parade on the morning of July Fourth, and, that night, fireworks concluding the celebration. In the whole history of Marquette this outburst of civic joy and pride stands unrivaled.[16]

Marquette Centennial Rotary Costume Dinner. Lottie and Robert Clark, great-grandson of Amos R. Harlow, a principal town founder, are in the foreground.

City Planning and Charter Revision

In the aftermath, the city's Rotary and other planners carefully and thoughtfully continued their deliberations. They held numerous meetings with city and school officials and with citizens of all ages. On July 18, 1949, George Skrubb appeared again at Rotary and with the aid of maps explained a new zoning ordinance.

On June 12, 1950, the Rotarians were invited to lunch at the new St. Michael grade school. There Msgr. Joseph Zryd discussed the problems of parochial schools and commented on the attractions of the building before taking the members on a tour of it. Clearly this meeting was to remind the city planners, as they surveyed public school requirements, that the Catholic portion of the community was continuing to make a substantial contribution to the education of Marquette children and youths.

Other interested persons addressed the club on how they believed the city should progress. In September, 1950, Willard Whitman stressed the need for more public elementary schools and at least an addition to Graveraet High School. Already Dr. Bernard Micklow had been chosen a Rotary representative on a citizens' committee to consider a new senior high building, and before the year's end faculty member Carl Bullock showed the Rotarians a film underscoring the pressures on existing facilities. By then the board of education was thinking of a two-million-dollar bond issue for school construction.

Early in 1951 Rotarian Claude Mosher, superintendent of the city's electric department, made a case for increased generating capacity, and Miss Phyllis S. Rankin, head of the Peter White Library, discussed its value and distributed copies of its annual report.

The final Marquette city plan[17] appeared in July, 1951, a little more than a month after Halverson, Allen, and Jenner had outlined it for the Rotary Club. Two chapters devoted to historical and population studies were followed by five on residential and neighborhood, recreational, industrial and commercial, transportation, and school and civic planning. A summary of city expenditures for the previous decade, zoning, and general conclusions rounded out the document.

A total capital outlay of $5,500,000, of which $2,000,000 would go for school construction and much of the rest to a sewage disposal plant, storm sewer system, street paving and repair, and to expansion of library, light, and power facilities, was recommended.

The most unique feature of the plan stemmed from a contest in which more than five hundred of the city's high school students, in March, 1948, had written essays on future community needs. The equivalent of a paragraph from each of twenty-five of these was quoted to illustrate "the type of suggestions that came naturally from the community."

The *Mining Journal* for October 6, 1951, praised the document as one containing "what every well-informed Marquette citizen should know." The paper continued:

> The board has taken a realistic approach to the city's planning problem and . . . every conscientious citizen who takes the time to read "Marquette, Michigan: City Plan" will set it down with a vastly improved understanding of his city and what is in store for it. (unnumbered front page)

Publication of the city plan occurred shortly after the voters approved a new municipal charter for Marquette in the fall of 1951. Among the nine men chosen in April, 1950, to revise the old one, six were Rotarians: Lincoln Frazier, Frank Russell, Jr., and Bernard L. York along with Allen and city planners Halverson and Jenner. York became the first mayor under the modernized instrument.

The charter and plan together constitute the supreme intellectual contribution of Marquette Rotarians, ten of them under official charge, to the governmental structure and orderly growth of the city. Inherent limitations preclude any charter's gaining fame as a literary masterpiece. It is sufficient praise for this one to say that when allowances are made for the passage of time and for the inability of anyone to have anticipated certain changes in state laws, also vicissitudes in the life of the town, it has served the people well for thirty years.

8
PROGRAMMED OPERATION

For a brief time after 1945 the United States, with its monopoly of atomic weapons, stood alone as the world's first super power. However, instead of exploiting its advantage by pressing on to Moscow as more bellicose citizens urged, the nation dismantled much of its conventional military apparatus and turned to the reconstruction of Europe and Japan and to promotion of international cooperation and peace.

The dawn of the Space Age ended American impregnability against attack. Neither land nor sea barriers could longer protect any nation from thermonuclear bombs and long-range missiles. Moreover, war, now fully industrialized, had become stripped of human and moral considerations. The Nazis had systematically exterminated four million European Jews by 1945. In the same year two American A-bombs wiped out 120,000 to 275,000 Japanese, civilian and military. In each case the justification was "necessity."

Small wonder that by the late forties, as Gregor Ziemer indicated, the United States was acting like an uncertain giant, inclined neither to lead nor to bludgeon. Beyond basic cultural ties with western Europe and the British empire, also with the newly-formed state of Israel, Americans continued to distinguish friend from foe according to economic importance and to the territorial propinquity of small satellite nations, whatever their ideologies or political systems. In Korea and Vietnam, where all was fluid and elusive, imaginary latitudinal lines alone were to suffice. Norman Cousins, editor of *The Saturday Review*, perceived a cumulative effect of ethical confusion when in the spring of 1952 he reported to a Marquette audience the feeling of American soldiers he had visited in Korea that they somehow were not "connected up" with the folks back home.

Depersonalization and mechanization, or, more precisely, homogenization, also were becoming characteristic of peacetime America. Limitations imposed by the great institutions of business, labor, agriculture, education, and government; by a vast network of transportation and communications systems; and by nationwide standardization of taste and behavior were replacing the old restrictions of nature, immediate economic necessity, religious beliefs, and powerful individuals and elite groups. Escape was impossible, although people had become so physically restless that since the fifties one of every six or seven employed persons in the United States has been directly or indirectly involved in motor transport.

Largely ignored were the danger signals raised by increasing population pressure upon the natural resources not only of the United States but of the free and nonaligned nations elsewhere, by perpetually growing indebtedness, and by an insidious but relentless air, water, and soil pollution, not to mention a debasement of language and taste. George Orwell's *Nineteen Eighty-four*, Rachel Carson's *The Silent Spring*, David Riesman's *The Lonely Crowd*, and Al Capp's comic strip, "Li'l Abner," were widely read, but their messages seldom heeded. The public shrank from moral options without realizing that failure to choose was itself a choice.

In the Upper Peninsula social and economic change lagged behind that in the rest of the country. The federal census showed that the region's population, down to 302,258 in 1950, rose but slightly to 305,952 in 1960. There were losses in ten of the fifteen counties; the only gains of consequence were in the county and city of Marquette. Here continuing employment declines in mining, lumbering, and supporting enterprises were offset by expansions in construction, service industries, and government. Although Marquette went from 17,202 to 19,824 inhabitants during the decade, its growth rate was considerably below the national average. Most of the peninsula remained essentially wilderness and economically depressed.

Even in Marquette traces of frontier existence persisted into the early fifties. Wood-burning stoves, home deliveries of ice, and horse-drawn milk wagons were yet common. Oil was supplanting coal as residential fuel, but natural gas did not become available until 1966. Dial telephones arrived in January, 1955; local television station WLUC, a year later. Commercial airline service started in 1949, but nothing like a modern air terminal was built for another eight years. This came shortly before the Duluth, South Shore & Atlantic Railroad, after more than a century of passenger service to Marquette, discontinued its remaining train No. 1. Not until the winter of 1958-59, when a four-lane divided highway was completed to Negaunee, can it be said that the area was perceptibly tinged with big city appearance.

Patriarchs and Neophytes

That Marquette was slow to experience the full impact of scientific and technological advances does not mean that its social outlook was unaffected. Here, too, the scale was tipping from rugged individualism to life adjustment, among Rotarians no less than among the townspeople generally.

Members of the Marquette Rotary Club simultaneously were shifting their interest from the mechanical innovation and invention which had intrigued Austin Farrell, Maxwell Reynolds, and other associates in times past; also from creative speculations of the kind which had inspired George Shiras to do so much for the cultural enrichment of the city. The task of second generation Rotarians was not to establish family names and enterprises, but to perpetuate them. Like Americans similarly situated everywhere, they were perfecting their managerial skills and techniques of friendly persuasion, particularly as these might induce investment of outside money and talent in Marquette commercial and industrial ventures and in public improvements.

Never has the Rotary Club had so large and distinguished a nucleus of patriarchs as, despite attrition through death, during the 1950s. In July, 1951, the number of honorary members stood at three: Adm. Clifford Swanson, Elmer Jones, and Russell E. Horwood. Within the next five years these men were joined by nine more: charter member Joseph Gannon, Percy G. Teeple, Arthur K. Bennett, Reynolds, Whitman, Ed Wilmers, Harlow Clark, Parker, and Tape. Ernest Pearce preferred senior active to honorary classification. Several of the honorees died soon after election: Reynolds and Parker in 1952 and Jones, Whitman, and Clark in 1955.

Nearly a dozen of the club's aging members had joined before 1926; others had entered late in life. The most casual visitor could not help noticing their presence—Edward Bice, Samuel Buck, Frederick Burrall, Charles Drury, Charles B. Hedgcock, August Syverson, Teeple—all sitting with a "revolving fund" of younger men at a long table placed at a right angle to the left of the officers and speakers in the Clifton dining room. Pearce and a half dozen others anchored or distributed themselves among the group at large.

Samuel H. Buck

The June 28, 1954, meeting was given entirely to the eulogizing of "Doc" Buck for his thirty years of perfect attendance. The district governor and governor-elect and the president and president-elect of the Ishpeming Rotary Club were present for the ceremony in which Buck received a thirty-year attendance pin and a testimonial album with greetings from every club in the district. All local Rotarians were invited to autograph it.

When in 1965 the club shifted its meetings to the L-shaped room in the basement of the Northland, where only tables for four were available, the oldest members lost their cohesiveness. However, Buck and Syverson still sat together week after week; both remained peppery well into their eighties. (One noon Buck dismissed rock and roll with a snort—"whorehouse music.") On January 4, 1965, Buck was accorded honorary membership in recognition of his forty-one years of perfect attendance and his many services to the club throughout. Since joining in 1920 he had missed one meeting, in May of 1924. Even this absence was never noted, perhaps because, according to legend, the session was adjourned to his hospital bed in an attempt to keep his record intact.

New members continued to be introduced to the club at the first meeting they attended, and were formally inducted later by Closser, Emery Jacques, James Wilson, or W. H. Treloar. Biographical sketches came before or after at intervals. On December 30, 1963, when the unusually large number of ten new members had accumulated, past Presidents Don Pearce, Robert Ling, Closser, and Treloar spoke, respectively, on what International, Community, Vocational, and Club service meant to him.

Perpetuating Tradition

Still striving for identification with a larger circle of Rotarians, the Marquette, Ishpeming, and Munising men continued for a time to hold annual tri-city meetings—on Grand Island, at the Marquette Golf and Country Club, and at Ishpeming's Mather Inn. The year 1951 was exceptional in that two meetings took place that spring and summer. In May, Gene Ronzani, head coach of the Green Bay Packers, spoke to the group in Munising. Three months later, representatives from Manistique, Gladstone, and Escanaba joined their neighbors for an outing at Grand Island, as they had not done for many years.

The latter meeting prepared the ground for an intercity assembly on Thursday, July 31, 1952, at the Marquette Golf Club. Early in the morning District Governor Ralph M. Reece of Menomonie, Wisconsin, met with two dozen officers, directors, and committeemen for a club assembly in the lounge of the Union National Bank. After that, 173 Rotarians from eleven Upper Peninsula clubs participated in golf matches; boat trips on the Reynolds-Frazier yacht, *Yankee Girl*; tours of the prison; and a dinner meeting at the clubhouse. This gathering was the last of its kind during the fifties. Representation from outside the host club had been small, and the minority of zealous cooperationists were unable to sustain the momentum.

The toastmaster at this concluding 1952 dinner was W. H. "Waba" Treloar. Although a native of Marquette, where he had lived throughout his youth, Treloar during the 1930s and early 1940s had been manager of the Ishpeming and Negaunee news bureau of the *Mining Journal*. After reassignment to the main office, where he eventually became general manager and publisher of the paper, Treloar transferred from the Ishpeming to the Marquette Rotary Club in February of 1947. His first talk, in observance of the old Armistice Day on November 11, was on "Freedom of the Press."

Since his return to Marquette, Treloar has been involved in almost every phase of Rotary's functions. At the regular weekly meetings he has been a fixture. Late in 1950 or early in 1951 he started giving five-minute newscasts. These received instant acclaim and were at once incorporated into the meeting schedule: prayer, "America," the Pledge of Allegiance, introduction of guests, songs, announcements and business—"and now Waba with the news." No speaker, panelist, or entertainer could ask for a more stimulating warm-up.

During the first few months of 1951 a lively repartee developed between Treloar and Frazier. As noted in The ROTATOR for June 11, "The running battle of words heard each Monday between Linc Frazier, program chairman, and Waba Treloar, newscaster, increases in interest." In 1952 and 1953, when the latter had greater program responsibilities, the two men shared the news spot, but since then the journalist has had the field to himself.

Following Lew Chase's retirement and final departure to California, he sent a wire recording of one more summary of world events, for the year 1948. Although this was greeted nostalgically, the transcribed voice was no substitute for the man. After a lapse of three years Treloar provided the digest for 1951. Then Richard F. O'Dell of Northern's history department gave the annual two-part summaries for twelve of the thirteen years they were scheduled between 1953 and 1969. On the other occasion, in 1967, Treloar and he shared the podium. Since 1971, when O'Dell left the club after a decade of membership, Treloar has delivered the yearly along with the weekly summations.

Like Treloar, with whom he often competed in storytelling, Closser engaged in a great many club activities. While Louis Hildebrand, T. Ray Uhlinger, William E. Wright (son of William S.), Pat LaFreniere, or he himself led in song, Closser played the piano in the manner of one accustomed to a less sedate setting. A straw hat, elastic armbands prominent above the elbows, and a stein atop his instrument were the only things lacking for this otherwise compleat honky-tonk performer.

It was Closser who in 1963 complained to President Fred Sabin that if the piano were not tuned by the next meeting, he would resign his position as accompanist. It was probably he, too, who suggested a few weeks earlier that the club sing "Jingle Bells" before adjourning right after lunch due to 100-degree heat.

Closser by exhortation and example perpetually urged club members to become more personally involved in service projects. He was one, along with Leonard Smith, Richard Barry, Ben Knauss, Carl Martin, and Vern Holgate, who took on the thankless job of producing the weekly ROTATOR. More than that, when he was chairman of the magazine committee, Closser gave his own five-minute talks, monthly, on articles in *The Rotarian*.

These are among the vivid memories of contemporary Rotarians for whom the fifties were "the good old days," even with annual dues increases from sixty-five to seventy-two dollars in 1952 and from ninety-two to $112 in 1965.

Even though developed around a single theme, the Christmas programs of the Marquette Rotary Club by their very nature have afforded greater variety in cast and character than have the reviews of secular happenings.

In December, 1950, a group of Graveraet High School students presented the second act of *The Birds' Christmas Carol.* Two years later Willard Whitman, appearing for the last time, "held the entire group spellbound with his superb and moving" rendition of "the Birth of the Christ Child." From 1953 through 1960 Ray Uhlinger, who in the forties had become a member of Northern's faculty and of the Rotary Club, directed the Collegiate Chorale in musical selections at the first or second meeting of the final month.

In 1953 Earl Closser gave a Christmas reading. The next year, he chose passages from Lew Wallace's *Ben Hur*, then followed in 1955 with his own abbreviated version of Dickens' *Christmas Carol.* Except for departures in 1959 and 1961, the first of them for Dylan Thomas's "A Child's Christmas in Wales," Closser until his death in 1974 stayed with his immensely popular condensation of the Dickens work. In this he recreated, through voice and manner, all the characters.

Fun and Games

Rotary Club deer hunters who went west of Marquette continued to have their November roundups at Big Bay throughout the fifties, while those who traveled east congregated sporadically at Atono, a revamped lumber camp near Deerton owned by men both in and out of the club. From six to a dozen Rotarians frequented this place, whereas the Big Bay meetings sometimes attracted twenty-five or more members and guests—at St. Mary's Church in 1951 and at the Big Bay Lodge for the next several years.

An almost simultaneous practice, from 1952 to 1962, was the holding of annual breakfasts in May or June at the Marquette Golf and Country Club. Despite lowered attendance due to distance and the serving time of 7:30, these were treated as regular meetings. Guest speakers sometimes forgot that the men were not ready for heavy intelectual or spiritual fare so early in the day.

The Rotary board of directors continued to meet monthly right after lunch on Monday or at a dinner meeting the same night in the Clifton or the Northland. New and old officers and board members were entertained annually at a member's camp or, occasionally, at Atono. This was also the site for several fellowship parties and for at least one club assembly with a district governor, although the customary place for the latter was the Union National Bank lounge or a room at the Northland.

On Labor Day of 1953 about fifty Rotarians and guests enjoyed outdoor sport and a barbecue at Camp Atono. Fortuitously, after the cycle of recreational meetings there had run its course, the Huron Mountain Club, through the good offices of Marquette Rotarian William A. Todd, extended its hospitality to the group for a regular luncheon meeting each or every other spring.

Ladies Nights always have been highlights of the Rotary Club's social seasons. In the early 1950s two of these featured a Lawrence College student, whose illustrated talk on his travels through "Lilliputia," the smallest principalities in Europe, was so enjoyed that he was invited to give another on Spain. At the 1954 party a visiting Rotary Fellow described life in Scotland as she had witnessed it. Clowns entertained at the following two. After a lapse of several years, the festivities resumed in 1962. The most unique in the new series involved an excursion to Big Bay on the Marquette and Huron Mountain Railroad in July of 1964.

There also were lighter programs at the regular weekly meetings. Students from the Marquette and John D. Pierce high schools provided dramatic readings and sketches. Vocalists from the Saturday Music Club continued to perform, as did the Collegiate Chorale and instrumentalists from Northern. The Howard Junior High School boys' glee club entertained on two occasions. Without question, the most famous musician ever to demonstrate his talent before the club was David Rubinoff,

RELAXING AT
CAMP ATONO

Left to right: Robert Ling, Robert Jean, Jack Ziegler, Edward Stratton, Ray Nelson, Fred Sabin, Earl Closser.

An Informal Board Meeting

David Rubinoff chats with Warden Emery E. Jacques (left) and Rev. Arthur C. De Vries (right) after entertaining prison inmates. Alexander Makofka is at the far right.

by whom, with his "magic violin" and his accompanist, Alexander Makofka, "a very interesting and beautiful program was rendered" on May 21, 1951.

Within a two-year span, three Walt Disney programs were arranged for the group. Through the courtesy of the Northern Dairy Company, Clarence Nash of Glendale, California, the "voice of Donald Duck," in June, 1953, exhibited his skill via a model of the "lovable" cartoon character. Dr. Ernest Nichol, who gave up medical practice to become a whistler for Disney films and whose parents were from the Upper Peninsula,[1] on November 30 gave "a most fascinating series of well-known musical selections and bird imitations, including the canary, thrush, meadowlark and many others." Two Disney films were shown at a meeting in 1955.

Local speakers dealt with many cultural themes. Uhlinger discussed his work at

LADIES NIGHT 1962

Clockwise from left: Gerald and Virginia Grundstrom, Lincoln and Anne Frazier, Roy and Helen Fletcher.

Left to right: Anne Heath, Beatrice McKichan, Roy Heath, Amy Hecox, Muriel Closser. Les Corey (standing) in background.

the National Music Camp at Interlochen, Michigan. Mrs. Abby Beecher Roberts reminisced about her early life in Marquette and the Upper Peninsula. James L. Rapport of Northern's speech and drama department compared classical and modern plays. Mrs. Robert E. (Shirley) Moore stimulated the member's interest in nineteenth-century naturalist Henry Rowe Schoolcraft. Mrs. George Spear, Jr., related the history of the Lake Superior Creative Arts Association.

Northern ornithologist Rollin Thoren, with appropriate visual aids including some of the equipment originally used, analyzed the photography of George Shiras who, according to the minutes, "was once a member of this club." Displaying his characteristic genius for enlivening his talks, Thoren suddenly "set off an early model flash gun, which startled the members and filled the room with smoke."

Many local Rotarians were golfers, some of them excellent, and were devoted members of the Marquette Golf and Country Club, but Rotary talks seldom featured golf, other summer sports, or hunting. Early in 1950 the club did witness a film on professional baseball's 1949 World Series. Four years later Robert Brebner showed a Remington Arms Company film titled *Gunning the Flyway*, on the hunting of water fowl. In August, 1963, he also gave an illustrated account of his participation in a recent Chicago to Mackinac yacht race. Morgan Gingrass, Marquette's recreation director, in 1957 discussed the city's plans and activities in this field.

One of the Upper Peninsula's most proficient and versatile athletes, "Muggs" Gingrass thought first of becoming a professional hockey player, but while a collegian at Northern, North Carolina State, and Michigan State was drawn to football. In his first season as a halfback with the Detroit Lions (1942), injury forced his retirement from that sport. Following graduation from Northern, Gingrass played semiprofessional baseball downstate and years later, in 1973, won the U.P. senior men's golf championship. During two decades with the U.P. Office Supply Company, he became the firm's senior partner. He is a longtime member and past president of the Marquette Rotary Club.

Most of the sports presentations concentrated on football, basketball, skiing, and ice hockey. Over the years several Northern football coaches—Money, Lloyd Eaton, F. L. "Frosty" Ferzacca and his assistants, Burt Gustafson and Roland Dotsch—offered previews and postmortems on the "Wildcats'" fall seasons. Gustafson and Dotsch went on to become assistant coaches for the Green Bay Packers. The latter now is with the Pittsburgh Steelers; Gustafson and Eaton are Packer scouts. In the early 1960s Northern basketball coach Stan Albeck gave accounts of his teams. He has lately been head coach of the San Antonio Spurs.

In 1949 Joe Perrault of Ishpeming, the national Class A ski jumping champion, "gave a very interesting talk on the Olympics and the various hills he had competed on." At the same meeting a fellow townsman, Class B champion Clarence Rasmussen, also spoke. Brebner in 1955 showed a Swiss National Ski Association film. Brebner, Roy Fletcher, Jr., William Anderson, and others participated in programs relating specifically to the Cliffs Ridge Ski Area south of the city.

Members of the Marquette Sentinels professional hockey team were guests of the club in 1956. Five years later Weldon "Weldy" Olson of Marquette, an Olympic gold medal winner as a member of the champion U.S. hockey team of 1960, described its training at Squaw Valley and progress toward ultimate triumph over Soviet Russia's best.

To Geneva and Beyond

It may have been more than a coincidence that most of the Rotarians' emphasis on sociability came before the Eisenhower-Khrushchev summit meeting in 1955 at Geneva, after which the postwar pall on Soviet-American relations lifted somewhat. Until then the cold war, with its profound suspicions, also the Korean conflict and McCarthyism, affected Marquette no less than the rest of grassroots America by encouraging much thought and planning for civil defense and even experimentation with bomb shelters. Some lightheartedness was essential in this otherwise grim period.

In any year, however, most of the Rotary Club's programs dealt with serious business. Particularly grave were those presented by a distinctive group of newcomers to the town and Upper Peninsula—European wartime and postwar refugees or "displaced persons."

In the spring of 1949 Fr. David Spelgatti, who had charge of the facilities of the Catholic Diocese of Marquette to aid these people, traced the passage of congressional legislation permitting their entry and regulating their relocation. He stated that at the time seventeen of them were in the peninsula. Over the next four years an Estonian, a Finn, and a Ukranian resident of Poland, all of whom had been caught up by the Russian invasions of their countries, related their hardships while living in, and escaping from, occupied areas.

Their message was the same. People who have lost or who have never known personal freedom are unusually appreciative when they achieve it. In April, 1962, Fr. Wilbur M. Gibbs spoke to the Rotarians about the unaccompanied children coming to the United States from Cuba every day, most of them from middle-class families. He talked of the approximately twenty teenage boys of this description at the local orphanage. About twelve of them were guests of the club that day, and one, speaking for the rest, told why they had left Cuba.

The Korean War years were the most anxious. Congressman John Bennett addressed the Rotary Club on the conflict's relationship to defense and the national budget. Gunther Meyland, local director of civilian defense, informed the members that Marquette was one of three crucial Michigan targets for atomic bomb attacks. The now Lt. Col. Stanley Long was one of three military men to relate their battle experiences. William J. Grede of Milwaukee, president of the National Association of Manufacturers, worried that complacency could lead to inflation, communism, and dictatorship in the United States.

The peaceful applications of atomic energy along with the possibly deleterious effects of bomb tests in the American West furnished material for several programs on radiation. Lincoln Frazier in 1952 suggested that extremely small amounts of uranium might soon heat homes and power planes in flights around the world. In the summer of 1955 a Michigan National Guard officer, in "one of the most popular programs we have ever had," showed color slides of test blasts in Nevada. Shortly after, meteorologist Laurel Dahlin assured the Rotarians that atomic bomb explosions had negligible effects on the weather and that two of them would be required to release as much energy as the sun bestowed upon one square mile in Nevada in a day.

The Rotary Club members were intensely interested in the establishment in 1957 of the K. I. Sawyer Air Force Base in Sands Township south of Marquette, in relocation of the county airport to its former site between Marquette and Negaunee, and in the social and economic effects of these developments. In April of 1955 Earl Closser noted as a realtor that Marquette and its environs should anticipate a fifteen percent increase in population and a need for one hundred new housing units annually over the next three years in order to accommodate 250 officers and their families.

The first base commander, Lt. Col. Robert L. Brockelhurst, joined the Marquette Rotary Club in January, 1956, and kept the members informed of construction progress. On August 19, 1957, Brig. Gen. W. H. Wise, the commander at Truax Field in Wisconsin with jurisdiction over Sawyer and several other installations in the Midwest, spoke on "Air Defense" and the wisdom of military-civilian cooperation for the sake of national survival.

In 1960 Gen. Harold Humfield, commander of the 40th Air Division, addressed a joint meeting of local service clubs on "Peace Insurance," as he termed the work of the Strategic Air Command. The next year, Col. Leon H. Berger, Semi-Automatic Ground Environment (SAGE) commander at the Sawyer base, "gave a very frank

Airmen at the K. I. Sawyer Air Force Base

talk on atomic bombs" and their effects, "and it doesn't present a very comforting picture"—so the Rotary minutes read.

In another program dealing with defense, the Rotarians in the summer of 1959 toured the U.S.S. *Warrington*, a destroyer anchored in the lower harbor, and heard a lecture on the importance of the Navy. The launching of Russia's earth satellite "Sputnik 1" in 1957 persuaded U.S. Sen. Charles Potter of Michigan to report to the club the next spring on America's effort to catch up. In 1963 the Rotarians were delighted by a color film on Col. John Glenn's orbital flight in "Friendship 7."

Programs emphasizing hopes and strategies for peace were few. In July of 1950 Mrs. Chase S. Osborn, widow of Michigan's only governor from the Upper Peninsula, asked the Marquette Rotary Club to address a resolution to Congress requesting a meeting of Atlantic Pact nations to organize an Atlantic Union. Nonplussed, the board decided to follow protocol and write Rotary International for advice.

Rev. James Wright observed Armistice Day in 1951 with one of his most eloquent talks to his fellow Rotarians. Agreeing that appeasement of Russia anywhere would be "sheer folly," he nevertheless stressed the importance of unceasing efforts for peace and the spread of democracy "even though the theme of world affairs seems to be war and preparation for war." Science, education and culture were not enough to guarantee peace, for with all of these Germany came to resemble Mirabeau's perceived flaw in Napoleonic France—"not a nation with an army, but an army with a nation." Atomic bombs could not halt communism; freedom could.

Speakers from within and outside the Marquette Rotary Club returned from extensive stays or travels abroad with most interesting reports on the lives and problems of peoples almost everywhere in the non-Communist world. Lecturers divided into three groups—men whose business or professional careers encouraged travel, persons who had lived for many years in foreign lands, and tourists.

In the first category was local Rotarian Russell E. Horwood, who in 1949 talked about Japan as he had come to know it while with the then Michigan State College agricultural research and extension service following World War II. In 1953 he again addressed the club after having spent two intervening years helping to establish the University of the Ryukyus. He stated that the Japanese had completely dominated the islanders for so many centuries and had "so stifled their initiative and capacity for leadership that they were practically incapable of self-government." Even so, he insisted that Americans "must work *with* rather than do something *to* these people," a dictum he applied to relations with all similarly situated folk.

Northern's Luther West in 1953 described his tour of the Mediterranean under United Nations auspices to promote insect control. Guest Rotarian F. Albee Flodin, president of the Lake Shore Engineering Company, and the club's own Max Nunemaker noted after trips to Europe such phenomena as business climate, labor costs, and devaluation of the British pound sterling. Henry St. Onge, a former Marquette Rotarian who had become a Far Eastern representative of the Harnischfager Corporation, in 1956 recalled time spent in the sixteen countries comprising his territory.

In 1952 Mrs. Earl (Miriam) Hilton of Marquette, who had been born in Iran to

American missionaries, "gave very interesting word pictures of the exciting life [there] . . . both political and religious." In that year also, a former State Department employee, Elisha Greifer of Ishpeming, reviewed conditions in Germany and events leading up to them. Willard Whitman, Jr., who had returned to Roberts College in Istanbul after the second world conflict, during two visits home in 1956 and 1960 described conditions in Turkey. In the late 1950s Miodrag Georgevich, a native of Yugoslavia and a political scientist at Northern, appraised the Tito regime and on a second occasion talked about the United Nations.

Rotarian Ferdinand Friedensburg IV, a German diplomat stationed in Detroit, in two appearances expressed his conviction that Germany was America's greatest ally in Europe. In 1958 Lt. Gov. Philip A. Hart spoke to the club on the role of the United Nations as the guardian of world peace. Three years later the now U.S. Sen. Hart addressed a joint meeting of the Marquette service clubs on Africa.

Local Catholic priests and Protestant clergymen also contributed to the Rotarians' understanding of postwar Europe. Following a two-year assignment at the Vatican, Fr. Robert Chisholm in 1950 discussed Italian politics and the importance of Marshall Plan aid to Italy. In the early sixties Msgr. Edmund Szoka of Ishpeming and Fr. Dominic Zadra of Marquette gave their impressions of the Vatican II Council.

In the fall of 1955 Rotarian Paul Cargo, pastor of the First Methodist Church, reported on his study and travel seminar in four European countries the previous summer. A guest from outside the northern peninsula, Rev. Michael Krietzky, in 1954 told of his problems behind the iron curtain while employed as a missionary for the Seventh Day Adventists. Ten years later Otis Gatewood, a Church of Christ missionary, spoke to the Rotarians and Kiwanians on religious life in European communist countries.

Northern Michigan College (the name was shortened in 1955) faculty members Holmes Boynton, Gunther Meyland, and Flora Loubert reported on their travels in Iceland, Europe, and Africa. Miss Loubert returned from a two-month tour of the latter in 1958 especially impressed by the desire of Africa's blacks for freedom from foreign domination and for equality with whites. Lincoln Frazier, in a talk titled "A Practical View of Europe—1958," shared his memories of the Brussels Universal and International Exhibition, the first world's fair since 1939. This he termed a great success. He also alluded to European transportation, construction, wages, taxes, and interest rates.

By 1964 Ernest Pearce had become the foremost world traveler then in active association with the Marquette Rotary Club. In eight speeches over six years, he described his tours of Europe, South America, and Africa, and his 1961 trip around the world. He dwelt especially on Spain, Portugal, the Holy Land, ports of call in the South Pacific and the Orient, and eight safaris he had made in Africa. Journeying separately, Harvard Jean and he both had Rotary meeting make-ups on board the *Queen Elizabeth* in 1956.

E. L. Pearce and Friend. Landmark at left is *not a* Union National branch bank night deposit box.

Harvard Jean, Boulevardier (Paris)

Commerce, Industry, And Agriculture

At the March 19, 1956, meeting of the Rotary Club, Jean Worth, veteran editor of the *Escanaba Daily Press*, was the speaker. Secretary William C. Anderson summarized his message:

> Mr. Worth talked on the great potential that the Upper Peninsula has in store, and the economic growth we can expect. He cited the vast reserves in copper, iron, timber, and good farm lands, and pointed out that the Straits bridge, the St. Lawrence seaway and the availability of natural gas will all result in expansion in the U.P. It was an interesting, convincing talk, pointing to a bright future for this country.

Most people at the time would have agreed that Worth's optimism was justified. With evidence of much material progress nationally and stirrings of it in Marquette, the Rotarians were buoyed by the dazzling diversity rather than dismayed by the baffling complexities which came at them through the many weekly programs devoted to local and regional problems.

In May of 1955 Paul Bagwell of Michigan State University had pleased a large audience at a joint service club Michigan Week meeting when he enumerated a long list of products in which the state had led the Union.

At a similar event on May 22 of the next year, Michigan Governor G. Mennen Williams spoke on the beneficial effects of automation in increasing leisure and the demand for recreation related goods and services. He believed tourism in the Upper Peninsula had a bright future. Pursuing the same theme in a speech that evening at St. Peter's Cathedral Hall, he said, "In the long run, I am confident automation will be good for everybody if we use our heads about it. . . . To maintain our lead in economics, we've got to automate . . . to keep our system better than others."[2]

As presentations on specialized topics became more technical and their implications more difficult to grasp, a du Pont Chemical Company spokesman warned in 1959 of problems confronting society through a combination of increased production and leisure time, better living standards, and diminishing natural resources. About the same time, Gerald Johnson, head of the Upper Peninsula Development Bureau's industrial division, suggested to the Rotarians that improved air connections and advertising were helping to bring more manufacturing to the area.

Management of natural resources was always in the minds of thoughtful people living close to receding wilderness. For many scientists the "balance of nature" was not a fictional term but a phenomenon which, however elastic, could not be ignored. Rotary programs on the weather, air and water pollution, lumbering and reforestation, deer and other wildlife control, all in the face of growing population and special interest pressures, indicated this concern. Together, the presentations demonstrated a real need for objective data and for precise, specialized techniques to promote understanding and reduce conflict among competing groups.

One noncontroversial issue, the depredations of sea lampreys among the Lake Superior trout and whitefish, severely challenged the ingenuity of the U.S.Fish and Wildlife Service. Leo Erkilla of that agency appeared before the Rotarians four times to explain the use of electric weirs and other means to combat the parasites. A desperate battle had subsided into a tolerable war of attrition by 1961 when one of Erkilla's successors informed the club that the chemical TFM had proven much more effective than weirs.

Mechanized agriculture, which contributed heavily to higher investment costs, larger and fewer holdings, and a shrinking farm population, led the Rotarians to make a special effort to understand the problems of the farmers remaining in the area. Between 1950 and 1957 the club invited farmers to luncheon meetings annually. About twenty attended the March 27, 1950, session, which stressed the desirability of rural-urban populations "becoming acquainted and working together for the betterment of all." Sixteen farm guests came the next year to a panel discussion by seven Michigan State University staff members on rural education.

In the ordinary course of events, the Rotarians in 1955 viewed a Ford Motor Company film titled *The American Farm*, which described ways machinery had made agricultural operations easier and more efficient. A representative of the Michigan Milk Producers Association talked in 1960 about the problems of Upper Peninsula dairymen and farmers.

Ben Westrate, director of the 4-H clubs in the peninsula, in 1949 presented a brief history of the movement nationally. At the 1957 rural-urban meeting, the Rotarians honored the youthful king and queen along with six adults involved in 4-H work. Toward the end of the decade the Rotary Club made two financial contributions to that cause.

Money and banking were topics of unceasing interest to the Marquette Rotarians. In December of 1949 Ernest Pearce repeated for their benefit a speech on "Savings" which he had given in Chicago before bankers from thirty-five states. During the fifties and early sixties E. J. "Pat" LaFreniere gave six talks on fraud, Michigan taxes and tax reform, the history of accounting and auditing, and "Why Pick on Me?"—the settlement of federal income tax cases. On March 4, 1963, the club observed the centennial of national banking in the United States with talks by three local bankers—Homer Hilton, James Braddock, and Ellwood Mattson.

New Technology

Technical change was the theme for many other vocational programs from 1949 to 1966. Roy W. Fletcher, Jr., narrated a film showing improvements in oil drilling equipment. Local and out-of-town speakers considered innovation, invention, and new products in the fields of wood distillation, diamond drilling, rubber and synthetics production, and cement block and helicopter manufacture.

In two meetings late in 1957, eight Rotarians each spoke briefly on "What's New in My Business?" LaFreniere discussed changes in income tax regulations; W. J. Weber, in collection and credit agencies; Victor Holliday, in Cliffs Dow operations; Edgar Harden, in the education of high school science teachers; Don Pearce, in his travel agency; Dr. Norman Matthews, in pediatrics; Robert Brebner, in construction; and Robert Clark, in law.

The club members paid more than a dozen visits to industrial firms—to the Lake Shore Engineering Company, the Lake Superior & Ishpeming Railroad shops, and to the Cliffs Dow Chemical Company, Munising Wood Products, and Vollwerth meat processing plants. About six programs were devoted to the telephone and to new inventions, the solar battery, for example, connected with it. In March, 1954, John L. Farley of the Michigan Bell Telephone Company office in Menominee suggested that a big obstacle to nationwide dial service was duplication in phone numbers. Other officials, including local Rotarians John Gerling and Edward J. Stratton, related the telephone to national defense, presented a film on the Telstar satellite put into orbit by AT&T, and considered the pervasive influence of the telephone.

The linking of sound and light reproduction and transmission begun commercially in the 1920s with sound movies and culminating after World War II in a second connection through television did not, as has been noted, reach fruition in Marquette until the opening of station WLUC-TV in 1956. After that, the central Upper Pen-

Cliffs Dow provides lunch at Presque Isle Pavilion, 1961

insula began to feel with the rest of the nation the broad and penetrating influence of audio-visual aids upon daily habit and upon written words and syntax once limited to books, periodicals, and newspapers. The impact was as powerful as that of motor conveyance upon steam transportation and its undergirding rails.

The changes occurred so gradually that their enormous effect upon life and language was not to be appreciated for another twenty years. The slow, almost imperceptible buildup to television in Marquette is well illustrated by the rising frequency of color slide and motion picture presentations at the Marquette Rotary Club's weekly luncheons.

During the fiscal year 1954-55 almost half of all programs employed these aids. Ten of the thirteen between November 15 and February 7 were semi-automated. There was some subsidence about the time Treloar in October of 1955 described the progress being made on the construction of WLUC. The novelty had pretty well worn off when Fred Lieberman, president of the Iron Range Cable Corporation, came before the group five years later to discuss plans for cable television in Marquette County. At present about one in four local Rotary programs utilizes slide or motion picture projections.

After the discovery of uranium in Baraga County, A. K. Snelgrove, a professor of geology at the Michigan College of Mining and Technology, in April of 1950 spoke on its possible significance for the Upper Peninsula.

Aided by a multimillion-dollar loan from the Reconstruction Finance Corporation,[3] the Copper Range Company and its subsidiary, the White Pine Copper Company, built a new town of White Pine and resumed copper mining in Ontonagon County. In the spring of 1953 the Marquette Rotarians were treated to a program of color slides showing the development of the White Pine community and of mine building and shaft construction.

Fourteen local club members on August 25, 1959, visited the copper mine site in lieu of attending the regular meeting at home. The next week, Jerry Warner, a civil engineer connected with White Pine, came to Marquette to solicit the Rotarians' support for opening fringe areas around the Porcupine Mountain State Park to mining. He assured the group that this could be done without seriously affecting the scenic beauty of the Porcupines.

The iron mining companies were able to offset a lessening demand for production workers in Marquette County with increased employment in the construction of new facilities and the installation of more modern equipment. As early as November 20, 1950, Francis Tartaron, manager of iron ore research for the Jones & Laughlin Steel Corporation, offered hope that the life of the Marquette Range could be extended greatly through beneficiation of low grade ores.

In September, 1957, Munro Tibbitts showed an Erie Mining Company film on taconite ore, open pits from which it was being extracted outside the Upper Peninsula, processing mills, and railroads and docks for handling. According to club Secretary Elmer Carlson, "Not fully developed yet, this taconite mining will have a great deal to do with the future of the iron ranges in the Great Lakes area." Early in 1959 Dwight C. Brown, assistant director of research for Jones & Laughlin, speaking on "Whither Michigan Ore," moved Secretary Robert Brebner to record in the minutes, "It is conceivable that open pit mining would, in the future, replace our shaft mining, and that we could look forward to large developments of sintering and pelletizing plants in Upper Michigan."

A few meetings later, Ned Johnson, director of research for the Cleveland-Cliffs Iron Company, spent almost all of his time "familiarizing members of the club with the terms 'beneficence [*sic*],' 'up-grading,' 'agglomeration,' and other technical terms."

H. Stuart Harrison

H. Stuart Harrison, president of CCI, on March 27, 1961, gave a major address before the Marquette Rotary Club.[4] In it he stated that by 1970 the annual production of low content iron ore on the Marquette Range could reach 6,600,000 tons if, according to the *Mining Journal* summary the next day, "the company has the right industrial climate for expansion." This would require, quoting from the same source, "the cooperation and understanding of labor, the Legislature and the public."

Of the problems confronting the company and its partners—competition from foreign ores, high domestic labor costs, and taxation—Harrison judged the first to be the most formidable. He said that in 1947, when foreign ore imports stood at five million tons, domestic production was ninety-two million, of which seventy-eight million were from the Lake Superior region. By 1960 foreign ore production had increased to thirty-five million tons, whereas total United States yield was down to eighty-three million and that of the Lake Superior region to sixty-eight million tons. "The Marquette range," he emphasized, "is not competing with the Mesabi Range, but with Africa, India, South America and Canada."

Harrison noted a rapid increase in hourly wages to $3.29 for miners in the employ of CCI as contrasted to an average daily wage of from $1.25 to $1.50 in Africa and South America. He also pointed to lower income taxes and more liberal depreciation allowances in foreign countries. He urged revision of the tax equalization system, delegation of some of the state's power of eminent domain to mining companies, a specific instead of an ad valorem tax on ore, and public sympathy for the mining companies' water problem—"low grade ore properties require a tremendous amount of water."

Several years before, on June 23, 1958, Jack Powell of the United Steelworkers of America local in Negaunee had presented his organization's views on wages and working conditions. In March, 1964, Robert S. Thompson of Marquette, a professional labor mediator, addressed the Rotarians on the arbitration of disputes.

Transportation—The St. Lawrence Seaway and the Mackinac Bridge

Rotary programs during 1954 and 1955 revealed the alarm of railroad representatives over the rapid decline of their industry due to competition from motor transport—truck, bus, automobile, and airplane. The club viewed a color film titled *The Story of American Railroads* in March, 1954. The next fall Roobe H. Allie of Detroit, secretary of the Michigan Railway Association, told the Rotarians that the railroads did not fear competition but would like regulations to apply equitably to all forms of transportation. The following summer George Wyatt, chairman of the same organization, reiterated this position and lamented the railroads' inability to acquire capital for renovation.

Highway development and safety were subjects of a half dozen Rotary programs. In response to a request from the Marquette Chamber of Commerce, the club's board of directors in August, 1955, submitted a resolution to the State Highway Department favoring construction of the four-lane divided thoroughfare which eventually was built to Negaunee. A film, *The Road Ahead*, revealed in 1958 the scope of the interstate system and the use of federal tax dollars in its behalf.

The long-awaited completion of the St. Lawrence Seaway in 1955 was of great interest locally. While work was in progress, C. Ver Duin, the mayor of Grand Haven and secretary of the Great Lakes Harbor Association, in 1954 discussed its advantages for Marquette, as did U.S. Sen. Homer Ferguson in a wide-ranging talk on September 27 of the same year at a joint meeting of the men's service clubs. Ferguson dealt with the pledge of allegiance to the flag, communism, thermonuclear weapons secrets, Korea, the FBI, President Dwight D. Eisenhower's $50 billion highway program, and federal tax policies along with the waterway.[5]

In May, 1957, the Rotarians enjoyed *The Eighth Sea*, a color film portraying the long history and final success of the project. Two years later a director of the St.

Lawrence Seaway Corporation, John Beukema, reminded the local group that the facility must be improved perpetually and extended even to remote port towns like Marquette.

The Sault Canal Centennial celebration in 1955 furnished another occasion for showing, on August 1, a color film produced by the University of Michigan on the historical, economic, and military importance of the canal system at Sault Ste. Marie.

Another long heralded achievement in Michigan was the spanning of its two principal peninsulas with the gigantic bridge across the Straits of Mackinac. On October 24, 1955, Prentiss M. Brown of St. Ignace, chairman of the Mackinac Bridge Authority, covered the history, financing, physical dimensions of the structure, and progress made to that time. Nearly four years after its official opening in November, 1957, Larry Rubin, executive secretary of the Bridge Authority, in June of 1961 reviewed for the club its early years in operation.

Social Trends

While life was being made materially easier through technological advances, the gain seemed to be counterbalanced by psychological pressures, if the Marquette Rotary Club programs can be regarded as accurate measures. In 1949 past President Emery Jacques, now warden of the prison, traced the history of penology and concluded that Americans "are still a hundred years behind the time in trying to rehabilitate a man for release to society." Five years later, having obtained several millions of dollars in legislative appropriations, he talked about new construction projects and subdivided the Rotarians into groups for prison tours.

In the early fifties Police Chief Donald McCormick praised the local chapter of Alcoholics Anonymous, Judge Carroll Rushton spoke on "Red Tape and the Law," and George Blue of the Marquette FBI office discussed the work of his agency. Men from the sheriff's department called for greater patriotism and responsible citizenship. City Attorney John J. Walsh considered estates, wills, and trusts in relation to taxes.

Michigan's Chief Justice John R. Dethmers in March, 1953, stressed the importance of an impartial, independent judiciary, and three years later Associate Justice Talbot Smith cautioned against loss of individual rights, particularly if committee appointment should ever replace election of state supreme court members. State Treasurer D. Hale Brake on September 21 declared that "government should be administered by the smallest unit capable of performing the necessary public service functions in a reasonably competent manner."

Municipal Judge Edward Dembowski in 1958 described his duties and noted in passing that half of all automobile accidents could be attributed at least in part to alcohol. The next year, Donald Small, probation officer for the circuit court, presented the case histories of two boys involved in crime—their attitudes, family background, and proposals for rehabilitation.

Also in 1959 Harold M. Dorr, a professor of political science at the University of

Michigan, was quoted in the Rotary Club minutes as saying at a joint meeting of local service organizations that "the voting population of this country, in general, was becoming less interested in its stake in government," adding that we Americans have "no one to blame but ourselves if we feel that the government's influence is, on both state and national scenes, lopsided or top-heavy." The *Mining Journal* pointed up Dorr's scolding of business and professional leaders for their political apathy.[6]

In September of 1962 Republican Leslie Richards and Democrat Charles Follo, both delegates to the recently concluded state constitutional convention in Lansing, agreed that the new constitution produced there was basically a good one and should be ratified, as it soon was.

The contribution of good personal health to a sound society also received attention from the Marquette Rotarians. In March, 1949, Harry Haeffner, moderator of Detroit's Forum and Town Hall, made clear, however, his attitude toward what he termed the evils of socialized medicine. Thereafter, seven of the club's physicians reported on new knowledge and techniques in medicine and surgery.

James R. Acocks, in several programs spread over a decade, described treatment of tuberculosis at the then Morgan Heights Sanatorium (since 1971 the Acocks Medical Facility) and in the United States generally. Using X-ray photographs, he instructed the group on the diagnosis and cure or alleviation of tuberculosis and lung cancer. In 1958 he discussed prescription drugs, noting the existence of about four hundred in the sulfa family alone, of which a half dozen were in use at the time; also five thousand antibiotics, about twenty of which he judged "very good" and five or six "out-standing."

T. Boyd Bolitho, radiologist, in 1951 gave an illustrated talk on X-rays and twelve years later indicated that the dangers from radiation fallout to that time had been exaggerated. Charles P. Drury, again the city health officer, spoke in 1951 on the fluoridation of drinking water and, later in the decade, on the state program for handicapped children. In October, 1964, Dr. Stewart Erhard of Eaton Rapids, Michigan,

Dr. James R. Acocks (right)

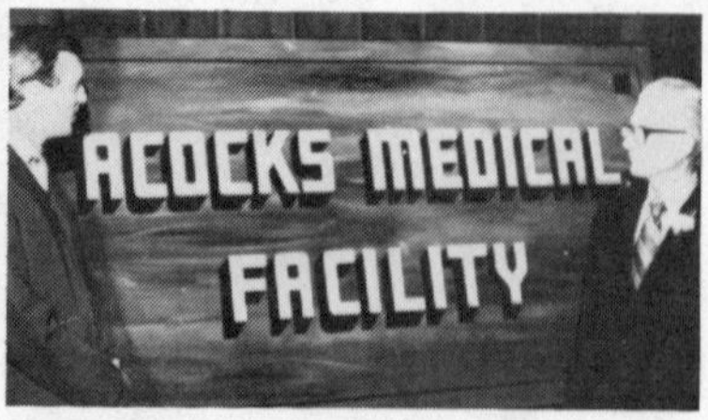

and Pastor John Erhard of Escanaba showed a movie and talked on "Smoking and Cancer" in promoting their "5 Day Plan to Stop Smoking."

In February, 1959, Matthew C. Bennett spoke on "What's New in Surgery." He was followed two years later by pediatrician Norman Matthews and internist E. R. Huffman, who informed the club of developments in their fields. In January, 1964, George M. Wilson, Jr., Huffman, and K. Charles Wright formed a panel to advise on coronary heart disease—"How One Gets It," "What To Do If You Have It," and "How To Keep From Getting It." The minutes state that "the meeting adjourned when Pat LaFreniere announced that he wasn't feeling well."

Occasional programs on aging and the Social Security system encouraged those Rotarians who were looking forward to retirement. In April, 1951, club member Paul Chamberlain called attention to new schedules affecting old age and survivors' benefits. In the early 1960s Rotarian George C. Franzen, Marquette district manager of the Social Security Administration, reported national findings on how pensioners over one hundred years of age were enjoying life. He stated in 1965 that in his eight-county area total payments, including those for Medicare, had reached eighteen million dollars annually.

Talks on inspirational and ideological themes occurred with some frequency. On November 24, 1952, Fr. John Vinson Suhr, radio director for the Catholic Diocese of Marquette, gave "an inspiring address on his thoughts of what a real Thanksgiving Day should represent." He believed it would be termed more appropriately "Sacrifice Day" because true happiness comes through self-denial. Almost all of the Rotarians stayed on to compliment him. In a talk on "The Living Years," Msgr. Joseph Zryd emphasized the need for daily prayers. On Washington's Birthday in 1954, Albert Burrows reviewed the Anglo-American quest for liberty in a presentation titled "Heritage of Freedom."

In a practical vein Ogden Johnson and Ralph Huhtala of the Cleveland-Cliffs Iron Company in 1954 described "How Our Business System Operates." In that year also, at a joint meeting of Marquette men's service clubs, Louis C. Turner of Akron, Ohio, a past president of the Toastmasters Association of America, asked, "Do You Have What It Takes To Be Successful?"

Although almost no black people were living in Marquette at the time, the civil rights controversy nationally and the approach of the Civil War Centennial observance moved the local Rotarians to review in a contemporary setting the greatest cataclysm in United States history. In August, 1955, Sidney Samuels, a Dallas lawyer, appeared before the club to discuss racial desegregation. Wrote Secretary William Anderson, "He didn't like it." Anderson continued:

> Mr. Samuels was a very fluent and dynamic speaker. He held the interest of the group as he discussed in detail the historical background of segregation, and the effects of the Civil War on the South in general.
>
> The subject of desegregation is a very controversial one, indeed, an explosive one. Mr. Samuels, in very dramatically presenting the traditional viewpoints of

a Southerner, demonstrated very clearly that there is a great deal of work to be done before this problem is solved.

Rotarian Richard P. Sonderegger, a member of the Michigan Civil War Centennial Commission and professor of history at Northern, spoke in the fall of 1960 on the significance of the conflict. The next week, Kenyon Boyer focused attention on Presidential elections. Rotarian Norbert Smith, pastor of the First Methodist Church, much later gave the club "a most interesting report" of his participation in the famous August 28, 1963, Freedom March in Washington, D.C.

In 1961, when social protest was about to erupt nationally, Ernest Pearce recalled again "The Meaning of Rotary."

9
CLUB-COMMUNITY-YOUTH

The city of Marquette during the fifties and early sixties developed much as George Skrubb and the Rotary and other planning board members had anticipated. Though not without a struggle, the public school system expanded to meet the needs of local children and youths even as the Bishop Baraga and John D. Pierce high schools closed. The Peter White Public Library added a wing. New municipal sewage and power plants, a Marquette Armory building, and a marina were constructed. Downtown lighting was modernized. Additional bleachers were raised at Memorial Field, and ski facilities were installed in the Mount Mesnard (Marquette) area.

More local government projects led naturally to more city employment. In 1952 Rotarian Claude L. Mosher, superintendent of light and power, had warned the club of Marquette's need for up-to-date lighting, and John Seeley, architect, had described progress on the new sewage disposal plant on the Carp River. Two years later Mayor Bernard York, also a Rotarian, "presented a most interesting talk on the six-year budget under which the City of Marquette now operates." City Manager George Meholick spoke in 1958 about the lamentable condition of the town's antiquated water distribution system and emphasized the difficulty of multiplying municipal services without a broader tax base. Nevertheless, by the summer of 1961 the city had received enough support to employ a yearly average of 224 people, an increase of forty-nine from 175 a decade earlier.

Simultaneously the branch prison, local medical facilities, Northern Michigan College (University in 1963), tourism, and new or enlarged county, state, and federal government offices and payrolls became the principal economic reliance of a community suffering industrial decline.

Marquette Rotarians still engaged individually in almost every phase of community development, but together they had become a nurturing agency rather than a crucible for ideas and projects. Soon gone were the days when the club members had almost monopolized city government and planning, when they had decided in regular meetings or in smaller but identifiable Rotary gatherings that a swimming pool, Palestra, golf course, or hotel should be built, and then, as men whose financial and political authority was unchallenged, had taken whatever steps were needed to bring it to fruition.

Consistent with a national trend, initiative and control were passing to administrators and specialized technicians. Many of these were agents of large corporate or government entities whose directives came from Washington, Lansing, or other cities much larger than Marquette. Major financing now came through taxes, loans, outside investment, local gifts from the Shiras and Kaufman funds, and contributions from still well-to-do individuals who preferred to remain anonymous behind "quiet money."

By 1966, the golden anniversary year of the Marquette Rotary Club, members and townspeople at large could find considerable satisfaction in the material and cultural progress of the city. If social malaise and urban blight were nibbling at even so small a town as Marquette, and if numerous but impecunious latter-day Shirases in and out of the club still dreamed of a "Queen City" worthy of its truly magnificent natural setting—complete with a natural history and marine museum, convention center, downtown mall, and a coherent scenic harbor and shoreline development—this, it could be argued plausibly and amiably, might yet be realized—all in good time, and by someone else.

The prestige of the Marquette Rotary Club and its members remained high. Whether or not financial support was sought, almost every proposition affecting the common good was brought to the attention of the group in carefully prepared and delivered presentations. James Scanlon, Marquette County welfare director, must have welcomed for public relations purposes alone the opportunity to inform the Rotarians about the work of his department, as he did in June, 1958. When in November, 1964, Vern Dahlquist, executive director of the Upper Peninsula branch of the Michigan Children's Aid Society (now the Child & Family Services of the Upper Peninsula), talked about the history and program of his agency, he noted that the president of its board always had been a Rotarian.

Late in 1964 the Rotary board of directors gave five hundred dollars to a Marquette Youth Foundation established by Judge Michael De Fant and other citizens to buy and renovate a house for a distressed family. The work was done and the family benefited for about ten years.

Although organizations like the Children's Aid Society, Catholic Social Services, and the Salvation Army continued to provide exceptionally valuable assistance, the great bulk of social work, once almost entirely in the domain of private philanthropy, by the fifties had been taken over by the federal Social Security and state welfare agencies.

Giving Continued

Efforts in Marquette to systematize even private charity date from 1924, when the local Community Chest (United Way) was established. In the fifties, as in many years past, the Rotary and other men's service clubs continued to sponsor its annual kickoff luncheons and dinners, but after 1946 Rotary had ceased making club donations. W. H. Treloar was among the toastmasters at the introductory meetings, and Rotarians Elmer Carlson and Wesley Jenner headed the drives for 1957-58 and 1958-59. Occasionally a club member addressed his fellow Rotarians on Community Chest benefits to a participating organization with which he was affiliated.

In November of 1954 the Rotary board informed the Chamber of Commerce, Community Chest, and Veterans Council that donations were at the discretion of the club members individually. However, at a dinner for Rotarians at Camp Atono in the spring of 1956, the club raised three hundred dollars for the Community Chest during a special "Fill the Gap" campaign.

At a joint meeting in the new Chamber of Commerce building in February, 1960, the Rotarians and Kiwanians appealed for continuing citizen support for the Chamber. Four years later Rotary President L. Wallace Bruce appointed Wesley E. Perron an official club representative on the reorganized council of the Greater Marquette United Community Chest.

Except for small and irregular donations to Community Chest, Salvation Army, and cleanup campaigns, the Marquette Rotarians as a body contributed for more than fifteen years only to youth and health related projects, particularly the Bay Cliff Health Camp. When the Graveraet High School band gave a concert in the spring of 1950 to raise money for drum majors' uniforms, the club made up the difference of $150 between costs and proceeds. Three years later another hundred dollars went to the Bishop Baraga school for playground equipment.

One financial gift to the club deserves special mention here. In 1955 President Roy W. Fletcher, Jr., who during his term bought and liquidated the stock of a local hardware store, turned over a large remnant of it to the club so that members could hold a rummage sale for the benefit of the Bay Cliff camp. The return of approximately $2,650 from this source proved to be the most substantial sum received by the Rotary group since the acquisition of its hotel stock in 1929.

Also in the mid-fifties Rotarian J. H. Kline, president of the Lake Superior & Ishpeming Railroad Company, solicited club endorsement of the offer of a steam engine for the use of children at Presque Isle Park. However, the board of directors took no action, and the city declined to accept because of maintenance and possible liability costs.[1]

For several years beginning in 1951 the directors augmented the Children's Clinic lunch fund and, from 1952 through 1955, supported the agency's monthly film program to the extent of one hundred dollars annually. During the decade there was no break in club sponsorship of Marquette delegates to the Wolverine Boys' State as the Rotary youth committee worked closely with the American Legion on the project. The Rotarians showed little interest in Scouting although the board did appropriate money to help a local representative attend the 1959 Girl Scout national encampment at Colorado Springs.

From 1949 through 1951 the Rotary Club and other men's service organizations held annual dinners to honor athletes of the three high schools. At a regular meeting on April 3, 1961, the Rotarians entertained Coach Victor Hurst and all the members of his Class D state championship John D. Pierce High School basketball squad. The school closed permanently that June.

As early as 1940 the board of directors had received and declined a request from the Marquette Hockey Association to help support a local men's team, the Sentinels.

On October 6, 1941, however, the board endorsed the Association's appeal for city assistance and requested the boys' committee of the club to consider Rotary sponsorship of a junior boys' team. The war interrupted progress on that, but in December of 1950 the directors did donate a small sum for the midget hockey squad.

A few years later Allan F. Olson, chairman of the club's youth committee, pressed earnestly for sustained support of a Rotary junior hockey unit. Olson, a second team All-American while at the Michigan College of Mines at Houghton (now Michigan Technological University), is one of nine Marquette hockey-playing brothers, including Edward, a professional, and Olympic gold medalist Weldon. One sister has been a speed skater; the other, a figure skater and instructor. The Olson Arena in the Marquette Lakeview Arena is named for the family.[2]

The Rotarians on April 4, 1955, entertained the eleven members of the VFW Warriors hockey team after their participation in an international junior tournament at Duluth. The following year, Olson obtained a small Rotary donation for junior hockey and in 1958 persuaded the board to underwrite the cost of uniforms for the boys. After talks by Harold Alholm and Rotarian Morgan Gingrass on progress of the junior hockey program, Secretary Brebner commented in the minutes for April 6, "It was . . . interesting to discover how well organized and effective this junior league hockey has proven to be. . . ."

The degree of its effectiveness became evident when the National Bantam Hockey Tournament was held on March 18 and 19, 1961, in Marquette. Local Rotarians individually bought tickets and gave additional money to insure its success. Perhaps the club's purchase of new uniforms for the Marquette Rotary Club Juvenile squad helped stimulate them to become both the Marquette Industrial League and state VFW champions in the winter of 1963-64. Defeat by a Sault Ste. Marie team in overtime cost them the national title that season.[3]

The Rotary Club entertained its protegés at its regular meeting on March 9, 1964. "Earl Closser . . . really jazzed up his piano playing for the benefit of our youthful guests." The runner-up trophy was presented to President Fred Sabin for display, and each player received a team picture and a souvenir plaque.

Nevertheless, the favorite project of the Marquette Rotary Club was the Bay Cliff Health Camp. If any one person outside Rotary was more successful than any other in inspiring the men to live up to their ideal of service within it, that one was Elba L. Morse, superintendent of the Northern Michigan Children's Clinic and director of the camp. Gracious, kindhearted, and motherly, also determined and astute, Miss Morse over many years extracted more material and financial assistance than any other nonmember. This she did not so much by direct solicitation as through her infectious enthusiasm, industry, and dedication. When the Michigan Nursing Center Association chose her the Michigan Nurse of the Year 1952, Marquette and Ishpeming Rotarians and Rotary Anns turned out en masse for a community tribute on May 13, her birthday.[4]

Since the camp's inception, Marquette Rotarians habitually have gone out in groups to help clean it for opening in the spring and then, individually or together,

Rotary Club Championship Juvenile Hockey Team, 1964

have called with gifts of much-needed equipment or money, to make improvements, or just to see how the children and staff are progressing. At Miss Morse's behest, Cliffs Dow Rotarians several times sent crews of mechanics and materials for repair and maintenance. Numerous Rotarians have served on the camp's governing board.

A glimpse into the relationship between the local club members and Miss Morse and her staff is provided in one of her letters, dated August 18, 1952, and bearing the salutation, "My dear Dr. Buck." It was to thank him "for all the things that you did that made this camping season one of the best." The message continued:

> In the first place, the dishwasher and potato peeler were a godsend. The fact that we had 38 children under seven years of age will show you that we couldn't expect the children to assist in our camp capers like peeling potatoes and washing dishes, so the dishwasher and potato peeler were almost essentials this year. We want to thank you heartily for steering the ship and getting these for us. We also wish to thank you for the treat of popsicles for the children and for the loan of the freezer, to say nothing about the potatoes. . . .

This from the "grand old lady of Bay Cliff" to the "good old soul" of the Marquette Rotary Club.

At two summer luncheon meetings of the club, Miss Morse and other Bay Cliff camp staff members discussed their work. On July 19, 1954, Ernest Pearce summarized the camp's financial condition, and Mrs. Eva Burdick, educational director, described the variety of services offered the children, who were spending six to eight weeks at Bay Cliff without expense to their families. She counted among the staff one occupational and three physiotherapists; two student therapists from Wayne

University and one, a blind youth, from Michigan State College (University), all full-time; also six credit counselors from Northern. Following a talk by the sightless young man on life at the camp, a fourteen-year-old polio victim illustrated his own improvement by taking a few steps without braces—"a most apt and touching finish to the program."

On the second occasion, July 18, 1955, Mrs. Burdick identified the four principal functions of the camp as occupational therapy; physical therapy; speech, hearing, and sight-saving aid; and remedial instruction. Three of her associates then commented on their duties. Miss Morse received a standing ovation at the end of the meeting.

Meanwhile, the Rotarians on December 28, 1953, voted to assess each member five dollars on his birthday in order to raise $450 annually for Bay Cliff. As the club recovered from a membership decline, the "Birthdays for Bay Cliff" program reached the five-hundred-dollar level.

A Marquette Rotary-Kiwanis Aunt Jemima Pancake Day at the armory on May 22, 1957, netted a special $2,570 for Bay Cliff. A return engagement sponsored by all five of the city's service organizations on July 1, 1961, yielded $880 as the Rotary Club's share of the total proceeds for the camp. Rotarians sold tickets for the 1959 premier showing in Marquette of the famous motion picture *The Anatomy of a Murder*, which had been filmed locally and at Big Bay. The money from that also went to the health camp.

The Marquette Rotarians were much more interested in the physical than in the mental and emotional health of children. On August 26, 1946, Dr. Samuel W. Hartwell, psychiatrist, outlined plans for an Upper Peninsula Child Guidance Clinic to serve two hundred children for from six months to two years each. The agency was established with headquarters in Marquette and four branches in strategically located cities elsewhere in the peninsula. Although several Marquette and Ishpeming Rotarians became involved with this partnership between the state and volunteer citizens' groups, their clubs did not.

The local Rotarians were more receptive to plans for an adult mental health clinic. Robert Drew of the Michigan Department of Mental Health, who addressed the members in May, 1959, was the first of several speakers including Probate Judge De Fant; Roland Schwitzgoebel, professor of education at Northern; St. Mary's Hospital administrator George Mancuso; and Dr. Richard Cameron, superintendent of the Newberry State Hospital, who urged establishment of a facility in Marquette.

The club's board late in 1959 contributed a small sum to aid a Marquette Health, Welfare, and Education committee in promoting the enterprise. On July 1, 1963, the directors also donated five hundred dollars to St. Mary's Hospital, which was adding a mental health wing and enlarging its accommodations for older, chronically ill patients. In March of 1964 Dr. David R. Wall, psychiatrist for the newly established Upper Peninsula Adult Mental Health Clinic at St. Mary's, discussed progress in his field. He joined Rotary in 1966.

Numerous club programs during the fifties and sixties emphasized a persistent shortage of nurses and a need for hospital modernization to keep pace with medical advances. In the autumn of 1950 Miss Audrey Shade, superintendent of St. Luke's Hospital, spoke particularly about the importance of its school of nursing, as did Mrs. Irene Anderson and two student nurses from the staff several years later. Howard Lehwald, administrator at St. Luke's, when discussing financial problems in 1957, explained its organizational structure and the differences between a hospital and a business firm. The next year, Rotarian Victor Holliday noted that a new unit at the K. I. Sawyer air base would relieve some of the pressures on the local hospitals.

The Rotarians still dominated the St. Luke's board and continued to contribute time and money toward improvements. In June, 1965, the club gave five hundred dollars to a Greater St. Luke's Building Fund. About the same time, the Frazier and Reynolds families made a gift of the Hotel Northland to the hospital. They had purchased the landmark from Rotarian Edward L. Pearce, Ernest's eldest son, who in turn had acquired it in 1961 from Frank Russell, Jr. Beginning in 1949, Russell had bought up all of the Kawbawgam Hotel Company stock, including the shares his grandfather had given the Rotary Club.

Support for Education

Acting as program chairman on March 11, 1957, Robert H. Clark (son of Harlow), who with fellow Rotarian Clyde DeHaas was a trustee of the Peter White Library, introduced librarian Phyllis Rankin, speaker for the day. Following Miss Rankin's outline of proposals for building expansion, the Rotarians agreed to promote the bond issue essential to realization. Late in 1958 a new two-story wing containing an auditorium, children's room, and additional work and shelving space was completed.

Willard Whitman, who remained superintendent of the public schools until 1953, and, particulary, his successor, Rotarian Henry J. Bothwell, led drives in the fifties to construct and improve more elementary schools than at any time in the city's history. In this they were supported staunchly by Rotarian Herman E. Olson, executive vice-president of the First National Bank, and by the other school board members.

On May 11, 1953, one of these, L. D. Kooker, solicited Rotary help in a forthcoming millage and bond issue campaign. Early in 1955 Bothwell informed the club that the growing school age population in town and establishment of the air base soon would overwhelm existing facilities. Before another bond issue vote scheduled for December 13, Bothwell and a board member, Mrs. Mabel Leskee, urged the city's service clubs to support three proposals to build two elementary schools and to renovate a third. The drive succeeded. By the fall of 1957 Marquette could boast construction of the Whitman, Parkview, and Sandy Knoll schools and improvement of the Fisher building, all within four years.

While school authorities were contemplating their next project of a new high school to accommodate a cresting wave of enrollments at the secondary level, Northern Michigan College experienced a spurt which in the sixties was to culminate in

Willard M. Whitman Elementary School

a "quantum jump" to university status. For this the extremely vigorous President Edgar L. Harden (1956-67) was responsible.

In the early fifties President Tape had conducted the Rotarians through the new Lydia Olson Library at Northern. Leo Van Tassel, Northern's comptroller, had reminded the group of the college's financial importance to the city and had projected an enrollment increase to from twelve to fifteen hundred students within the next dozen to fifteen years.

Harden gave his first speech to the Marquette Rotary Club on August 6, 1956, the day he was elected to membership, on his educational philosophy and goals for Northern. From this time forth, the club's relations with Northern became increasingly cordial. Harden spoke on the institution's expansion program in 1958 and, as state chairman of Michigan Week, addressed the local Rotarians on "Education and Water Resources" in May of the same year.

Also in the spring of 1958, following a meeting of all Marquette, Ishpeming, and Negaunee service clubs at Northern, the guests were given a tour of the new field house, named for retired coach and athletic director Charles B. Hedgcock.[5]

Responding to the impetus Russia's Sputnik had given science education in the United States, two recipients of National Science Foundation grants at Northern reported to the club on their year of study at the universities of Texas and Michigan. Holmes Boynton, who headed a National Science Institute at the college in the summer of 1958, described the progress of fifty high school enrollees.

In the early sixties Roy E. Heath, Northern's director of research and development, acquainted his fellow Rotarians with teaching machines, arranged a visit of service clubs to the university's computer and data processing center, and discussed the uses of an IBM computer there. Northern's first director of educational television, Kenneth Bergsma, conducted the members through the campus television and FM radio studios. On July 23, 1962, Msgr. Nolan McKevitt, Rotarian, repeated at a luncheon meeting the baccalaureate address he had given at Northern the previous month. President Harden later compared his visit to Germany in 1962 with that in 1957.

On December 4, 1961, the Rotary board of directors donated one thousand dollars to Northern's "Goals for Greatness" campaign headed by Treloar. Harden on June 24, 1963, reminded the club that his prediction seven years earlier that Northern would have two thousand students by 1965 had been greeted with skepticism. He stated that now enrollment had reached thirty-one hundred in the fall of 1962 and that fifteen percent of Marquette's entire population was presently connected with the newly designated university. His latest projection was for an enrollment of six thousand by 1970. According to the minutes, "His talk was well received."

Involvement with Students

At the instigation of Allan Olson, the club resumed the practice of inviting students to its regular meetings during the first months of 1953, from late September, 1963, into March of the next year, and again in 1965-66. The first schedule accommodated twelve high school and college students, from one to four at a time. During the second cycle, they came in groups of two to five weekly from the Graveraet and Baraga high schools only. These boys and young men were chosen without regard to vocational interest. Occasionally, however, the club singled out business administration majors at Northern or members of Junior Achievement at Graveraet.

The club on April 2, 1951, welcomed ten Northern students to a roundtable discussion on railroad problems. The next year, it entertained another group at a business students recognition day. At a joint meeting of service clubs sponsored by the brokerage house of Paine, Webber, Jackson & Curtis in March, 1954, Rotarian Leo W. Bruce, manager of the local office, had as his personal guests members of the student Business Administration Club. The gathering was addressed by Roger LaCroix, a Duluth banker, who showed a film, *What Makes Us Tick*, illustrating the purpose and functions of investments. He also talked about business conditions generally. A month later, when eighteen members of the club again visited Rotary, a panel of students analyzed Northern's offerings in their field of interest.

Several Rotary meetings were given to the Junior Achievement program, a nationwide effort to afford high school students practical experience in organizing and operating miniature "companies." Marquette Rotarians J. H. Kline, Herman Olson, Allan Olson, Edward Pearce, Wesley Jenner, and Henry Bothwell were organizers and charter directors of the local organization. Elmer Carlson served later.[6]

In Marquette the Junior Achievers manufactured and sold snow scoops, decorative thermometers, and kitchen aids, for example—items young people could make or assemble themselves for a ready market. In September, 1957, the Rotary Club viewed a film explaining the national enterprise.

Late in 1959 Jack McDonald, a member of the student board of directors, reviewed the history of the operation at Graveraet, then called upon presidents of four units to describe the items currently being made and to give sample "sales pitches." At a joint meeting of service clubs in 1963, Herbert D. Soper of Milwaukee, a member of the national executive committee of Junior Achievement, spoke on the free enterprise system.

The Rotary Club kept in touch with high school activities in other ways. In the fall of 1957 it invited two Graveraet senior girls, Christina Carlson and Gretchen Lambert, to tell of their bicycle excursion to New England a few months before.

Longyear Hall

NORTHERN MICHIGAN
UNIVERSITY BUILD-
INGS NAMED FOR
MARQUETTE
ROTARIANS

Kaye Hall

Lynn H. Halverson
Residence Hall

Edgar L. Harden
Learning Resources
Center

Charles B.
Hedgcock Physical Education Building and Field
House

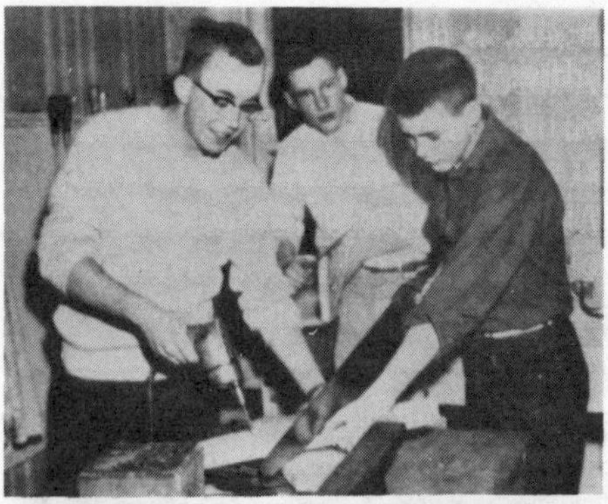

Junior Achievement at Marquette Senior High School

They came dressed for travel and with vehicles and gear. Graveraet instructor Milton A. Johnson on two occasions, the first time accompanied by students, described the annual senior trip to Washington, New York, and other cities of historic and current appeal.

In the spring of 1960 the club helped to defray the expenses of Roger LaBonte, a Northern senior, who went to Washington for a White House Conference on Children and Youth. As predecessors had done more than a decade before, Graveraet High School seniors repeated the talks they had given at their June commencement exercises. In the summer of 1962 Roland Schwitzgoebel alerted the Rotarians to a citizens' Better Schools drive he was heading.

Foreign Students

The Rotarians invariably were pleased to be visited by foreign youths. Most appropriately, the first to arrive were four French Scouts bringing greetings from Laon, the birthplace and ancestral home of Fr. Jacques Marquette. They appeared before the club on August 1, 1949, having deviated from their course while canoeing over the exact 1673 Marquette-Joliet route from Three Rivers, Quebec, through the waterways leading to the Mississippi—extended to New Orleans, beyond the farthest point of the original voyage. Rotarians were among the Marquette residents who housed six foreign students passing through the city in 1950.

Within a few years members of the Iron Mountain Rotary Club came in successive summers with one student from Pakistan and another from India to urge the Marquette men to adopt the neighboring group's custom of several seasons in bringing young people from different countries for six-week visits to the Upper Peninsula. Sverre Thorvaldson, chairman of the local club's international student projects committee, had charge of arrangements for a Rotary sponsored English exchange student, Stephen Taylor of Huddersfield, Yorkshire, who spent several weeks in Marquette during the summer of 1957.

Taylor stayed with nine Rotary families for one week each and attended several club meetings. He gave the group results of a questionnaire he had circulated among

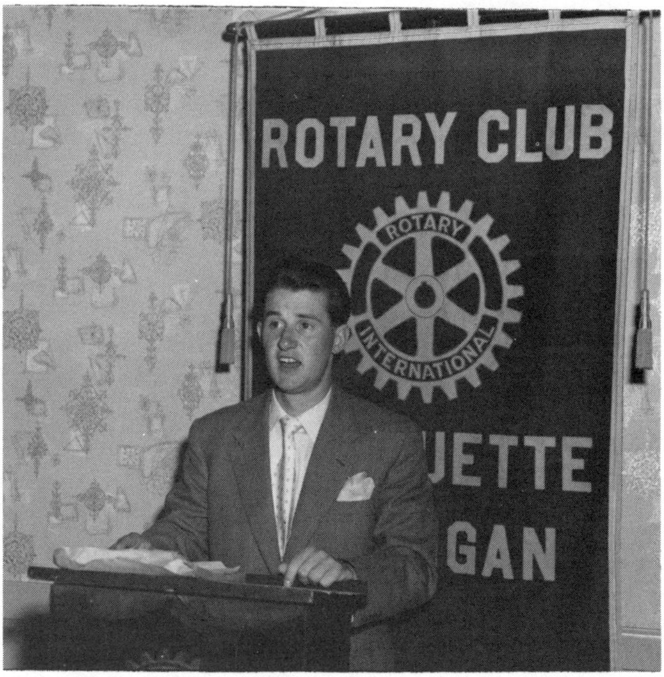

Stephen Taylor

friends and acquaintances in Huddersfield asking for their preconceptions about the United States, then distributed a similar one here for consumption at home.

By this time foreign students were coming to Northern on their own initiative or under the auspices of church groups. One was enrolled at John D. Pierce High School for a year. Most accepted invitations to speak at Rotary meetings. By 1959 students from abroad had become numerous enough to form an international relations club, which provided the Rotary program on October 19. Early in 1961 the Rotarians helped to pay the expenses of two foreign students attending Northern to travel to a student model United Nations conference in East Lansing.

Åke Ryhagen

The first foreign high school student sponsored by the Marquette Rotary Club for a long stay was Åke Ryhagen, son of a Rotarian in Uddeholm, Sweden. Young Ryhagen came to the city through Michigan Youth for Understanding. During the year 1963-64, he attended Graveraet Senior High School, from which he received a diploma, and resided with a Rotarian family. Upon his arrival he exchanged Rotary banners with President Fred Sabin. On April 13, 1964, he "gave an excellent report on his country and handled the question and answer period with great diplomacy."

German-born Helmut Kreitz, a Northern Michigan University faculty member and local Rotarian, assumed major responsibility in scheduling five students from the University of Saarbrücken to study at Northern the following year under the joint sponsorship of the local university and the Rotary Club. The Swedish and German students all lived with Rotarians in Marquette.

Financial Aid to Students

Until the fifties the Marquette Rotarians seldom gave money outright to local students. When they did, the sums were small and were taken from the general fund. The curiously named scholarship loan fund was limited strictly to loans for academic purposes; it was not used for grants.

However, a noticeable shift in club sentiment occurred in 1951. In that year the directors donated $363 to the Northern music scholarship fund and began a four-year practice of financing a Saturday Music Club scholarship for students attending the National Music Camp at Interlochen. The money in each instance came from the general fund.

When on April 20, 1953, the club sold its fifty shares of Kawbawgam Hotel Company stock to Frank Russell, Jr., at their par value of five thousand dollars, one-half payable at once and the balance within three years, the scholarship loan fund was enlarged accordingly. Although the first thought was to create a special Shiras loan category with this money, all of it was placed in this scholarship loan fund.

Another sizable accretion came in 1953-54. Several months before his death in December, 1952, Earle Parker, chairman of a short-lived board of trustees for the loan fund, disclosed that some time earlier a group of Marquette people and he had pooled their resources for loans of their own to Northern students and that he now held about fifteen hundred dollars. Undoubtedly with the others' consent, he announced his intention to will this sum to the Rotary Club with the stipulation that it be used more liberally than the restrictions then applying to the loan fund allowed.

When the club received $1,525 from Parker's estate, one of the first things the board members had to do was to recognize the distinction between "scholarship" as an adjective describing the purpose of a loan and as a noun embracing both the description and purpose of an award or gift. Since then, the term "scholarship and loan" has been applied quite consistently.

The main problem was to establish new rules for more flexible allotment of funds. After a spirited discussion on the merits of grants as opposed to loans, the board on May 10, 1954, resolved to utilize eighty-five percent of the income from the scholarship and loan fund for scholarships and to add the remaining fifteen percent to principal. The club ratified the change on June 7.

Through an undated letter from W. J. Weber to President Earl Closser (1946-47), the club's aims and objects committee had recommended that three one-hundred-dollar scholarships be given worthy seniors from the city's three high schools, with the understanding that the recipients attend Northern. The substance of this proposal, broadened to prohibit sex discrimination and to permit awards to students already enrolled at Northern, was adopted by the board of directors on August 30, 1954. At the same meeting, the board also voted to continue loans to a maximum of five hundred dollars per student, without regard to choice of college or university.

The first three scholarships went to two young women and a man already at Northern. During the next several years, the grants settled back to high school seniors. Special scholarships amounting to $292.50 in 1956-57 and to $150 in 1957-58 were awarded Northern students. Between the end of World War II and June 30, 1959, loans totaling $3,795 were made to eight men. Another of seventy-five dollars was converted into a grant.

From 1922 to the middle of 1959, twenty-three male students received thirty-four loans amounting to $7,095 and, after 1954, $2,042 was awarded in scholarships. Over a thirty-seven-year period the scholarship and loan fund increased from one thousand dollars to $12,756. By the end of 1959 only $450 in two loans remained outstanding.

Having noted the inactivity of the loan portion of the fund, Northern's President Harden proposed that some of it be transferred for administration by the college. Negotiations between Northern officials and the Rotary Club's scholarship and loan committee, headed by Allan Olson, culminated in an agreement effective March 28, 1960.

This established a three-thousand-dollar Earle M. Parker Rotary Loan Fund comprising the fifteen hundred dollars from the Parker estate and a matching amount from the rest of the club's scholarship and loan fund. The total amount was placed in trust with Northern, under the oversight of its comptroller, for loans to "eligible and deserving Marquette County students." The contract also stipulated that sums, "not to exceed $500 per person, would be made without distinction to program of study, sex, race, religion or other affiliation." Interest payments, at progressive rates, were not to start until after a recipient's graduation. The college promised the same protection to the Parker Fund as that given its own loan money. The agreement was made effective for five years, reviewable at the end of four, and, by mutual consent, renewable for another five. In 1965 it was extended to 1970.

The Rotary board made payment to Northern on April 9, 1960. The contract was amended on September 9 to permit loans to students in Northern's practical nursing program by waiving a minimum twelve-hour credit completion requirement to qualify. During the academic year 1960-61 eighteen students borrowed the near limit of $2,992, and a Northern spokesman stated that still more money could be beneficially distributed. The club's reaction was cautious, but on February 24, 1964, the members voted to transfer an additional three thousand dollars to the Parker Fund.

During the early sixties the club also supported the student aid program of Rotary International. At its October 7, 1963, meeting, the local board of directors voted to contribute two hundred dollars, also five dollars for each new member, to the Rotary Foundation. The next month, this action was construed to mean that the club in effect was donating ten dollars for each initiate, and on February 3, 1964, the directors formally committed the group to the 10 and 1 plan by which the club annually gives ten dollars for each newcomer and one for every existing member.

Late in 1965 the local Rotarians were gratified to learn that Phillip C. Muerhcke of Gwinn, a Northern Michigan University graduate, would become the club's first Rotary Foundation Fellow. He spent the academic year 1966-67 at the University of Sydney in Australia.

Major Controversy—The Electric Power Issue

A portent of the social and economic conflict so characteristic of the nation in the sixties and seventies involved the Marquette Rotary Club in 1962 and '63 in the most obviously divisive situation ever to confront it.

Even during the fifties, modernization and expansion by the Cleveland-Cliffs Iron Company and its partners began to require vastly more electric power. To meet the new demand, Cleveland-Cliffs and the Upper Peninsula Power Company formed an Upper Peninsula Generating Company, in which each held a half interest, and through it built a steam plant near the mouth of the Dead River and the ore docks at what was named the Presque Isle station. The new facility, with a capacity of 23,000 kilowatts, began operation in August, 1955. A larger unit was completed in the summer of 1962, and a still larger one of 58,400 kilowatt capacity came into use late in 1963.[7]

Meanwhile, burgeoning enrollments at Northern, increasing medical needs, and general population growth were overtaxing Marquette's diesel unit and its three hydroelectric plants in the same area. In 1962 the people of the city were faced with the question of whether to buy additional power from the U.P. Power Company or to expand their own holdings, also, if the latter, where to put their steam plant.

At this juncture the U.P. Power Company, whose president, John H. Warden, was a Houghton Rotarian with family and banking ties in Marquette, on October 4, 1962, offered to sell the city the additional power it needed.[8] For several years Warden and another of his company's officials, William Veeser, had been pointing toward this in talks to the Marquette Rotary Club.

With planning for a new municipal unit in an advanced stage, a Citizens Committee on Power Information on January 26, 1963, appealed to the voters to petition for a referendum on whether the plant should be built. The committee contended that city officials had embarked on an overly ambitious program, one which would cost the town $13,300,000, far more than it could afford. One thousand signatures would be needed by February 18 to get the matter on the ballot.[9]

Simultaneously, Commissioner C. Fred Rydholm addressed a communication "To the People of Marquette," urging them not to support the petition drive. To do so, he warned, would raise the interest rate on bonds for the project, would jeopardize federal aid to the amount of two million dollars, and might lead to a power shortage before a new steam plant could be completed.[10]

The always gentlemanly Lincoln Frazier, spokesman for the Citizens Committee, between January 29 and February 6 published four open "Dear Fred" letters to an equally courteous adversary. In these, Frazier argued that $13,300,000 was more than half of the city's assessed valuation of $26,000,000; that it had never been shown that taxes and light and power bills were lower in Marquette than elsewhere or that the existing municipally owned facilities were managed efficiently; that commitment to a huge bonded indebtedness would force delay or abandonment of many other much needed improvements; and that such a burden would impair the city's credit, for even though the bonds would be the direct obligation of the independent light and power board, they in effect would be the responsibility of the town. Frazier closed with the question, could not the city contract for its additional electricity?[11]

A fellow Rotarian, City Manager Thomas Moore, who was in addition the superintendent of power, noted in partial reply that the true cost would be $10,934,776, not $13,300,000, and that the total income of the light and power department over a ten-year period would be $19,178,400, sufficient to keep the indebtedness under control.[12]

Mayor James Smith deplored delaying tactics. City employees "and Friends" ran a full-page advertisement in the *Mining Journal* to refute an earlier claim that the U.P. Generating Company was the largest single taxpayer in Marquette with figures indicating that the city's light and power board contributed far more money to the town. The same notice listed electric rates for seven neighboring communities which relied on private sources of power. By comparison, Marquette's charges were held to be the lowest.[13]

While the debate for and against construction was going on, Rotarians Ling, Heath, Closser, and Jack D. McKichan were representing residents of Shiras Hills, Lakeview Heights, and the South Lake Street district who wished to have the proposed municipal steam plant located elsewhere—on a site farther north along the shore of the harbor or on the Dead River away from Lake Superior. A 250-foot stack to relieve them of air pollution was in their view unsightly, to say the least. It long had been hoped that the intended location would be developed as a recreation, not an industrial area. The critics were not mollified by promises of a "clean stack," tasteful landscaping, and a heated swimming pool.[14]

Within the Rotary Club the controversy peaked at the luncheon meetings of February 4 and 11 and at a board meeting on the fourth. At the noon gatherings Ernest Pearce and Thomas Moore each took an hour to summarize the opposing arguments. A judicious secretary called the contest "a draw." Almost all of the board's time in an evening session "was taken up with a heated discussion of the power problem facing the City of Marquette."

Warden announced on February 7 that his company was withdrawing its formal offer of the previous October but, pointing to the steadily increasing capacity at the Presque Isle station, suggested that in case of future city shortages an agreement could be worked out. Five days later, the Citizens Committee announced that it was abandoning its thrust for a referendum.[15]

The municipal steam generating plant, named for George Shiras, was opened in

1967 on the Lake Superior site at the foot of East Hampton Street to which such vigorous objection had been made. Private and public power officials have cooperated quite amicably since. However, in and out of the Rotary Club, people still remember that the city has never fulfilled its promise to construct a heated swimming pool on the premises, and complaints persist that the stack is not clean.

The Passing of Patriarchs—Ernest Pearce's "Big Year"

As the Marquette Rotary Club approached its fiftieth anniversary, it lost within six years five of its most distinguished patriarchs: Frederick P. Burrall, eighty-seven; Percy G. Teeple, eighty-nine; Edward S. Bice, ninety; J. Cloyd Bowman, eighty-one (in Florida); and Joseph C. Gannon, eighty-eight, last of the charter members, who died on February 16, 1965. Gannon had been in chronically poor health and had rarely attended meetings during his later years. His passing escaped official notice by the club.

Ernest Pearce died on June 30, 1964. In contrast to Gannon, he had remained robust until the last three years of his life and active in the club throughout. At a televised Rotary meeting on April 11, 1960, he had received a special charter member pin for forty-four years of service, but his most exciting days lay ahead. For him "The Big Year," as he called it, was 1961.

One of his greatest satisfactions ever came on January 31 when, at the age of seventy-five, after encouragement from Milton Johnson and a year's study for adult night courses, he was graduated from Graveraet Senior High School. Beyond that, W. H. Treloar several weeks earlier had received an enthusiastic reponse to his phoned suggestion to CBS that Pearce be invited to celebrate his accomplishment by appearing on Garry Moore's television show, "I've Got a Secret." With Henry Morgan substituting for Moore, who was on vacation, Pearce faced a panel consisting of Bill Cullen, Betsy Palmer, Johnny Carson, and Gretchen Wyler during a taping session on February 15 in New York.

The program was broadcast nationally on February 22 to upwards of twenty-five million viewers, according to a *Mining Journal* report. This is believed to have been the first time anyone from Marquette had received TV exposure of such dimension. An Associated Press release on Pearce's graduation, together with his television appearance, brought him newspaper clippings from thirty states and two foreign countries, also "scores of telegrams" and "hundreds of personal notes."[16]

Pearce next treated himself to "a graduation present of a '45 day Trip Around the World,' leaving New York on February 25, 1961." In April he attended an international conference of Masons in Washington, D.C., and on September 16 was honored at home by those of the Upper Peninsula at a testimonial dinner attended by four hundred persons. The next month, he entered St. Luke's Hospital for major surgery, the first of his life, but on October 27 kept an engagement to serve as chairman and toastmaster at an anniversary dinner of the First Methodist Church. "Back to work

E. L. Pearce on "I've Got a Secret" TV Program, 1961, with Host Henry Morgan and Panelists Johnny Carson, Bill Cullen, and Betsy Palmer

Oct. 31." In December he learned that he was to be awarded an honorary doctorate at Northern's June, 1962, commencement.[17]

For over forty-eight years Pearce had been a main support of the Marquette Rotary Club. It is probably no exaggeration to say that toward the end he was *The* Establishment. Physically quite large, he seemed still larger, He conveyed the impression of caged energy, in the manner of J. P. Morgan. Pearce undoubtedly was among the last of the American breed of "rugged individualists"—a man of conviction or prejudice, depending on the point of view. In today's delicate terminology, he was "controversial."

At the July 23, 1964, regular luncheon meeting of the Rotary Club, Earl Closser read a eulogy written by Treloar. It began and ended with the words, "Because a man walked here. . . ."

The Golden Anniversary

It was fitting that Robert J. Pearce, son of Ernest, should be chosen club president for its fiftieth anniversary year. He was the fourth member of his family to hold the office, his brothers Edward L. and Don having preceded him in the chair in addition to his father.[18] Indeed, Robert Pearce had been held back in the progression to permit the honoring of both his family and him in this fashion.

The anniversary meeting was held on January 17, 1966,[19] to mark the month in which the Marquette Rotary Club had organized and chosen its first officers. Some two hundred Rotarians, Rotary Anns, and guests—many past presidents among them—assembled for dinner in the Great Lakes rooms of Northern's university center to the

E. L. Pearce and Sons: David, Robert, Edward, and Don

The Golden Anniversary, 1966 President Robert Pearce cuts birthday cake while Toastmaster W. H. Treloar looks on.

accompaniment of popular music played by the local Jim Boerner dance trio.

President Pearce opened the program by calling upon Rev. Norbert W. Smith for the invocation and upon William E. Wright for direction in the singing of R-O-T-A-R-Y. Pearce then spoke briefly about the club's dedication to the Rotary motto, "Service Above Self," thereby establishing the theme for the evening before turning the meeting over to Toastmaster Treloar.

After recognizing the presence of August Syverson, the oldest living past president, and Dr. Samuel Buck, whose perfect attendance now was approaching forty-two years, Richard O'Dell gave the principal address of the night on "Historical Highlights," a summary of the Marquette Rotary Club's service record.[20]

To illustrate the organization's continuing devotion to service, Roy Heath made a 10 and 1 presentation to District Governor Clifford A. Lewis of Curtis, Michigan. Dr. Norman Matthews gave fellow Rotarian Roy Fletcher, a director of Bay Cliff, the annual contribution of five hundred dollars for the camp. Rev. Smith presented scholarship checks to two Marquette students enrolled at Northern. President Pearce gave Col. Peter Sianis, commander of the K. I. Sawyer Air Force Base, a plaque in recognition of his personal record of service and announced his election to honorary membership in the club.

Earl Closser read congratulatory messages from many organizations and individuals, including two from Vice-President Hubert H. Humphrey and Michigan's Governor George Romney, also a concurrent resolution from the Michigan legislature which had been introduced by Sen. Joseph Mack and Rep. Dominic J. Jacobetti. The Marquette Kiwanis Club sent a floral tribute and a message of esteem to "the grand old men" of Rotary.

The Marquette Rotary Club officers for the year 1965-66 were, in addition to Pearce, Edward J. Stratton, vice-president; William A. Todd, secretary; Ray A. Nelson, treasurer; and George Franzen, sergeant at arms. These men, along with L. Wallace Bruce, Charles T. Smedman, Vern O. Holgate, Dr. George M. Wilson, and Wesley E. Perron, constituted the board of directors.

Pearce and Closser Holding Congratulatory Resolution from Michigan Legislature;
Treloar and Peter Sianis at left and right

10
EXPANSION AND SERVICE

The "spirit of Geneva" and the consensus politics of the Eisenhower years wore off long before the mid-1960s. The continuing decline of Great Britain and France as world colonial powers encouraged greater Russian and American involvement in the Middle East and among the emerging nations of the Third World. Helping to maintain a precarious diplomatic and military balance, China in the sixties clashed sharply with Russia and during the Nixon Administration strove for a rapprochement, however tentative and tenuous, with the United States.

Meanwhile, the enormous burst of prosperity among the industrialized nations of the West, particularly the North American giant, began to strain the mineral resources of the world. Multinational corporations competed everywhere for raw materials, labor, and markets and in so doing became ever more capital and less labor intensive. In the seventies, leaders of once "backward" countries revealed an unsuspected astuteness in using their own huge stocks of oil and other basic commodities to advantage in international exchange. Consequently the United States, by far the most voracious consumer of world treasure, found itself reverting to the status of a debtor nation with no longer invulnerable currency. Once staunch European and Japanese allies started asserting their independence from American influence and control.

Immersed like everyone else in a caldron of world discontent, Americans who for a half century had felt as safe from unwanted immigration as from military invasion began to sense an inundation of foreign peoples and cultures which threatened traditional Anglo-Saxon values, concepts, and customs. The demands of continued world leadership required the United States to bring practice more nearly into conformance with its ideals of freedom and equal opportunity by starting, in the fifties, school desegregation programs and, later, by extending voting and other civil rights to its own black citizens and native Indians to a degree which otherwise might not have been done to this day.

Compounding the inevitable problems of an industrialized, urbanized society were the Kennedy and King assassinations, the abhorrent Vietnam War, and the Johnson and Nixon probings of the limits to the "Imperial Presidency" which culminated in the Watergate debacle.

For the first time, Marquette's rate of economic and social change truly became synchronized with that of the outside world, most evidently through the magnitude and rapidity of public and private construction: government office buildings, a municipal steam generating plant, shopping centers, educational structures, high-rise apartments for senior citizens, and greatly enlarged medical facilities, not to mention the nearby billion-dollar mining expansion program of Cleveland-Cliffs and its partners.

With or without Marquette's particular combination of construction projects and trends during the past two decades, most of the current problems of life would have afflicted the city in the ordinary course of events. But there can be no doubt that physical growth, promoted and financed mainly by or through enterprising outsiders, often contributed to social destabilization rather than cohesion.

Entrepreneurs, hired managers, and construction workers came and went, as did thousands of university students recruited from far beyond the Upper Peninsula. Many native and longtime residents of Marquette, whatever their economic and social status, became uneasy, resentful, and occasionally alarmed at a pace of existence much faster than that which always had characterized the town and region and with which, for good or ill, they had felt generally comfortable.

As community leaders became more committed to material growth, a large minority of citizens remained skeptical of all government economic and social programs, indeed of any new enterprises beyond the capacity of private local groups or individuals to finance. A few exceptionally vocal and durable populists, through their persistent opposition to school construction, municipal power expansion, and government funded projects for civic improvement, conveyed an "even if it was good I wouldn't like it" impression to the more optimistic, dynamic Marquette and outside planners and developers.

Changes In Philosophy and Personnel

A time-honored gentlemen's agreement whereby three Protestants and two Catholics, most or all of them Rotarians, had kept the city commission on a steady, conservative course ended during the 1950s. By the mid-sixties the Rotarians, mildly polarized on the issue of economic expansion, were in many other respects as caught up in social flux as the rest of the community. By 1970 death and retirement would have taken their toll of all but three or four club members whose affiliations antedated the early thirties, thus virtually completing a long philosophical drift from individualism and firm conviction to pragmatism. As much as any single event, the election of Social Security administrator George Franzen to the club's presidency in 1967 signaled the advance into a new era.

A dozen of Marquette's most prominent physicians and businessmen, whose Rotary membership averaged almost four decades, were lost to the club through death within little more than five years after its golden anniversary. In 1966 Dr. Arthur K. Bennett, a former chief of staff of both hospitals and for a time the city's health officer, died in Marquette at the age of eighty-five. While in retirement in Florida he had helped found the Rotary Club of Mt. Dora. Dr. Charles Drury, who had been the health officer for a total of twenty-five years, died in 1967 in St. Petersburg, Florida.

John D. Morrison

A month earlier, Dr. Buck had succumbed after a brief illness at eighty-eight. Past President Syverson followed him in death at the same age a few months later. George M. Altmann, founder and proprietor of the typewriter and adding machine service bearing his name, and Norman J. Dobson, founder and president of the U.P. Office Supply Company, died in 1968 and 1970. Clayton P. Frei, automobile dealer (1969); Harvard A. Jean, optometrist and owner of Jean's Jewelry Store, successor to Conklin's (1971); and Clyde DeHaas, long a manufacturer's representative selling industrial and construction supplies (1971), were other veterans who passed from the scene.

Gone, too, were past Presidents John Morrison, who had been the auditor general of Michigan in 1945-46 (1968); Edward Pearce, who had succeeded his father in the presidency of the Union National Bank (1966); and Robert Pearce, an insurance agency head (1970). The two brothers were still in their early fifties. L. Burton Hadley, a veteran of World War I and president of the club for the year 1937-38, was elected the first life member in 1970. He died in 1980 in Florida.

Despite the attritions of death, retirement, and resignation, service in Rotary lived on. Among the new members none had a more colorful as well as distinguished career than lean, soft-spoken, courteous Capt. David H. McClintock, USN (Ret.), who joined the club in 1966.

After coming to Marquette at an early age, McClintock was educated at the John D. Pierce School, Northern, and the U.S. Naval Academy. Peacetime duty as a submarine officer in the Pacific culminated in a Japanese aerial attack on his vessel, the U.S.S. *Plunger*, on December 7, 1941, while en route from the west cost to Hawaii. Seven wartime patrols on *Plunger* and *Cero* were followed by a brief assignment on the staff of Fleet Adm. William F. Halsey.

Then, while in command of two submarines, McClintock in October, 1944, closed with the main Japanese fleet of thirty-two warships moving to attack in the Philippine Islands. His own *Darter* fired the first shot in the Battle for Leyte Gulf, sinking the heavy cruiser *Atago*, flagship of the fleet commander, Vice Adm. Takeo Kurita. The companion submarine destroyed another enemy vessel of the same classification. After damaging a third cruiser so badly that two destroyers had to be assigned to guard it, *Darter* herself ran aground. Her crew were rescued several hours laters.

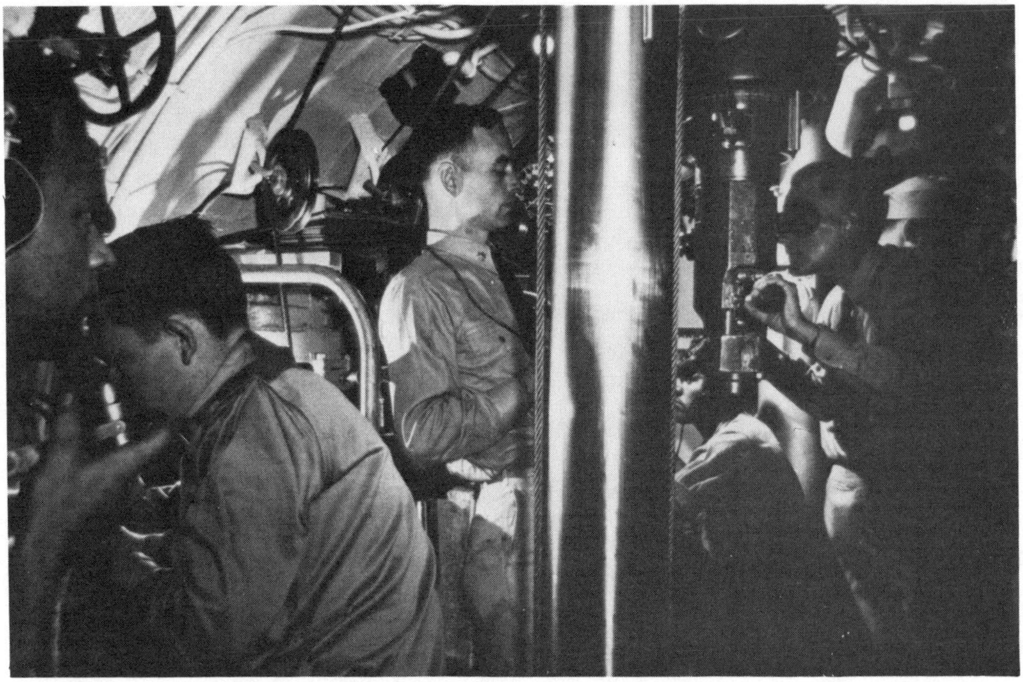

Lt. Comdr. David McClintock (center)
in U.S.S. *Cero* in Navy Recruiting Photograph, World War II

Thus the two submarines in McClintock's charge destroyed or immobilized five Japanese ships before the battle was fully joined. Adm. Samuel Eliot Morison, America's most noted naval historian, has described what developed into three-part action as the "greatest sea fight of this or of any other war." World War II ended as McClintock was returning to the Pacific with a new submarine, *Menhaden*.

For his wartime services McClintock was awarded the Navy Cross, Silver Star, and two Bronze Stars. From 1945 until his retirement in 1965 he was given many command, staff, and administrative (ROTC, National Security Council, National War College) assignments. At intervals he commanded Submarine Division Twenty-One, Squadron Eight, and Flotilla One. The latter, based in San Diego, embraced all American submarines operating from the west coast of the United States.[1]

A commercial movie, *The Two Davids and Goliath*, made with Navy Department cooperation, became one segment in a series, "The Silent Service," which was televised nationally in the 1950s and 1960s. Shown twice to the Marquette Rotarians, the film starred Murray Hamilton as McClintock and Dennis Weaver as his teammate in the Leyte Gulf operation.

Community Service

Determined to build on the record of their first fifty years, the Marquette Rotarians immediately after their golden anniversary celebration sought as a group to enter the mainstream of civic improvement in the city. As in the late 1940s, their aim was not to compete with any existing agency. But this time they proposed to offer material as well as moral support for a variety of worthy projects. To this end President Robert Pearce in February of 1966 informally solicited ideas from friends and business associates as to community needs and ways the club could assist in meeting them.

The signs seemed favorable. Against the background of war in Vietnam and of unrest and assassination at home, the desirability of morale-building community endeavor appeared self-evident. Although primarily in a nurturing role still, the Rotarians nevertheless might assume responsibility for a few modest tasks while providing "seed money" for the development of ideas whose fulfillment would require much larger commitments from other agencies. Conceivably, too, from club investigation and reflection might come a homogenizing influence reminiscent of that contributed by the Rotarians through the first city planning board.

Already, as part of the Johnson Administration's War on Poverty, the U.S. Office of Economic Opportunity was sponsoring a nonprofit, charitable Alger-Marquette Community Action Board (AMCAB) with headquarters in Marquette. Northern Michigan University had secured, or was about to obtain, federal grants to institute a Volunteers in Service to America (VISTA) program and to establish a Women's Job Corps Center on Northern's campus. The latter was to help three hundred young women from the inner cities of Chicago and other metropolitan areas acquire more useful vocational and social skills than they could achieve in their home environments.

As early as the spring of 1962 the city, aided by three federal grants, two private land use studies, and establishment of a Marquette office of the U.S. Department of Housing and Urban Development (HUD), had begun seeking ways to halt deterioration in downtown Marquette and to construct adequate low rental housing units for senior citizens. On January 11, 1966, George Howell, urban renewal director for Marquette, discussed at a Rotary luncheon plans for clearing and renovating an area in the heart of the city. In 1966 and '67 Women's Job Corps, AMCAB, and VISTA representatives explained their operations at weekly Rotary meetings.

During the same period, private individuals and groups kept the club informed of their efforts toward civic and social improvement. William F. Wilson described the structure and functions of Operation Action, conceived by Edgar Harden and Detroit Edison Company Board Chairman Walker Cisler to encourage industrial and commercial growth in the Upper Peninsula. Vern Dahlquist returned to review the work of the Child & Family Services of the Upper Peninsula. Ben Martin of Northern showed a Mott Foundation film titled *The Community School*, a pictorial narrative of a movement in Flint, Michigan, to open its schools to a range of adult as well as youth activities. Early in 1967 Donald F. Vreeland of Iron Mountain explained the northern peninsula program of the YMCA, which he served as district secretary.

Marquette Community Projects, Inc.

Among the persons consulted by Pearce was Jerry Pulliam, executive vice-president of the Marquette Chamber of Commerce. In a three-page letter dated February 19,

1966, Pulliam proposed that the Rotary Club consider the possibilities for: 1) acquisition of a building for an art gallery or museum of local culture (though not in competition with the Marquette County Historical Society) to serve as a work and display area for local artists; 2) development or construction of a harbor street "as a replica of the old Marquette with the atmosphere of the lumberjack, the miner, the fisherman, the sailor, the landowner preserved with the taverns, offices, shops and services they required"; and 3) establishment of a fund for inquiry into the prospects for a public auditorium or arena, shoreline cleanup and beautification, medical research, construction of a marina, and implementation of the first two numbered suggestions.

Shortly afterward Pearce appointed an exploratory Rotary committee headed by Wesley E. Perron, director of the club's committee on community service. Following extensive discussion at regular weekly meetings, during which the members at large contributed numerous suggestions for projects, the committee recommended establishment of a nonprofit Marquette Community Projects corporation within the club, funding to be by voluntary contributions of Rotarians. Robert Clark drafted a constitution, bylaws, and articles of incorporation.

In June the Rotarians approved the new instruments and, accordingly, elected nine trustees for staggered terms of from one to three years: Clark, Perron, Patrick L. Bennett, Lesley Cory, Wesley Jenner, E. J. LaFreniere, Richard O'Dell, Rev. Norbert Smith, and William Wright. The trustees chose O'Dell and Smith chairman and secretary. As club treasurer, Ray Nelson was given custody of the corporation's funds.

Edward J. Stratton, successor to Robert Pearce as president of the Rotary Club, announced in August of 1966 that his principal objective would be to "Build For the Future." Simultaneously, the trustees of Marquette Community Projects, Inc., informed the parent group that they had decided upon two specific tasks for the coming year—"the furnishing of a Rotary Room for the temporary Marquette Community Center and the sponsoring of a Youth Community Projects Fair."

Several months before, the Shiras Institute, through a gift of sixty-three thousand dollars to the city, had made possible the purchase of the old Soo Line Railroad Company depot on Main Street for conversion into a community building. Included in the agreement was the stipulation that proceeds from any second sale should go toward construction of a similar facility.

Patrick Bennett, manager of Northern Stationers, Inc., acted as purchasing agent for a pool table, tennis tables, lounge and folding chairs, and several other items for the Rotary Room. The building opened in the fall and remained in use until 1969, when the city did sell it and moved the center to the gymnasium of the recently closed Bishop Baraga High School.

In October, 1966, the Rotary Club announced to the public that, in cooperation with Northern Michigan University, the Marquette Public Schools, Bishop Baraga High School, and Marquette Youth Services, and with the endorsement of the city commission, it was sponsoring "Projects Unlimited," a prize contest and youth fair for all Marquette students between the ages of fourteen and twenty-one. There would be two categories of competition: 1) Audiovisual projects graphically representing through drawings, sculpture, or scale models ideas for necessary or desirable improvements in Marquette; 2) Essays "on some phase of urban planning or community life." Up to three thousand dollars in prizes would be awarded within two age groups for each classification.

The one-day fair was held on Saturday, May 13, 1967, in the Brule Room of the Northern Michigan University Center. Marquette architect Howard G. McKie, Rev. Norbert Smith, and Earl Closser chaired citizens' committees which judged the projects and essays and handled physical arrangements. Mrs. Betty Lou Kitzman of the *Mining Journal* provided excellent news coverage, as she had through several months of preparation.[2]

First prizes of five hundred dollars were awarded to Daniel J. Trotochaud, a Northern student, for his model of a youth center, and to Patricia L. Savitski and John S. Price jointly, of Marquette Senior High School, for a Presque Isle resort display. Lesser sums were granted designers of city-county building, blood bank, and Presque Isle improvement exhibits and the sculptor of *Youth*, a nearly life-size plaster statue. The few essays submitted were so lacking in quality that a token payment only was made for one entry, "The Drinking Problem vs. the Good Student."

The considerable student and town interest evident in the early stages of development had dwindled during the winter and spring until few more than a couple of dozen hardy contestants and their families and friends attended the fair. Its "incomplete success" inevitably invites comparison with the remarkably productive essay contest among the Marquette high school students in 1948. This, of course, had been

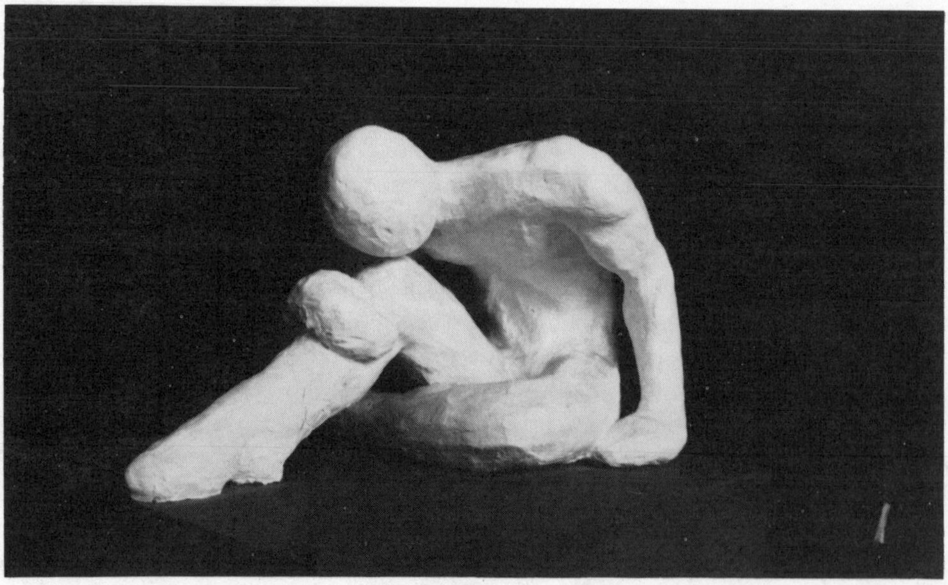

Youth
Rotary "Projects Unlimited" prizewinning statue by Brian Dragon, Marquette Senior High School student, now owned by Miodrag and Militza Georgevich of Marquette.

held just as the outline of an ambitious school construction program was becoming discernible. The Rotarians of that day were firmly in charge of city planning, the whole town was looking forward to its centennial celebration, and youthful writers stood a good chance of seeing extracts from their work in print.

In 1966-67, by contrast, the city was socially fragmented and contentious. Vested government and private interests were leading people in different directions instead of uniting them in support of a coherent pattern for development. High school and university students, worried about Vietnam and about the insecurities of family life, took their now excellent educational facilities for granted. They sought release from frustration in dubious recreational pursuits and various forms of protest. The younger ones vented a good deal of their displeasure upon dress codes and hair length limitations. Convinced that in these uncongenial circumstances anything more that Marquette Community Projects might attempt would not be worth the effort, the Rotarians in July of 1967 dissolved it.

Urban Renewal

Illustrative of the depth of feeling about community matters was the controversy over urban renewal. For several years during the mid- and late sixties, city commissioners gained or lost seats according to their stand on the issue. Briefly stated, the question was whether the city should avail itself of an already earmarked federal sum of $1,067,438 to buy and clear almost all the land of structures within a two-block downtown area bounded by Front, Washington, Fourth, and Bluff streets, plus a strip on the south side of Washington between the *Mining Journal* building and Third Street, then sell the land back to former owners or to new purchasers. The city was to contribute several hundred thousand dollars in electrical installations and improvements and, perhaps, a small amount of cash.[3]

Proponents of the project reasoned that retail sales dollars leaving Marquette for other communities in the Upper Peninsula and Wisconsin would be retained and tourist trade increased. Renovation of a relatively small district, to be done by private developers, would mark the start of a citywide face-lifting which would enhance greatly the prosperity and beauty of the town, particularly if a pedestrian mall were included in the plans for reconstruction.

Critics—small business people and impoverished homeowners and renters in the affected area along with commercial interests outside it—dwelt on the hardships of temporary or permanent dislocation; the feeling that enterprises in the designated zone would benefit from government assistance to the detriment of those outside it, also that, wherever located, bankers, realtors, and landowners would be the ones who would profit most; the conviction that local private groups could accomplish what should be done without the aid of federal funds and outside planners and workers; and on the contention that the proposals were not comprehensive or specific enough to insure the results desired.

Two defeats at the polls in 1969 terminated the urban renewal project. Although there was considerable diversity of opinion within the Rotary Club, the members gave the issue little formal attention. On October 27, however, just before the second balloting, Earl Closser spoke in favor of a modified plan, Lincoln Frazier on the feasibility of a public parking area on South Front Street.

Outward Thrust

Continued growth and dispersion of population and businesses into the townships led the Union National Bank to replace its downtown structure, the First National to remodel part of its building, and both to establish branches around the perimeter of Marquette. The sale and conversion of the old city hall into an architecturally distinctive office building through private initiative and funding set a high standard for similar though smaller undertakings. The greater amount of community renovation remained to be done.

In rapid succession the Shopko center, the Marquette Mall, University Shopping Center, and Westwood Plaza were constructed between 1969 and 1976 away from the heart of town. The Clark family provided the site and has retained managerial control of the second of these. On September 10, 1973, the Marquette Rotarians toured the complex, several weeks before its opening.

Dissolution of Marquette Community Projects, Inc., did not detract permanently from the Rotary Club's practice of contributing to enterprises undertaken by other agencies, particularly those in which Rotarians had major roles.

For many years Allan Olson headed a citizens' committee to plan a convention center or arena to replace the Palestra. A week after City Manager Thomas McNabb gave a progress report to the Rotary Club, the board of directors on August 7, 1972, pledged three thousand dollars over a three-year period to the arena's construction fund. The full membership approved the decision and voted to raise the money by assessing each Rotarian ten dollars annually. Within a year after the Lakeview Arena was completed farther east on Fair Avenue, largely through the efforts of several Rotarians, the old Palestra was razed in September of 1974.

Important, perhaps indispensable, to construction of the new center was a gift of one hundred thousand dollars from the Shiras Institute. By the spring of 1977 this source, whose assets had been augmented by additional bequests, had disbursed over one million dollars for Marquette area projects. Details of its benefactions were recounted on May 2 of that year at a community luncheon at which three hundred persons honored the Institute at the Northern Michigan University Center. In the presence of Frank Russell, Jr., and the other trustees, two of them Rotarians Herman Olson and Allan Olson, the chairman, W. H. Treloar, introduced Kenneth S. Lowe, former editor of the *Mining Journal*. With the aid of slides, Lowe reviewed forty years of Shiras philanthropy.[4]

The *Mining Journal* had stated succinctly three days before:

> Shiras grants helped build or improve the tourist park, Marquette golf course, Harlow and Lakeside parks, the Marquette County Historical Society building, the Palestra, Shiras Zoo, the tennis courts and planetarium at Marquette Senior

Lakeview Arena
Its 60,000 square feet (accommodating two ice rinks) have been utilized for hockey, figure skating, and ice shows; also for circuses, concerts, conventions, banquets, and trade shows. Attendance of 50,000 were expected at 1982 Logging Congress here.

Northern Michigan University hockey team defeats the University of Minnesota for division championship in Lakeview Arena prior to becoming NCAA Runner-Up for 1979-80.

High School, Marquette's Lakeview Arena and Presque Isle marina, and countless other projects.

A recent gift to the city helped it to acquire downtown lakefront property which it intends to develop for public use.

The institute also has supported junior hockey and junior baseball; Boy Scouts, Girl Scouts and Sea Scouts; Bay Cliff Health Camp . . .; Brookridge—the Marquette residential facility for emotionally disturbed children; the cobalt treatment center at Bell Memorial Hospital and the National Ski Hall of Fame in Ishpeming—and a host of recreation-oriented groups. . . .[5]

On April 30 the paper had recalled Shiras grants for the purchase of the Soo Line depot, for Northern scholarship and cultural purposes, and in the late forties, for partial payment of the Palestra's artificial ice plant.[6]

Since the recognition luncheon, the Shiras Institute has continued its grant program with taste and discrimination. It has provided, for example, funds to the Peter White Public Library to help prepare and furnish its Local Heritage rooms, a project begun as part of Marquette's Bicentennial observance.

To this as well as to almost all similar improvements, Rotarians, past and present, or their families have contributed. Club members were largely responsible for construction of the small boat marina at the neck of Presque Isle. On March 14, 1977, Mayor Holly Greer came before the Rotary Club to report suggestions and plans for the city's new lower harbor site. As noted in the second of the three *Mining Journal* paragraphs quoted above, the acquisition was facilitated by a Shiras gift. It should also be mentioned that the Spear family had offered the property at considerably less than market value. During her talk, Mrs. Greer recognized the work of Rotarians David McClintock and David Allie, the first a consultant to, the other a member of a special committee planning for the area's development.

Social and Educational Services

In addition to a small monetary gift by the Rotary Club to the Marquette Health Planning Council, individual contributions by Rotarians and Rotary Anns in time, knowledge, and money to the multimillion-dollar hospital construction program in the city have been too numerous to list. Lincoln Frazier and Wesley Jenner, representing St. Luke's and St. Mary's respectively, were two members of a four-man committee which in 1973 negotiated a merger of the two units into one Marquette General Hospital in order to eliminate duplications in service. Expansion in the wake of this has brought an increase in the number of area physicians and surgeons from approximately thirty in 1972 to about eighty in 1981, has introduced the most modern, sophisticated equipment available, and has made Marquette the undisputed medical center for the Upper Peninsula.

In connection with hospital development there was an ironic turn which surely would have saddened George Shiras had he lived to see it. After having held title to the Hotel Northland for five years, St. Luke's Hospital in 1970 sold it to Rotarians Don Pearce and Richard A. Lutey. They refurbished and renamed it The Heritage House. When they transferred it to a Milwaukee purchaser in 1975, the old landmark for the first time passed from Rotary ownership or control. Although now back in local hands under the name Old Marquette Inn, the break from the club and its members appears to be permanent.

Patience, industry, and determination over many years have characterized Rotary and other citizen support for the public schools. Following two unsuccessful bond drives, split shift sessions at Graveraet High School, and loss of North Central Association accreditation, a third vote had authorized construction of a new Marquette Senior High School building, which opened in the fall of 1964.

In May, 1969, guest speaker Roland Schwitzgoebel successfully appealed to the Rotarians for their endorsement of yet another bond issue proposal, this one for $7,655,000. Citizen approval at the polls on June 9 made possible an addition to the still new high school, remodeling of the Graveraet building, and construction of the Henry J. Bothwell Middle School.

Opening of the Bothwell school in 1972 brought to a most gratifying conclusion

James Couzens Memorial Building (St. Luke's Hospital Addition of 1938)

St. Luke's Hospital Board of Trustees, 1941 (Rotarians All) *Standing*: Harlow A. Clark, Eugene G. Day, Lincoln B. Frazier, Maxwell K. Reynolds. *Seated*: Peter White Phelps, John D. Morrison, Edward S. Bice.

Marquette General Hospital

Henry J. Bothwell Middle School

a more than twenty-year effort to provide the children and youth of Marquette the best public education the taxpayers felt they could afford. Superintendents Whitman and Bothwell, trustees Herman Olson and Mrs. Richard P. (Marion) Sonderegger, also Frazier and numerous Rotarians in unofficial capacities, had worked strenuously to improve and expand the schools' programs as well as their physical facilities. The combined service of Olson and Mrs. Sonderegger as school board members and officers totaled thirty-six years.

In 1966 the Upper Peninsula branch of the Michigan Children's Aid Society and the Family Service Society of Marquette merged to form the Child & Family Services of the Upper Peninsula. During 1968 the enlarged organization assisted 574 clients. Today it categorizes its functions under six headings: "family counseling, foster home care, adoption, marriage counseling, problem pregnancy services, residential treatment."[7] Rotarian Albert Burrows had been president of the Family Service Society for ten years, and two Rotary Anns, Mrs. Frank B. (Rachel) Spear, Jr., and Mrs. Lincoln B. (Anne) Frazier, had headed the organization for six and eleven years, respectively. Mrs. Frazier has served the consolidated group as president from 1977 to 1979.

Since the club's golden anniversary, four Rotarians have received community-wide recognition for their contributions to the city. The Marquette Junior Chamber of Commerce chose businessman Robert Ling "Young Man of the Year" for 1966 and attorney Thomas P. Casselman for the same distinction in 1974. W. H. Treloar was honored in 1967 and Lincoln Frazier in 1976 at appreciation dinners in the Great Lakes Rooms of the Northern Michigan University Center.[8] In 1977 the Rotary board of directors appointed a committee to consider establishment of a Marquette citizens hall of fame, but no action resulted.

Since 1970 several changes have occurred in the Rotary Club's policies governing gifts, exclusive of student loans and scholarships. There has been greater personal involvement in fund-raising and service projects. Donations to area agencies have been more varied and in greater amounts. Most significant have been the increased payments to the Rotary Foundation, made possible in part by a weekly lottery.

Support for the Greater Marquette United Community Chest (since 1974 the United Way of Marquette County) has been continuous. Marquette Rotarians Kenneth S. Hogg, Jr., and Robert Pearce were council president and campaign chairman in the same year of 1967. Two years later Robert C. Neldberg and George P. Petry were cochairmen, and in 1978 Robert B. Glenn headed the drive. In the latter years, under the immediate direction of John Weting, seventy-seven Rotarians each made at least one solicitation visit.

While waging a campaign against trash widely strewn in and around the town, Colonel E. "Bud" Weesen proposed that the club acquire a suitably labeled Rotary "Litter Trailer." This was obtained and displayed on Ladies Night in June, 1969. For a decade groups of Rotarians headed successively by Weesen, James R. Sesslar, and Edward N. Locke put the trailer to good use—the last time during "Operation Clean Sweep" in May, 1979. The vehicle has been sold, but Rotary participation in the annual city cleanup continues.

Beginning in 1971 the Rotary Club has participated with other service organizations in annual Salvation Army Christmas bellringing competition. In 1971, 1977, 1979, and 1980 the Rotarians have won the traveling trophy awarded the group raising the most money. Irvin W. Horton and his sixty-one fellow Rotary bellringers in 1979 filled their kettles with a record $1,341.78. After hearing a talk by Lt. James McLean on "The Salvation Army in the Marquette Area" in May, 1978, the Rotary board made a special donation to the Salvation Army Boy Scout troop.

Since 1972 the Rotary Club has given Christmas parties for handicapped children. The first of these was held for more than forty physically impaired youngsters who

Arvid Savola and Bill Owen, Bellringers for Salvation Army

gathered at noon on Tuesday, December 19, 1972, at the Heritage House. The next year two parties were sponsored, one at the Heritage House for children in the Marquette-Alger Intermediate School District special education program, the other at the Charcoal Pit for multihandicapped preschoolers. More than sixty guests attended the two affairs. At both, Rotarian Willard C. Evert was Santa Claus, and Helmut Kreitz, accompanied by "Mario" on the accordian, played the viola and led the caroling. The 1973 events established a pattern for a single party the following year and for two more in 1975. In 1976, at the Holiday Inn, the local Ellen Clement Singers, a high school group, helped entertain.

Willard Martin and fellow Rotarians arranged the club's annual party on December 16, 1980, at the Holiday Inn for about sixty children and twenty-five MAISD staff members. After lunch came greetings from President Burt Parolini, a magic show by Dan David, caroling led by Tim Brimmer and Harold Wright, and Santa's distribution of gifts to all of the youngsters. "Another reason to feel good about being a Rotarian," reported Matthew Surrell in The ROTATOR.

After termination of "Birthdays for Bay Cliff" in 1969, the Marquette Rotary Club's monetary contributions to the health camp were reduced in amount and frequency. Nevertheless, when on August 16, 1971, camp director John Vargo conducted District Governor Ralph Noble of Houghton and twenty-one Marquette Rotarians on a tour of the facility, Noble expressed complete satisfaction with what he saw, and the next month the local Rotary board appropriated $250 for Bay Cliff.

On November 29, 1971, Dr. Patrick T. Kelly, a Marquette dentist and Rotarian, at a regular meeting of the club lamented the termination of a Mott Foundation dental program at Bay Cliff. The next year, the Rotary board voted three hundred dollars to help perpetuate the work. At the suggestion of Rotarian Rico N. Zenti, the club sponsored four Rotary Golf Days from June 26 through 29, 1973, at the Marquette Golf and Country Club. A surcharge of one dollar per round netted the Rotarians $261 for Bay Cliff. From 1975 through 1978 the Rotary Club and other local

Lloyd Steinhoff as Santa Claus at Children's Christmas Party, 1981

service organizations sponsored a Bay Cliff Benefit Carnival staged by an outside company. In 1977 the Rotary contribution from this source amounted to $532. During the past two years, the club has relied solely on cash donations from its general fund.

Following its golden anniversary, the Rotary Club gradually revived its interest in the Boy and Girl Scouts. On May 1, 1967, the board of directors contributed a small sum to the girls' organization. Richard Showalter, the Hiawathaland District Scout executive, appeared before the club on March 3, 1969, with a fifteen-year-old Boy Scout. However, a real resurgence of enthusiasm was evinced when the board on September 13, 1976, voted to contribute one thousand dollars over a three-year period toward renovation of the Boy Scout camp. The board called upon Allan L. Niemi, director of community service, to name a committee to determine how this sum should be raised, considering first the prospects for a pancake breakfast for which the manager of Sambo's already had offered batter at cost.

On January 16, 1977, Niemi, his committee, and other Rotarians—fifty-eight in all—served more than twelve hundred persons at such a breakfast in the National Guard Armory. So successful was this event that the club more than fulfilled its long-term pledge by donating $1,450 to the Boy Scouts by April 6. Niemi again had charge of the project, this one principally for the Girl Scouts, in January of 1978. The agreement was that the girls should receive fifty percent of the proceeds up to one thousand dollars. From a net of twenty-two hundred, the Rotarians easily met the maximum and in addition were able to allot sizable amounts to the Boy Scouts and the children's Christmas party of that year.

During the spring of 1978 Rotarian Gordon A. Johnstone assisted in arranging a successful Marquette Senior High School All Sports Booster Club pancake breakfast. In anticipation of the third annual Rotary Club meal early in 1979, the board decided to apportion half of the proceeds for community projects and to divide the other half equally between the Boy and Girl Scouts. Under the direction of Frank Allen this, too, was distinctly profitable. The disappointment in the series came in 1980 when proceeds dropped about forty percent below those of the preceding year. In 1981 the affair netted $1,637.

The Marquette Rotarians also have utilized what for them have been two inno-

Boy Scouts at Camp Red Buck

Glenn Stevens, Milton Soderberg, and Alfred Hunt await rush at annual Rotary Pancake Breakfast, 1980.

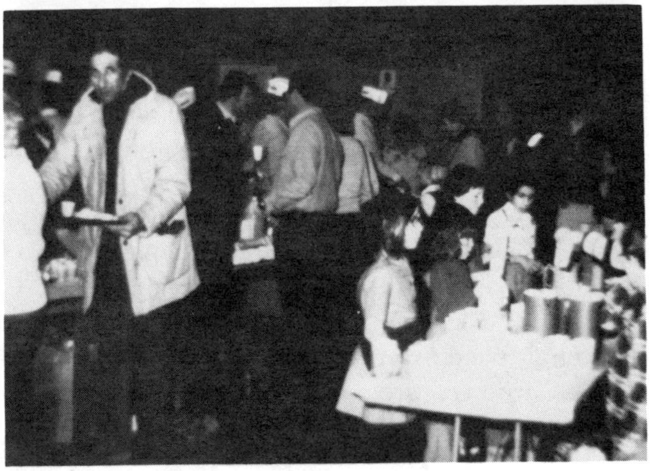

vative fund-raising techniques in recent years. In 1975 the club began selling lottery tickets for small sums—twenty-five cents each at first, now fifty cents or three for one dollar—at regular weekly meetings. The proceeds from these are split evenly between the winners and the Rotary Foundation. Remittances to the latter are made in five-hundred-dollar amounts. On August 18, 1978, the club sponsored a "Las Vegas" Night in the Great Lakes Rooms of the Northern Michigan University Center. Administered by four group chairmen—Thomas L. Gagnon, Donald E. Hooper, George E. Lott, Jr., and Johnstone—this event yielded eleven hundred dollars for club projects. Like the pancake breakfasts, this also has become an annual event.

Since 1966 the one object for which the Marquette Rotary Club has made contributions without a break has been the sending of delegates to Boys' State. Four donations have been made to the junior hockey program, the last for $250 in 1978.

Many recent gifts have been to different groups on a one-time basis: to the Northern Michigan University Arts Chorale, Norlake (a facility for the rehabilitation of delinquent and neglected children), the Marquette-Alger County Day School program, the NMU band for a trip to California to attend the 1976 football game in which Northern won the national NCAA Division II championship, the Northern student center for card tables and chairs, the Marquette County Historical Society for museum expansion, the Marquette Majestics Drum and Bugle Corps, the League of Women Voters to help pay for publication of their "Know Your Marquette County" booklet, the Humane Society, the Senior Citizens Fund, the Michigan State University Extension Service for purchase of a nutrition film suitable for elementary school showing, and Sundara House (a home for retarded young people).

The club also has purchased a freezer-refrigerator for Nu-Way House (a residential facility for alcoholics) and a portable television set for students in the Intermediate School District's special education program. The Rotarians in 1973 and 1974 helped support the Summer Day Breeze Camp sponsored by Northern Michigan University and by Marquette area schools and districts. In 1974 the Rotary board paid the tuition of a prison inmate to enable him to graduate from Northern, and the next year made it financially possible for him to take a postgraduate course.

During the year 1978-79 the Rotary Club gave money to nineteen different organizations including Little League baseball and the Big Brothers and Big Sisters. Taking into account an additional fifteen hundred dollars for scholarships, total contributions amounted to $4,592.

In 1979-80 the club expended $3,615 for Marquette and foreign Rotary Youth Exchange students (inbound and outbound); fifteen hundred dollars for Rotary International's Health, Hunger, and Humanity (3-H) Program; slightly less than thirteen hundred for Paul Harris Fellowships; one thousand toward the expense of a Pittsburgh Wind Symphony concert in Marquette; seven hundred for the 1979 children's Christmas party; and five hundred for a scholarship. Including smaller gifts to twelve other individuals and agencies, contributions totaled $10,056.

11
CHANGING TIMES

Some features of the Marquette Rotary Club's weekly luncheon meetings remain constant. Induction ceremonies for new members, memorial tributes to the deceased, the district governor's annual visit, Rotary information days, and club elections, all are perpetually vital to successful operation.

A few of the program stalwarts, too, seem durable to the point of immortality. Pat LaFreniere leads in song, as he has for a quarter century, with a voice so powerful as to make his hands and arms unnecessary. When he is absent, the veteran Bill Wright fills in for him. After thirty years, Waba Treloar continues to deliver the news at a drumfire pace and intensity hardly less than when he began. Following one of his yearly summaries, the secretary reported a member's comment: "Best program for 1972, even though it is only the first week and first program!" At the January 7, 1980, session President Allan Niemi presented Treloar with a plaque in recognition of his many contributions to meetings.

Treloar's very success has been a source of club embarrassment for which no solution has been found. Each week after his newscast a dozen or more members abruptly depart from all over the room, leaving some of the less self-assured speakers wondering if they have been victims of a bad advance press.

There have been meeting and related changes, of course. In 1971 the location shifted from the basement to the main dining room of the Heritage House, and, five years later, to the Holiday Inn. The long series of outings at the Huron Mountain Club ended with the spring of 1979. Dues and luncheon costs have risen steadily. Since the resignation of Vern Holgate, The ROTATOR has been edited by a half dozen men, among whom Allen D. Raymond III served the longest. Late in 1976 Raymond proposed that the club's directory be issued in a small loose-leaf binder with one page, including photograph, for each member. The first of these appeared in the spring of 1976. A second edition followed in 1980.

During the past dozen or more years, the Rotary Club has suffered the universal impact of instant audio communication. This, along with the equally pervasive ease with which printed material can be duplicated, has diminished respect for the written word and, at the same time, has made it difficult to escape being deluged with paper. Previously, except for the period from April, 1936, to June, 1937, the minutes of both the board and regular meetings for fifty years were remarkably complete. Through World War II they were hardbound.

Clockwise from below: Pianist Hal Wright, Presidents Burt Parolini and Allan Niemi (past), Clyde Hecox Making Announcements and Introductions, Song Leader Pat LaFreniere, Newscaster Waba Treloar, Song Leader Bill Wright

Beginning in 1967, however, a serious record-keeping problem arose. Although the board's minutes have been kept reasonably intact, overburdened secretaries have been inclined to delegate to the editor of the bulletin the task of keeping track of the regular meetings. Through lack of coordination and adequate manpower, the records for from twenty to twenty-five percent of the weekly meetings for about seven years to 1975 have been lost or never were kept.

Having recognized the problem in the incipient stage, the board appointed past President Edward Stratton assistant secretary in October, 1968. A modest improvement lasted about three years. The records since 1975 have become fairly complete if The ROTATOR can be considered an adequate substitute for official minutes of regular weekly meetings. On April 2, 1979, the board appropriated eighteeen hundred dollars for a part-time secretary, but no action followed. Creation of a separate office of corresponding secretary is needed.

Women and the Club

Ideally, the board might offer a free membership, including meals, to a professional woman who would take care of the routine chores of recording secretary and bulletin editor. However, the rules of Rotary International do not permit female membership, and, unfortunately, women are not so complaisant about uncompensated work as they used to be.

Even so, the prospect for a woman's becoming secretary, indeed president, of the Marquette Rotary Club probably is better than it seems. For most of a decade women have been seeping gradually into the regular meetings through a process much like osmosis, not just in the traditional role of program participants, but as luncheon guests.

On March 6, 1972, Ms. Jean Albrighton and a women's liberation group provided "an interesting program on women's advancement in the world from the dark ages to the present time." This event seems to have had no immediate effect although it may have helped pave the way for a landmark joint meeting of the Marquette Rotary and Zonta clubs on March 19, 1973. Observed Patrick T. Kelly, secretary of the former: "When Rotary begins to accept women as members, we probably will find that the best are already Zontians."

Since October 20, 1975, possibly before, both girls and boys have been guests at the weekly luncheon meetings of Rotary as part of the longstanding practice, continuous since the fall of 1971, of giving high school students firsthand acquaintance with the club. Inbound and outbound Rotary exchange students, male and female, have attended meetings frequently. On March 31, 1980, Dr. and Mrs. Jean Jacques Schott and their son Jacques, parents and brother of Eric, a French exchange student living with past President Busharat Ahmad and his family, came to the regular luncheon meeting. In observance of National Secretaries Week, about a dozen Rotarians attended on April 21 with their aides, some of whom turned out to be their wives.

The fact that so many Marquette Rotary Anns, particularly wives of officers, do so much unpaid club work for their husbands, also that as homemakers they naturally have most responsibility for the welfare of foreign student guests, unquestionably has had the effect of bringing spouses closer together in Rotary.

In anticipation of Rotary Ann Night, July 7, 1975 (during the seventies the term "Ladies Night" came to be less frequently used), Mrs. Patrick (Jacqueline) Kelly reproduced material—SO YOUR HUSBAND IS A ROTARIAN!!!—from a booklet prepared by Mrs. Gordon (Mary) Keyes, wife of a Shewano, Wisconsin, former district governor. This answered basic questions Rotary Anns most frequently ask.

Rotary Ann Caroline Treloar was a guest of the club along with two sons on August 15, 1977, the Treloars' golden wedding anniversary. When the club's second Paul Harris Fellow, Pat LaFreniere (W. H. Treloar was the first), attended the May 1, 1978, luncheon meeting with his wife Gertrude, he was presented with a portrait of the couple. Six Marquette Rotary Anns were guests at District Governor Terry Cowan's noon visitation on August 14, 1978. In another departure from tradition, Mrs. Patricia Cowan appeared with her husband.

Over the past twelve years the local Rotarians have shared more and more meetings with their Rotary Anns in addition to inviting them individually to the luncheons. Instead of holding its regular session for December 16, 1968, at noon, the club met for dinner, without wives, then adjourned for a Christmas program at the Shiras Planetarium. However, the Rotary Anns and other guests a week later attended a party at which Helmut Kreitz and his viola and Mrs. Keith (Martha Closser) Semenak at the piano ("gad! what an improvement over father Earl," remarked the secretary) provided dinner music and accompaniment for seven club carolers. The climax, as usual, came with Closser's readings from Dickens' *Christmas Carol*.

The Rotary Anns were invited to a combined Christmas party and International Night in December, 1976. The cast from a high school production of *Oklahoma* entertained at a yuletide event a year later. In addition to separate Christmas and International Nights, the Rotary year 1977-78 was notable for a third evening with wives on July 10, at which the outgoing officers were honored and the new ones inducted.

Since 1978 some thought has been given to formation of a Rotary Ann auxiliary, but nothing has been done about it. On February 26, 1979, during World Understanding Week, twenty-seven wives attended the regular luncheon meeting. Iranian born Ardeshir M. "Ardi" Payan, now a Marquette Rotarian, spoke on "Iran: Yesterday-Today-Tomorrow."

Fellowship

An event unique in the annals of the local club occurred on October 14, 1977, when thirteen past presidents met with Lee R. Luff, secretary at the time, to explore ways in which they could make their experience more useful to the organization. Among numerous suggestions were some for fund-raising, vocational counseling for high school students (concern over teenage theft having been expressed), projects to aid senior citizens, more programs about business, and greater use of local Rotarians for Christmas and talent presentations. At the same time, participants voiced feelings that the club needed to concentrate on a few good projects—the Bay Cliff Health Camp, for example—and that the group was becoming too large and too heavily weighted toward the university. It was from this meeting that the proposal for a Marquette citizens hall of fame emanated together with the suggestion that the club might salute one Marquette resident each week or month.

Except through district conferences and assemblies, fellowship with Rotarians outside the city has been mostly with those at the air base and in Ishpeming. The local club was preparing to sponsor an organization for the servicemen at Gwinn until informed by headquarters in 1975 that the prospective members were too specialized vocationally. Treloar was the principal speaker at a joint meeting held on August 22, 1968, at the Wawonowin Country Club to celebrate the thirty-first anniversary of the Ishpeming Rotary Club. On this occasion Robert Clark read a poem he had written "with a nautical theme" and with the names of all charter members woven into it.

Michigan Week observances have inspired annual joint service club meetings in Marquette. Honorary Rotarian Edgar Harden, state chairman for 1967, arranged a dinner on June 26 of that year at which five former Michigan governors were present. On display were twenty-one paintings by Robert Thom of Birmingham on the state's history which had been commissioned by the Michigan Bell Telephone Company. Other joint meetings in the Michigan Week series have featured the appearance of downstate mayors on Mayor Exchange Day. In 1978 Dr. Daniel S. Mazzuchi, a Marquette Rotarian, was the Upper Peninsula regional chairman for the state celebration.

Michigan Governor William G. Milliken spoke at a countywide service club meeting at the K.I. Sawyer Air Force Base on April 1, 1973. A few months later, on October 29, Mayor Roman Gribbs of Detroit addressed the four Marquette men's service groups on "Revenue Sharing." After the Seney fire of 1976 (q.v.), U.S. Secretary of the Interior Thomas H. Kleppe on September 22 reviewed the costly event for the men in joint session and outlined plans for development of the national parklands. On its Meet the Candidate Day in the fall of 1977, the Marquette League of Women Voters presented to all of the service organizations the eight aspirants for four vacant seats on the city commission. French exchange student Eric Schott gave a slide presentation on his home city of Strasbourg at another Rotary-Zonta meeting on November 5, 1979.

City Management

During the seventies many Marquette Rotarians, confident that the community was in capable hands with Thomas McNabb as manager, became less attentive to municipal affairs. They also began to disfranchise themselves in town by moving to the suburbs. Despite a million-dollar cost overrun in construction of the Shiras steam plant, also periodic demands from townspeople that power facility control be restored to the city commission, most club members seemed satisfied that plant operation and expansion were being soundly administered by the independent board of light and power. McNabb briefed the Rotarians annually on the city's budget and major projects.

Otherwise, greatest club interest focused on local real estate tax increases. In August, 1970, James McDonald of the city assessor's office outlined policies and procedures for keeping assessments up-to-date. School superintendent Henry Bothwell and the system's chief budget officer, Bond Perket, the next month explained why, due to a complicated legislative formula to equalize educational opportunities statewide, tax millage was not being reduced even though property valuations were increasing. Perket and another school representative, Julius Tiziani, returned in March, 1977, to repeat this message and to add that school millage must be increased to stay even with inflation. On February 5, 1979, a new superintendent, Richard Klahn, appeared with Perket to discuss school planning and finance.

Meanwhile, Frederick Sabin and Robert Ling were among the founders of a Marquette taxpayers' association which in the mid-seventies promoted property tax limitation or reduction. On May 8, 1978, McNabb, in presenting the 1978-79 budget for the city, noted that the millage for governmental purposes had decreased from 18.65 to nine mills over the past thirteen years while the assessed valuation of Marquette property had risen to more than two hundred million dollars. He pointed out that the largest increase in the budget was for a new water pumping and storage station and for a water treatment plant.

Northern economist Phillip A. May, at a joint meeting of the Rotary and Zonta clubs in October of 1978, did a "wonderful job" of analyzing the Headlee and Tisch tax proposals for property tax relief in Michigan. May favored the first of these as a measure which would limit total state spending and help curb inflation, whereas the latter would only shift the burden from property to some other unspecified source or sources.

On May 14, 1979, during an all-Rotary program featuring City Commissioners William F. Wilson and Robert Ling along with the city manager, McNabb noted that the tax millage for local government again would go down, but that property valuations would rise thirteen to fifteen percent. Ling said he was inexperienced in government but not in paying taxes. Wilson blamed "big government" for "strangling" local units and added, "We need a return to local government control, especially in matters such as the unneeded water filtration plant."

A year later, in a strange, unprecedented situation for the Marquette Rotary Club, Ling, by that time the only Rotarian on the commission, sided with the majority of the governing body in forcing the resignation of Rotarian McNabb from his post after fifteen years as city manager.

Law and Order

Social unrest and increased crime inspired the Marquette Rotarians to schedule local lawyers for programs on or about May 1, Law Day, from 1967 through 1970. Early in 1969 Maj. George Hansen of the Michigan National Guard described new techniques in dealing with civil disorders. In July, 1972, a former Marquette resident, David Guilland, an FBI agent stationed in Reno, described an airplane hijacking in Nevada. The club gave the Watergate scandals no formal notice beyond a talk on impeachment and impeachable offenses by John R. Ashby of Northern's political science department—on March 3, 1974.

Detective Joseph Levandoski of the Marquette police department dealt with local crime at the June 17, 1968, meeting of the Rotary Club, and McNabb, Jenner, and Paul LaFreniere, a city commissioner at the time, comprised a panel to discuss police personnel and other problems in June, 1970. In the late summer of 1972 William Lasich, another local detective, and Khairati L. Sindwani, a Northern sociologist, considered national and local crime patterns. Several programs by Probate Judge De Fant and law enforcement officers during the early seventies concerned juvenile delinquency.

A few club programs were devoted to alcoholism, and on December 2, 1974, Capt. Marvin Gauthier of the Marquette police department discussed, for the first time in the group's history, "Drugs in Marquette." Commented the secretary, "While not one of those pleasant things we would rather hear, it is an unfortunate fact of life we must face." Shoplifting and check forgery have been topics for two or three programs since 1974.

Early in 1970 Robert Redmond, director of classification at the prison, showed an "excellent" film, *The Odds Against*, on life behind bars. On July 18, 1977, Thomas Skoog, assistant registrar at Northern, discussed the university's degree programs at the prison. Begun in 1972, these were the first in the United States to be offered within a penal institution, according to Skoog.

In February of 1978 Michael Anderegg, De Fant's successor as county probate judge, enumerated his options in "making the punishment fit the crime" up to designating a young offender a ward of the state. Anderegg suggested that Rotarians help relieve the shortage of foster parents by taking children into their own homes. (In the early sixties one Marquette Rotarian had done this; others may have.)

Apparently by pure coincidence, the Rotary Club meeting immediately following that at which the more than two dozen wives had shared in the observance of World Understanding Week was devoted to "Spouse Abuse." On March 5, 1979, Ms. Ann Henderson of the state board for abuse and treatment pointed to over 167 police reports of such occurrences during the previous year in Marquette County and to the need for a facility (since established) for something beyond "Band-Aid" treatment for victims. Fellow panelist Officer Greg Crays of the Michigan State Police stated that policemen are confronted by few situations more dangerous than those arising from family quarrels.

Boosting Marquette and the Area

Since the inclusion among the charter members of the Marquette Rotary Club of John D. Mangum, secretary and publicity agent for the Commercial Club, the Rotarians have maintained a cordial and intimate relationship with that organization and its successor, the Marquette Area Chamber of Commerce. When the volunteer Marquette Ambassadors Club was organized in 1963 as a public relations arm of the Chamber, about half of the new agency's members were local Rotarians, as they are now.

More than three years elapsed before Robert Polzin and William Wright, Ishpeming and Marquette Rotarians, in November of 1966 formally explained the Ambassadors' aims and functions to the local Rotary club. At another meeting in February, 1968, Robert Pearce described a visit of the emissaries to Flint, where they met with philanthropist Charles S. Mott at his home and toured the Mott Children's Health Center.

David Allie, then president of the Chamber of Commerce, on March 1, 1976, gave a "most informative presentation" on its past, present, and future. On August 8, 1977, Allie's successor, Dr. Daniel Mazzuchi, explained its goals for the year, and Allen

Marquette Ambassadors Club, 1965
Rear: Clayton Dahlke, Richard Bur, Jack Ziegler (R), Jack McCracken, Robert Pearce (R), Ray Nelson (R), William Wright (R), Clyde Hecox (R), Wesley Roberts, Robert Moore (R).
Front: Harlan Larson, Patrick Bennett (R), Larry Fredrickson, Robert Ling (R), Robert Luke, Richard Myers (R), James Luke.

Rotarians Ray Nelson and Robert Ling pose with Harlan Larson, Clayton Dahlke, Michigan Governor George Romney, Richard Angeli, and Robert Luke during attendance of Marquette Ambassadors at opening of the Internaional Bridge at Sault Ste. Marie, 1963.

Raymond, recently appointed executive vice-president, told his Rotary audience, "The Marquette Chamber of Commerce NEEDS YOU!"

Vocational Programs

Also in 1977 Colonel Weesen, a member of the Chamber's tourism and convention committee, described efforts to bring outside groups to Marquette, especially to the Lakeview Arena. He noted that in 1976 tourists and other travelers had spent seventy-three million dollars in Marquette County. On April 1, 1974, William Wilson, executive manager of Operation Action UP, stressed the continuing need for "Industrial Growth of the Upper Peninsula."

Few programs during the seventies dealt with agriculture or farm-related activities. One in 1976 was devoted to cooperative extension, particularly 4-H work. On August 15, 1977, Mrs. Ruth Butler, vice-chairman of the board of managers of the Upper Peninsula State Fair, spoke on the heritage theme of the forthcoming annual event. Richard Leep, a Michigan State University agronomist, in June, 1978, discussed potato production in the northern peninsula. He noted that 110 growers were producing crops worth from six to ten million dollars on five thousand acres of land.

In 1966 the club viewed a film on timber operations in British Columbia and listened attentively while Eugene Cole and Harold Sloan described the manufacture and marketing of Cliffs Dow Chemical Company products. On May 23, 1977, two timber producers representatives, Henry Bannach and Carl Theiler, gave the Rotarians advance notice of the thirty-second Lake States Logging Congress to be held in September at the Lakeview Arena. They expected more than 125 exhibitors and forty thousand visitors. Richard Black, general manager of Champion, Inc., on March 12, 1979, discussed plans for its Quinnesec Paper Mill to be located between Iron Mountain and Norway at a cost of six million dollars and with a labor force of eight hundred.

In the field of energy production and regulation James Wilkins, a spokesman for the Marathon Oil Corporation, in May, 1970, gave an illustrated talk on Alaskan oil and on regulatory and other problems confronting the petroleum indudstry. In April, 1975, the Marquette Rotary Club unanimously approved a resolution to support dredging at the mouth of the Dead River as part of an expansion project of the U.P. Generating Company at the Presque Isle station. The Rotarians toured the facilities there a few months later.

On September 11, 1978, Ishpeming Rotarian Burton Boyum, manager of administrative affairs for the Cleveland-Cliffs Iron Company, pointed to the problems created by foreign competition, high domestic wages, declining steel prices, and rising energy costs in an address on the state of mining on the Marquette Range. He emphasized that the Upper Peninsula Generating Company was paying thirty-nine cents of every tax dollar collected in Marquette. Manager O. E. Anderson soon afterward singled out government regulation and the low price of copper as the greatest obstacles to profitable operation of the White Pine Copper Mine. On March 9, 1970,

Ernest H. Ronn, staff representative of the United Steelworkers of America, had discussed difficulties facing miners.

Nostalgia and discouragement marked the few Rotary programs on railroads. Rotarian Francis Cardoni in 1967 commented briefly and showed a film, *Stop-Look-Listen*, on railroad safety. On March 22, 1971, George Von Kovering of Zeeland, Michigan, gave a slide presentation entitled "Countdown for America's Railroads." Frank Bourke of Escanaba, speaking on "Take a Train to Anywhere," on February 9, 1976, described railroading at its peak in the early 1900s.

Both lore and practical information were contained in talks relating to Lake Superior. In March of 1968 Chief G. C. Daugherty spoke about the functions of the U.S. Coast Guard Station in Marquette, as did Chief Carl Larson four years later. Two local men, District Commodore Arthur B. Neiger and Flotilla Commander (and Rotarian) Jon N. Kukuk, in September, 1979, acquainted the club with the Coast Guard Auxiliary's education, courtesy inspection, and search and rescue services to the boating public. Frederick Stonehouse discussed "Shipwrecks on Lake Superior" at an April, 1974, meeting.

Rotarian Kenneth Hogg interested the mariners in the local group with his narration in the spring of 1969 of English horologist John Harrison's success in measuring longitude on the high seas. Hogg appeared one week before Walter North, comptroller for the Mackinac Bridge Authority, discussed the history and future of the "Mighty Mac."

At a joint meeting of all Marquette service clubs arranged by Rotarian Gerald E. Grundstrom for May 10, 1976, Richard L. Terrell, vice-chairman of the board of General Motors Corporation, gave "A Progress Report on the Automobile Industry." Terrell predicted one of the best years ever for production and sales, but pointed to the difficulty of meeting government emissions standards while attempting to improve gasoline mileage. In the spring of 1978, A. J. Marusich, district engineer for the state Department of Highways and Transportation, showed a film on Michigan's transportation system.

Although Marquette Rotarian Arthur L. Hiebel was unable to win support for a Rotary "fly-in," aviation and space exploration were popular program topics during the decade following the club's golden anniversary. Part of the interest related to the Vietnam War, as indicated by the appearance of Peter W. Frazier, son of Lincoln, on November 21, 1966. A warrant officer in the U.S. Air Force, the younger man interspersed a slide presentation with remarks on his battle experiences.

The local Rotarians shared fully the national excitement attending the successful moon landing of Neil Armstrong and Edwin Aldrin, Jr., from Apollo 11 on July 20, 1969. Absorption in this historic event caused poor attendance at the luncheon meeting the next day, also a program adjustment through which those present witnessed a simulated take-off from the moon and listened to comments by Don Ryan of WLUC-TV on the contemporary role of television nationally and locally. Four years later Ron Goe, chief engineer of Rockwell International's California rocket plant, described NASA's space shuttle project.

Marquette Rotary Club airplane pilots were especially attentive to talks such as that on "Aviation in General and the FAA in Particular," given by Guy J. Blakely, district chief of the Federal Aviation Administration, in September, 1966. Regular patrons of the North Central Air Lines were intrigued by two programs in the late sixties on the new Convair 580 propjet plane serving Marquette. In 1970 Blakely showed a film relating the advantages of a good terminal in attracting new business and industry. Three years later Ernest Medina of the Engstrom Corporation, an F. Lee Bailey enterprise in Menominee, presented a film on helicopter manufacture and use. Other programs related to private plane operation and air safety.

Over the past fifteen years, representatives of the Michigan Bell Telephone Company have kept the Rotarians informed of its technological progress, and spokesmen for WLUC-TV have discussed many facets of television: transmission problems, program ratings, and local news, political campaigns, and election coverage. On October 1, 1979, Panax publisher J. Eugene Chambers, presently a Marquette Rotarian, and three of his associates gave the club a chance to "Meet the Press."

A sampling of additional programs suggests the diversity of vocational commitments and interests of the local Rotarians. Clothier Richard H. Myers once showed a Hart, Schaffner and Marx film, *Behind the Seams*. In 1971 Clyde W. Hecox gave the club a tour of the Bunny Bread establishment, and Richard Lutey conducted members through the remodeled Heritage House. Burt Parolini and Paul LaFreniere have talked on financial investments; Raymond S. Camilli, on taxes. Always concerned with general economic trends, the Rotarians consistently have paid close attention to the analyses of guest speakers Phillip May, Edward Powers, and Thomas Holmstrom from Northern's economics department.

Health

Now that medical care has become one of Marquette's major "industries," it has added to the keen interest of the Rotarians in health problems. During years of rapid growth culminating in the 1973 merger, hospital administrators Anthony B. De Lape and Donald J. Giesen of St. Mary's and Robert Johnson and Donald H. Carros of St. Luke's (all but Johnson were Rotarians) addressed the club on the operations of their respective units. During the seventies the Rotarians visited St. Mary's and the hospital facility at the prison. Since 1974, Rotarian Robert C. Neldberg, executive director, has spoken at three meetings on expansion plans for Marquette General.

Dr. Richard J. Potter, head of the Marquette County Health Department and long a Rotarian, addressed the club several times on the role of his agency in dealing with public health problems. Guest speaker John Diebel of Blue Cross-Blue Shield dealt with health insurance, and Dr. Daniel Mazzuchi, with reference to "Malpractice Insurance," warned of increased medical fees and a shortage of doctors due to higher premiums for protection against the increased number and expense of patients' lawsuits.

Specific physical ills along with mental and emotional ailments also have been topics for the weekly Rotary meetings. Representatives from the American Cancer Society and, in 1972, a panel of guest specialists have come before the club. One of the latter predicted that one of every four persons will be afflicted with cancer. Dr. Patrick Kelly in 1971 showed a color film on *Cancer of the Mouth and Throat*. Dental and respiratory problems also have been featured.

Alcoholism, particularly as alleviated through Alcoholics Anonymous and the special unit at Marquette General, has received due attention. On August 9, 1971, Ronald Collins, who was in charge of the alcohol safety program of the county health department, ascribed half of all highway deaths to liquor. He added that "if the truth were really reported," the statistics would show seventy-five to eighty percent. He branded the combination of alcohol and driving a "national menace."

Dr. David Wall for several years kept the concept of community mental health and the need of facilities for treatment at this level before the Rotarians. On March 18, 1973, during an appeal for funds, Thomas Heinonen of the then Alger-Delta-Marquette Community Mental Health Clinic and David Schubert, a senior at Northern Michigan University, described the Reach a Person (RAP) telephone line to deal with persons in crisis.

During 1978 the Rotary Club gave extraordinary attention to the drug problem. In January the board asked Burt Parolini to investigate this. After meeting with school and law enforcement officials and with Rotary's own Dr. Busharat Ahmad, he reported a need for clearer identification.

Northern psychologist Steven Platt subsequently appeared at two luncheon meetings of the club, on March 6 and 13. At the first of these he made a confidential survey of the Rotarians themselves, then at the second session shared his summary of the results and made several observations and suggestions. He noted that among the members liquor was the "biggie" and naiveté about other drugs was prevalent.

Categorizing drugs broadly to include alcohol and the nicotine in tea, coffee, and tobacco, Platt made these recommendations: 1) the use of a specific drug should be gauged by the tolerance of the user; 2) people should be taught to observe the rights of others; 3) they should be educated to perform efficiently and constructively in society; and 4) they should be brought to the realization that "they can feel good without drugs."

With reference to the treatment of certain specific difficulties, guest speaker Paul Young, a clinical psychologist, in June, 1969, had talked on hypnosis and had given the club members a partial demonstration of how it is achieved. His approach was so soothing and insidious that those Rotarians who did not fall asleep on the spot undoubtedly left preferring an afternoon nap to a return to work.

Looking to the future, Rotarian Ronald W. Richards in April, 1977, discussed the aim of the Upper Peninsula medical education program to encourage more physicians and surgeons to settle in the region. A year later Phillip Watts of Northern spoke on "Adult Fitness," noting the role of physical exercise in preventing heart disease and high blood pressure.

Welfare

Apart from appearances to solicit financial aid, spokesmen for area welfare agencies many times have continued to come before the club out of a general public relations desire to keep the Rotarians aware of their activities. During 1967 a particularly close connection existed between the Rotary Club and the Michigan Children's Aid & Family Services when Marquette Rotarians John Morrison, Lesley Cory, and Kenneth Hogg served that organization as president, senior vice-president, and as a board member. Early in the 1970s Victor Holliday, Jr., was acting director of Catholic Social Services.

Less intimate have been Rotary's relations with the Head Start day care center in the Messiah Lutheran Church building, the Big Brother movement, the Northern Michigan University Skill Center, Marquette Social Services, the Alger-Marquette Sheltered Workshop, and the Marquette County Humane Society. Nonetheless, by the mid-seventies each had been featured in one or more programs.

Recreation

The many meetings devoted to sports since the club's golden anniversary have borne ample testimony to the perennial enthusiasm of the Marquette Rotarians, as participants and spectators, for physical activities of a recreational nature. On numerous occasions the Rotarians have honored local high school athletes for outstanding performance, particularly in hockey and basketball. The club's junior hockey team concluded its 1968-69 season with a third-place finish in the state tournament. On April 14, 1969, the Rotarians entertained the Bishop Baraga Royals basketball team which, like that of the John D. Pierce Warriors eight years before, won the state Class D Championship a few months before their school went out of existence.

In 1966 C. V. Money spoke to his fellow Rotarians on the operations of the NMU health, physical education, and recreation department which he headed, and again in 1973, on the Upper Peninsula Sports Hall of Fame, of which he was executive secretary. Three years later the club members toured Northern's impressive new physical education building.

Devotees of golf, scuba diving, sailing, motorcycling, harness racing, and mountain climbing, all had their days at weekly luncheon meetings of the Marquette Rotary Club. In April of 1972 Mr. and Mrs. George Tomasi, skin diving instructors, offered a slide presentation on "Bare Boating & Diving BWI," which proved to be an account of their sailing and snorkeling during a ten-day vacation in the British West Indies. Four years later Thomas Casselman described his climb of Mt. Ranier.

In 1974 the Rotary Club provided a trophy for a national orienteering meet held at NMU and won by the South East Ohio Orienteering Club from Athens, Ohio. On September 15, 1975, Allen Raymond of Northern's military science department gave the Rotarians a preview of another such event and of the Army's Golden Knights skydiving demonstration simultaneous with it, both sponsored by the department early in October.

Automobile dealers Gerald Grundstrom, Daniel Hornbogen, Jr., and Willard Evert—Rotarians all—made seven sedans and a van available to the Knights, and Colonel Weesen and his staff at Cliffs Ridge furnished a staging area for the 235 orienteers. The Knights jumped at halftime during Northern's homecoming football game.[1] Edward Locke was to have presented the Rotary trophy to the winners of the meet, but no team qualified for it.

Hobbies, some involving a good deal of physical exertion, others little or none, also have been described for the Rotary Club by both members and outsiders. In November, 1970, Lee Erck, president of the Marquette Kennel Club, came to a meeting with several associates and three show dogs to demonstrate how the animals are judged. In October, 1975, Richard Lutey discussed some of the fine points of "Antique Auto Collecting," an avocation which has absorbed Frank Oatley, Ronald Garberson, and perhaps other local Rotarians as well. In 1977 Kenneth Hogg instructed the members on "Wine Making."

Two programs in 1979 featured talks and a film on *The Confederate Air Force*. In February of that year John Weting gave a "brilliant slide presentation" covering five most picturesque miles of his "Colorado River Float Trip." On March 19 Rotarians Robert Stow, Jon Kukuk, and James P. Grundstrom, spokesmen for "the rest of the crew," gave a slide account of their 1,187-mile trip through the "vast network of canals and bargeways that link Atlantic City, N.J., with the Great Lakes."

Over more than a decade Northern football coaches Roland Dotsch, Rae Drake, Gilbert Kreuger, and William Rademacher have briefed the Rotary Club annually on the schedules, prospects, triumphs, and disappointments of the Wildcat gridders, as have coaches Stanley Albeck and Glenn Brown for the basketball teams. Wrestling coach Ed Brown and swimming mentor Donald Trost have appeared less frequently. The Marquette Rotarians have entertained visiting basketball squads from Sweden and Yugoslavia, and in the spring of 1977 quarterback Greg Landry of the Detroit Lions, under the sponsorship of the Marquette County Cancer Society, discussed his team's modest prospects for the next season.

Winter sports always have had a special economic value for the area as illustrated by an Upper Peninsula Tourist Association film John Taylor showed the club in 1971. Colonel Weesen and other Rotarians have continued to present programs on snowmobiling while representatives of Cliffs Ridge Ski Area have kept the Rotarians informed of that facility's progress. Ski flying at Ironwood also has been duly noted.

Roy Heath for several years has encouraged club and community support for location of a Midwest Olympic Training Site near Marquette. Reminiscent of George Shiras in the imaginativeness and scope of his appeal, Heath on February 28, 1977, proposed that Northern Michigan University, the Marquette and Ishpeming Ski Club, and other area organizations "produce the best general winter training site in the region, and in some sports, the world." He noted that about $216,000,000 in federal money soon would be appropriated for construction of such a facility and another eighty-three million dollars annually for its operation. If successful in its bid, Marquette stood to gain eleven million yearly at an initial planning cost of fifty-three thousand. Little has developed.

The city continues to be a source of strength for ice hockey. Austin "Ozzie" O'Neill of the Marquette Iron Rangers was a member of the U.S. National Hockey team which in 1970 won the world championship at Bucharest. Although the professional Iron Rangers have passed from the scene, Northern now is a national collegiate power.

The Ishpeming Ski Club dates from 1870, and the National Ski Hall of Fame, about which Burton Boyum has spoken twice in recent years, is located at Ishpeming. When in August, 1977, Hal Dorf from that town's Hematite Travel Agency presented a slide program on the 1976 Winter Olympics for the Marquette Rotarians, he was helping to nurture an area interest in that event which in 1979-80 was lively indeed.

Military Preparedness

By 1966 the connection between sports and war had been irreparably broken in the public view, and the term "games" applied to military field maneuvers was passing from popular usage. Industrialized warfare had become too massive and indiscriminate for battlefield heroism and skill to have much effect on the outcome of a conflict. The new war games involve mathematicians, computers, and parlor game manufacturers under government contract in cerebral rather than physical exercise. Several Marquette Rotary Club programs dealing with dangers which exceedingly sophisticated weapons systems pose for all people, even those they are designed to protect, have strongly implied the change.

On July 1, 1968, Lt. Lee Smith, nuclear safety officer of the K.I. Sawyer Air Force Base, narrated a film on precautions attending the use of nuclear weapons. Early in 1970 Rotarian Robert T. Wagner, an NMU physicist, gave "an extremely interesting" talk on the American antiballistic missile system; two years later he discussed nuclear fusion before the club.

Capt. Arthur Bennett, brother of Dr. Matthew Bennett, in August, 1971, stated that "Russia now has a first-class navy by United States standards. . . . We must maintain our technological superiority at all costs." Eight years later Col. Al Dugard, USAF Wing Commander, 410th Bombardment Wing, stationed at the Sawyer base, was to warn again when discussing "The Soviet Threat," "We have a long way to go" in military preparedness.

The environmentally controversial Navy Project Sanguine, Seafarer, or ELF, as it has been named progessively, has been the topic of at least three presentations at Marquette Rotary Club luncheon meetings. At one of these, held jointly with the Kiwanis Club on December 1, 1975, Assistant Secretary of Defense Thomas Reed stated that Sanguine would be essential to national security in the 1980s, but that the Navy aimed to get "all the facts" before deciding where to locate it.[2] In May of 1976 James Barron and George Brandshaw of TGE-Sylvania considered only the engineering aspects of Seafarer. The question of whether a Navy extremely low frequency underground communications system will be installed in the Upper Peninsula has been alternately live and dormant in recent years.

On March 26, 1979, visiting speaker Col. Palmer McGrew described the Pentagon center for "The Hot Line to Moscow." He stated that translators practice daily to be ready for emergency messages which might allow the President as little as five minutes to decide whether to launch retaliatory missiles in a "doomsday" war.

That the human factor still has a place in field operations was the contention of Lt. Cols. James R. Sesslar, Allen Raymond, and Frank Allen, all from Northern's military science department and all Rotarians, who talked during the seventies on the importance of ROTC training in universities and colleges. On January 21, 1974, when asking "Where Are Our Leaders Coming From?", Raymond stated his conviction that the grave danger is not that the military will dominate the institutions of higher learning, but that the latter may fail, for lack of support for the ROTC, to provide the quality and breadth indispensable to leadership in the armed services.

In August, 1978, Cadet Dwight Raymond, son of Allen Raymond, informed the club of "Changes at West Point in the Wake of [the] Cheating Scandal of Spring '76." He stressed, however, that the honor code is so vital to the education of future officers that the Military Academy would not abandon it.

Early in 1979, in a sensational program arranged by Gerald Grundstrom, intelligence agent Johann Wolfgang von Reinhardt (alias), who had participated in a number of the episodes described in William Stevenson's *A Man Called Intrepid*, addressed the topic, "I.Q.: Without It We're Dead." At the last meeting of the year Colonel Allen returned to "The Soviet Military Threat."

12
A BROADENING VIEW

During the past sixteen years the Marquette Rotarians have shared the growing sense of limitation felt by Americans generally. Diplomatic and military reverses, the increasing inaccessibility of vital raw materials, and the adverse environmental effects of massive industrialization have stimulated among the group a still greater interest in the external world.

Programs by representatives of the Michigan Department of Conservation (now the Department of Natural Resources), the U.S. Forest Service, Northern Michigan University, and the Michigan State University Extension Service have made clearer than ever the interrelatedness and interdependence of all life, and spokesmen for industry and for environmental interest groups have demonstrated the need for great care in determining land use.

The Natural Environment

After Glenn Gregg, regional director of the Conservation Department, in the spring of 1966 outlined the structure and responsibilities of the divisions under his authority, game biologists Ralph E. Bailey and Henry Vondett the next year spoke to the club on deer management and on fish stocking programs in the Great Lakes, and David M. Frimodig, department naturalist, gave a color slide program on "Ghost Towns of the U.P." In the latter part of 1973 Bailey described attempts of the Department of Natural Resources to attract geese back into the region, and commercial fisherman Jerry Thill, who was followed soon afterward by a DNR representative with a contrary position, criticized state restrictions, especially on the use of gill nets.

During 1968 Gordon Huber, a Northern Michigan University graduate assistant in biology, with the aid of slides narrated his travels in Alaska; graduate forester Rodney Jacobs discussed the work of the Northern Hardwoods Research Laboratory; and Hugh P. Beattie spoke on the objectives of the National Park Service in developing the Pictured Rocks National Lakeshore Park, of which he was superintendent. The following year Lawrence Haack from the Escanaba office of the U.S. Forest Service showed a color film on wildlife in the area's national forests. In 1972 regional park supervisor Grant Wykhuis called attention to state campsite problems, and the year after that, NMU biologist Maynard Bowers catalogued the wildflowers of Michigan.

In 1968, also, Dr. Richard Potter discussed air and water pollution in the Pennsylvania coal fields, and Ralph Bailey described Conservation Department efforts to control water contamination through careful sewage disposal. Three years later NMU geologist John Hughes showed a film titled *The Beaches Are Rivers of Sand*, which called attention to difficulties arising from man's interference with the natural flow of sand.

Of special interest in 1973 were the appearances of James Scullion, vice-president of the Lake Superior & Ishpeming Railroad, who favored construction of a controversial coal unloading facility, since completed, in Marquette's upper harbor, and of Mrs. Munro (Julia) Tibbitts, representing Superior Public Rights, Inc., who opposed it. Scullion argued that the facility would improve the lower harbor shoreline by transferring the downtown stockpile of coal to the Dead River power site, whereas Mrs. Tibbitts dwelt on its adverse impact upon the scenic beauty of the Shiras and Presque Isle parks.

Marquette Rotarian Kenneth R. Saari, Upper Peninsula manager of the Michigan Power Company, in February, 1974, analyzed the energy crisis of that winter. A month later fellow club member Chester Briggs, manager of the Consolidated Fuel and Lumber Company, showed a film on reforestation. In the late spring Northern biologist William Robinson discussed his efforts to reestablish a wolf population in the Upper Peninsula. Robert McHugh of the U.S. Forest Service in July, 1977, considered land use in relation to wilderness areas. The following October, Rotarian David Olson, Michigan State University district forestry agent for the Upper Peninsula, gave a slide presentation on its forests. He noted that forty percent of the region's timbered land was publicly owned and that the rest was divided equally between large and small private owners.

Within the past five years two disasters, one natural and one man-made, have been topics for Marquette Rotary Club programs. On July 31, 1978, John Frye, manager of the Seney Wildlife Refuge of the U.S. Fish and Wildlife Service, reviewed the thirty-day Seney fire in the summer of 1976. He reported that although lightning caused eight to ten million dollars in damage to seventy-three thousand acres of land, no lasting detrimental effects on fish and other wildlife had been detected. On April 17, 1979, Joseph Finck of NMU's physics department reported on the "Three Mile Island Emergency." After explaining the basic principles of a nuclear reactor, he pointed up the problem of disposing of contaminated water following the near melt-down.

Other Peoples and Cultures

Except for Rev. Ralph W. Janka's celebration of the Easter season in 1968 and, five years later, Fr. Dan Rupp's report of progress toward canonization of Fr. Frederic Baraga, the nineteenth-century Catholic missionary and bishop of the Diocese of Sault Ste. Marie and Marquette, treatment of religious themes before the local Rotarians has related to Christian ministry in the contemporary world. On October 3,

1966, Rev. Norbert Smith and Msgr. Nolan McKevitt, both local club members, spoke on ecumenical cooperation in Marquette. In the spring of 1967 Rev. J. Eugene Kunos, pastor of the Bethel Lutheran Church in Ishpeming, discussed his missionary work in China. Early in 1974 Rev. Samuel F. Stout, another Marquette Rotarian, narrated his experiences in England as a participant in the exchange program of the United Methodist Church.

Seldom if ever in peacetime have so many Marquette Rotary Club programs related to foreign travel as in the decade ending with the close of the American Bicentennial year. In 1967 and 1968 West Germany was the focus for talks by visiting Rotarian Erich Weiss; by Georg von Pirch, that nation's consul general in Detroit; and by Helmut Kreitz, who compared the educational systems of his native and adopted countries. Lincoln Frazier's slide presentation following his visit to East Germany in 1967 was the first of four travelogues by him covering a trip to Australia and New Zealand, a pole-to-pole flight following a Pacific route, and a culminating journey to Japan in 1973.

Australian-born Robert Hockey, a member of Northern's physical education department, and Burton Boyum, who had spent four years in Perth as a mining engineer, in 1969 and 1974 described life "down under" from their different perspectives.

On October 21, 1968, Marquette native Capt. Claudius G. Pendill, USN (Ret.), a veteran of the two World and Korean wars, spoke on the planet's population explosion. During the next several years, three club members and a guest speaker reported on their firsthand contacts with some of the most crowded portions of the Orient. Roy Fletcher and Harold Wright in 1973 and 1976 gave accounts of their trips to Japan. Wright's also took him to Hong Kong and Thailand. A third Marquette Rotarian, Lt. Col. Adam A, Komosa, USA (Ret.), in the fall of 1975 addressed the club on "Pre-World War II China" as he remembered it when stationed in Tientsin before the Japanese occupation in the 1930s. Komosa's colleague in the NMU history department, Jon L. Saari, who had studied in Hong Kong and Taiwan, in 1976 discussed China's contemporary role in international politics. Rev. Janka in the spring of 1971 described his contacts with Vietnamese in Paris while a member of an American delegation seeking ways to end the war in Southeast Asia.

In February, 1968, Al Mallory, an Alger-Marquette County vocational-technical education specialist, reported on and displayed artifacts from Nepal, where he had instructed people of that country in the use of textbook printing equipment. Newly elected Rotarian Busharat Ahmad, a native of Pakistan and a Harvard educated ophthalmologist, in the fall of 1971 enumerated the many causes of political and social turmoil within East and West Pakistan and of hostilities between that geographically divided nation and India. A few months later he charged the American media with biased reporting on conditions in the two countries.

Late in 1968 Rotarian Russell W. Adams, who recently had represented Northern on an educational mission to Saudi Arabia, spoke about life as he had witnessed it in that part of the Middle East. Northern's President John X. Jamrich in January of 1972 described his trip to Italy and Israel in the company of Ishpeming Rotarian

Donald and Beulah Zettle Bound from Helsinki for Leningrad

Harold and Bette Wright in Bangkok

Samuel Cohodas, a staunch friend and financial patron of the latter nation with entree into its highest political circles. In July of the following year Col. Shaul Ramati, consul general of Israel for the Midwest, reviewed for the Marquette Rotarians his country's "Twenty-Five Years of Independence." Rotarian Mohey Mowafy, chairman of NMU's department of home economics, late in 1976 provided the club with "an entertaining and informative contrast" between ancient and modern Egypt, his native land.

Nearly a decade before, in August of 1968, Marquette resident Clark Lambros had appeared before the club to compare the economic and political systems of Greece, his birthplace, with those of the United States. A year before that, James Pearce, son of Don, had given the members his impressions gained from a visit to Russia. In 1971 Princess Catherine Caradja of Rumania warned the Rotarians against political forces of either the extreme right or left within the United States. At the last meeting in 1976 Miss Mary Holliday, daughter of Victor G., Jr., made "perceptive observations on the quality and style of life" in Russia and Eastern European countries which she had visited the preceding summer.

Fred Sabin, Charles Wright, and three non-Rotarians—Douglas Treado, Pat Fassbender, and Bart Berg—between 1968 and 1973 described their impressions of sub-Saharan Africa while on safari, on tour, or in residence there. Wright told of his year with his family in Zaire, where he had served as a medical missionary.

In September, 1967, Fred Rydholm, demonstrating his usual good humor and gift

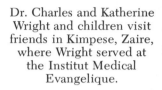

Dr. Charles and Katherine Wright and children visit friends in Kimpese, Zaire, where Wright served at the Institut Medical Evangelique.

Dr. Fred Sabin in St. Peter's Square, Rome

for storytelling, reminded the Marquette Rotarians of the surviving American Indian culture almost at their doorstep by relating his adventures with "Tom," an Ojibwa "bush Indian" from Ontario. Rydholm's display of canoe paddles, which he said his friend had made in two or three hours, drew admiring comments from his listeners. Four years later three Indian students attending Northern shared the podium at a Rotary meeting. One of them stated bluntly, "The Indian is interested in maintaining his old way of life and does not care about the white race gobbling up his reservations and disregarding past agreements and treaties."

Marquette's Third District Conference

Among the local Rotarians who traveled abroad in the early seventies was the effervescent Earl Closser, who spent more than six weeks touring the British Isles in the winter of 1971-72. Closser, through election at the 1973 conference at Shawano, Wisconsin, became Marquette's first district governor since Harlow Clark nearly fifty years before.

On July 16, 1973, Closser appeared before his fellow club members to deliver for the first time the address he was scheduled to give some seventeen hundred Rotarians in the thirty-three organizations comprising District 622 in the Upper Peninsula and Wisconsin.

Having chosen as the district theme "Involvement for Service," Closser called upon his associates to participate vigorously in the four official Rotary categories of club, community, vocational, and international service. He specifically urged support for the Interact program to organize high school boys and girls into Rotary-sponsored clubs, for Rotaract efforts to develop leadership among young people aged eighteen through twenty-eight years, and for Rotary Foundation assistance to collegians and to teachers of the handicapped as projects "to benefit, inspire, and motivate the young."[1]

Governor Earl in the fall of 1973 suffered one more in a series of heart attacks which had afflicted him over many years. He recovered sufficiently to delight the Marquette Rotarians again, on December 17, with his selections from Dickens' *Christmas Carol*. Then, to the immense sorrow of his vast number of friends, he died on January 28, 1974, at the age of sixty-nine. Past District Governor Gordon C. Keyes served the remainder of his term.

Due to Closser's passing, Marquette's third district conference convened in May of 1974 amid sadness and some confusion. Keyes and other past governors along with local Rotarians headed by Colonel Weesen had charge of the arrangements.

Despite vigorous external objections, Weesen, firmly supported by Lincoln Frazier and Allan Niemi among others, allotted over an hour to reports by Wisconsin and Canadian representatives and by visiting foreign students themselves on the value and potential of the infant Central States Rotary Youth Exchange Program. This was the first important exposure of Marquette Rotarians to a project which during the past decade has achieved worldwide significance.

Kenneth J. Shouldice, president of Lake Superior State College at Sault Ste. Marie, who during the previous year had visited the People's Republic of China, covering much the same ground as had President Richard Nixon, highlighted the proceedings with an illustrated lecture, "Observations on Modern China." Although cognizant of its less developed technology and critical of its stifling security measures, Shouldice perceived a contrast between the "egotistical hedonism" in the United States and the extraordinary discipline of the Chinese. He praised China as "the center of morality in the world" despite its prevailing atheism, adding that "the whole country is spotless. There is no litter in China." Shouldice spoke before three hundred Rotarians and guests.[2]

The Bicentennial

Even though the years 1974 and 1975 were among the gloomiest in recent American history, marked as they were by the Watergate scandals, the resignation of Nixon, diplomatic if not military failure in Vietnam, and economic recession, the Bicenten-

State of California
GOVERNOR'S OFFICE
SACRAMENTO 95814

RONALD REAGAN
GOVERNOR

March 4, 1974

Colonel Bud Weesen
Cliffs Ridge Ski Area
Marquette, Michigan 49855

Dear Colonel Weesen:

Thank you for your invitation to Mrs. Reagan and me to attend the Rotary District 622 Conference on May 11.

Unfortunately, a heavy legislative agenda prevents me from planning any out of state trips in May. I am very sorry that I am unable to join you. Perhaps at some future date we will be able to arrange a visit to Michigan.

Again, my thanks for thinking of us and best wishes for a most successful event.

Sincerely,

Ronald Reagan

RONALD REAGAN

Left to right: Colonel E. Weesen, Kenneth J. Shouldice, F. Wayne Graham (representative of the Rotary International president), Lincoln B. Frazier.

nial offered an exceptional opportunity for face-lifting, reexamination of the nation's ideals, and regeneration of its spirit.

For a decade this process had been under way at the Marquette County Historical Society. Its fund-raising campaign to renovate and expand its museum had brought that organization's representatives to regular luncheon meetings of the Rotary Club—staff members Ernest H. Rankin and Mrs. Orville (Esther) Bystrom and society Presidents Robert K. Richards and Wesley Perron, spanning the years 1967 through 1976.

Allen Raymond in the fall of 1975 introduced the Marquette Rotary Club's own observance of the two hundredth anniversary of the nation's birth by running a series of "Bicentennial Questions" and comments in The ROTATOR. On January 5, 1976, following a pessimistic assessment of the world's prospects, the veteran newsman W. H. Treloar "eloquently presented the urgent need to recapture the sense of individual worth and national purpose that had previously characterized this country." The next week, the board of directors voted Treloar the club's first Paul Harris Fellow by contributing one thousand dollars to the Rotary Foundation in his honor.

Rotarians figured prominently in preparations for "Town Meeting '76," a day of community discussion and entertainment at the Marquette Senior High School on Saturday, April 10. Committee chairmen for the event included Ronald Richards, program; David Allie (president of the Marquette Area Chamber of Commerce), attendance; and Barrington G. Ellis, food. Raymond, executive vice-president of the Chamber, was coordinator.[3]

Richard O'Dell returned as a guest in April and June to speak on the significance of the American Revolution and on the history of the club. Local Rotarians participated with members of other service organizations in the unusually vigorous annual Marquette "cleanup day" on May 1 and joined in selling tickets for an appearance of the U.S. Army Field Band and Soldiers Chorus at the armory the next month. A club invitation to President Gerald R. Ford to address all of the service groups in the Upper Peninsula at Marquette was declined.

District Governor A. M. Sterr, speaking to the club on October 4, emphasized that the distinctive contribution of Rotary is its creation of a climate of service. According to Raymond's report in The ROTATOR, "Amby concluded with a reminder on the importance of good public relations based on 'deeds' not 'words'. . . . He left us with many sound ideas and sparked a sense of purpose in what some members have observed is primarily a Knife and Fork Club." Robert N. Maust, who succeeded Raymond as editor of the bulletin early in 1977, concluded the club's observance of the Bicentennial with fourteen installments of "Rotary 'Roots'," based largely on Ernest Pearce's 1936 history of the organization.

The Marquette Rotary Club, which had shared the nation's malaise of the early 1970s—to the extent that attendance had drifted to an embarrassing low level—enjoyed a reversal of fortunes during the presidency of Dr. Busharat Ahmad, 1977-78. An exceptionally dedicated Rotarian, Ahmad immediately began to enforce the attendance rules, to improve the quality and balance of programs by making them a committee responsibility, and to encourage club participation in tangible projects such as the spring city cleanup. In association with Allen Raymond, Pryse Duerfeldt, Lee Luff, and others, Ahmad during the past several years has involved the local group in the international concerns of Rotary. By the spring of 1981 he had completed nine years of perfect attendance.

Education

Ever hopeful of the academic value of formal education to the young and confident of the economic advantages of schools and related institutions to the community at large, the Rotarians perennially have followed with interest Northern Michigan University's plans for plant and program expansion. A few months before his retirement, from which he later was to emerge to serve as acting head of Michigan State University, President Harden on October 19, 1966, addressed a joint meeting of the Marquette service clubs on Northern's continuing growth, and Thomas Peters spoke on the activities of the NMU Alumni Association, which he directed. Soon after his accession to office, President John X. Jamrich on October 28, 1968, summarized for the Rotarians his philosophy of education as it related to the university.

Meanwhile, William B. Stegath, director of the University of Michigan Alumni Association, and President Ralph J. Jalkanen of Suomi College kept the club members abreast of developments on their campuses. In August, 1971, during his official visit as district governor of Rotary, Ralph Noble of Michigan Technological University affirmed his faith in the current generation of students.

A casualty of Northern's progress was Kaye Hall, for decades the physical center of student and faculty life. At a joint meeting of service clubs in February of 1972, President Jamrich "presented facts and figures on why Kaye Hall must go." A month later Mrs. Bruce (Carol) Peterson and Max Putters appeared before the Rotary Club to argue for preservation of the old edifice, but the structure was razed before the year was out. So that the name of James H. B. Kaye, so revered by local Rotarians and Northern alumni, might nevertheless be perpetuated, the president's new home has been designated Kaye House.

Several Marquette Rotary Club meetings during the seventies dealt with contributions of NMU's business and vocational programs to the economy of the city and the Upper Peninsula. While results fell far short of Dean Donald Hangen's 1971 prediction that the number of instructors and students in the school of business would soon double, Jamrich, Peters, and Treloar, who still headed Northern's development fund, in February, 1973, described their efforts to raise three hundred thousand dollars over the ensuing five years, much of that sum to aid the school of business and management.

Early in 1977 NMU's Brian Gnauck described the courses offered in the department of management and marketing and its "overall analysis and problem-solving service" to business people willing to acquaint students with some of their practical difficulties. In January, 1980, Rotarian Glenn Stevens, Northern's associate provost, described the institution's new $18,500,000 skill center for non-degree students. A bus tour for the club members elicited the comment that the facility "should have a major impact on job development in the U.P."

Two years earlier, on January 24, 1978, Superintendent of Schools Richard Klahn, speaking on "The Economics of Education: A Non-traditional Point of View," stressed the impact of rapid technological change on elementary and secondary education, also the pressures for vocational training to satisfy the requirements of the private sector of the economy.

Toward the end of the seventies popular concern over the relationship between moral values and education was creeping into the purview of the local Rotarians. In November, 1977, Edward J. Powers of Northern's economics department "discussed the plight of American education, which he attributed to 'lack of leadership and honesty' throughout all ways of life, i.e. political, industrial, judicial, and academic and the concentration on 'the buck' and materialism. 'There are no heroes today. . . .' "

Perhaps as a counterweight to the Powers assessment, the editor of The ROTATOR reprinted in the May 22, 1978, issue a brief article by Rotarian Robert B. Glenn, provost and academic vice-president of NMU, on "The State of Things," which had appeared recently in the *Michigan Academician*.

After asserting that "the university . . . must provide an opportunity for the expression of diverse opinion, without becoming in the process the agent for *an* opinion," Glenn, with particular but not exclusive reference to the controversy over whether television nurtures crime, pointed to the importance of vicarious experience and to "the regenerating value of emphathic response and of catharsis, and the possibility that sex and violence might endow these with greater meaning." Before concluding with a strong implication that he himself was more Aristotelian than Platonic in his outlook, Glenn emphasized that "it is not the material, but rather what the artist does with it, that makes art meaningful."[4]

There is nothing in the written records of the club to show that during the past thirty years its members as a body have felt that the artist, educator, politician—or anyone else—has a moral obligation to society. The local men have not even tried to give the Rotary ideal of service an explicit moral connotation. Nevertheless, when in the 1960s a young Northern Michigan University instructor wrote and produced a play which reflected upon Christianity in a fashion which many people in Marquette believed to be blasphemous, only the personal charm and political adroitness of President Harden averted a "town and gown" explosion to which a number of Rotarians were prepared to make a major contribution.

The episode was a reminder that however reluctant they may be to draw a theoretical line between liberty and license, many club members, when their own fundamental values are threatened, still feel strongly that there is a real distinction to be made. When crisis looms, they are as ready as other men to impose and defend their determination of it.

The Arts

Most of the time the Rotarians as a group have concerned themselves mainly with the morale-building aspects of culture. In October, 1967, Mrs. Richard (Venetia) Boltz, representing the Marquette Community Theater, acquainted the club members with the history of that organization, then sang, as did two other cast members who also danced, selections from a forthcoming production of *Showboat*. Ten years later Thomas and Arthur Anderson, from the same group of thespians, covered the entire record of live theater in Marquette.

One memorable noon session of Rotary, in May of 1968, featured a wide range of club musical talent—diverse in instrumentation and voice and uneven in quality. The program was produced by Earl Closser, whose daughter Martha provided piano accompaniment for Robert Clark, violin; Lincoln Frazier, saxophone; Clyde Hecox, tenor; and Helmut Kreitz, viola. Three folk singers—Roy Fletcher, Matthew Bennett, and Don Pearce (guitar)—were "on their own."

Agreeing that except for the thoroughly professional Kreitz the club's instrumentalists might have gained from a few practice sessions since their last public performance (1935?), the listeners agreed, unanimously and enthusiastically, that these *intime* recitals should be continued. None has occurred since. The in-house musicians may have been discouraged by the standard the NMU Arts Chorale set at another luncheon meeting a few months later.

Early in 1974 principals from the Northern musical, *The Roar of the Grease Paint, The Smell of the Crowd*, favored the Rotarians with excerpts from their production. Three years later James A. Panowski, director of theater at Northern, reviewed five plays scheduled for the 1977-78 season. In February, 1978, the club members had a novel experience when Joann McGhee described the "energy-movement" and dance program of the Marquette public schools. She noted that Sandy Knoll, the core school, had received a National Endowment of the Arts grant.

In recent years the Rotarians not only have supported the 1978 appearance of the

Pittsburgh Wind Symphony in Marquette, by pledging the first thousand dollars toward it, but have shown continued interest in the local Community Concert Association and in the maturation of Northern's music education and television programs. Following a dazzling musical smorgasbord by university recitalists on March 31, 1980, some Rotarians began to speculate on ways to give NMU talent greater community exposure.

After George Lott, general manager of Northern's television and radio stations, on October 27, 1975, spoke to the club on "Public Broadcasting," local Rotarians and Rotary Anns helped in WNMU-TV's semiannual drives to raise funds for its Public Broadcasting Service. On the evening of March 13, 1978, ten Rotary couples and one "stag" received phoned pledges at the station.

Student Assistance

With some modifications and quite significant shifts in policy, the Rotary Club has persisted in its efforts to maintain personal contacts with young people and to nurture their educational aspirations. Its firm tradition of entertaining high school boys and girls at each regular meeting has been mentioned. Other overtures and gestures of support have been more sporadic and ephemeral.

Junior Achievement members from Marquette Senior High School seem to have made their final appearance on February 24, 1969, although the club made a small donation to the group as late as 1973. The September 25, 1972, accounts of faculty member Louis Taccolini and three high school students of their bicycle trip through western Europe during the summer were the last of their kind to be given the club.

Involvement with high school debaters endured somewhat longer. In June, 1969, the Rotary board of directors voted a small sum for Marquette and Bishop Baraga team members attending a workshop at Northern. In February, 1972, four students from the public high school's novice debate team, first-place winners in the Upper Peninsula and third in the state, came before the club to argue the question, "Should the jury system be abolished or changed?" The Rotary board in 1975 appropriated $225 to assist a later squad.

Toward the end of the sixties, members of the Rotary scholarship and loan committee were becoming dissatisfied with the arrangement by which Northern Michigan University administered six thousand dollars of the club's funds in making loans to students. Nearly half of the amount was lying idle, and about a third of the rest was proving difficult to recover. Consequently, at the expiration of the second five-year agreement in 1970, the Earle M. Parker Loan Fund was dissolved, and the remaining money, less several hundred dollars in bad debts, was repaid to the club. The Rotarians used five hundred dollars of the sum recovered to augment the thousand already on deposit with the St. Luke's Hospital School of Nursing loan fund.

Anticipating these actions, Allan Olson, on behalf of the scholarship committee, on May 25, 1970, introduced "the first Marquette Senior High School recipient of the Marquette Rotary Scholarship award, to be used at a college or university of his choice in the Upper Peninsula for the academic year 1970-1971." However, this option was soon discarded, and for most of the period since Bishop Baraga High School closed in 1969, a single scholarship in the amount of five hundred dollars has been granted each year, with renewals for complete undergraduate attendance at Northern only as merited. Outside this framework at least one other award has been made to a NMU student. In addition, during the past three to six years, the board has allotted one hundred dollars annually toward the expenses of a Marquette High School representative to a World Affairs Seminar in Whitewater, Wisconsin. On April 30, 1980, the assets of the scholarship fund (no loans have been made in recent years) stood at $16,043.

The widening attraction of Northern for students from outside the United States, encouragement from Rotary International, and a growing number of local Rotarians of foreign birth have been powerful stimuli to deep Marquette Rotary Club involvement with the programs of the Rotary Foundation to encourage international service and world understanding.

By the 1970s the practice of welcoming foreign students from the University and from Marquette High School to regular weekly meetings, along with Marquette area young people home from study and travel abroad, was well established. The five German students from the University of Saarbrücken had conducted a most interesting program on April 5, 1966. The club's own Rotary Fellow, Phillip Muerhcke, back from his year in Australia, attended the noon Christmas meeting on December 18, 1967. In May, 1969, four young women, students from Argentina, Brazil, Iran, and Thailand, showed slides and pointed out some of the distinctive features of their homelands. Late in 1970 Dirk Ahlers, by then a foreign language instructor at Northern, recalled his experiences as one of the University of Saarbrücken exchange students four years before.

The Rotary Foundation—Paul Harris Fellows and Rotary Scholars

The Rotary Foundation, outgrowth of an earlier Endowment Fund, came into being in 1928. The Depression hampered its progress, but the Rotary International board of directors in 1938 launched a drive to raise two million dollars to sustain it. The Second World War caused another setback. However, the 1938 goal was reached during a wave of sentiment to establish a suitable memorial to Paul Harris after his death in 1947.[5]

The Foundation first provided Rotary graduate fellowships. In 1965-66 its objectives were expanded to include group study exchanges, technical training, and what came to be known as special grants for many purposes. Along the way, undergraduate scholarships also were added. Due to confusion over the many types of awards which had evolved, the Foundation's trustees in 1979-80 brought all of them into five classifications of *Scholarships*: Graduate, Undergraduate, Journalism, Vocational (previously Technical Training), and Teachers of the Handicapped.[6]

Within the period from 1946 through 1982-83, the number of educational awards will have risen from eighteen to 1,294 annually.[7]

A few years ago the Marquette Rotary Club moved from the 10 and 1 plan to the "200 percent" level in contributing to the Foundation. This was attained in 1973 when the local organization gave $1,760, or twenty dollars per member, to the international agency.

Club and individual subscriptions for Paul Harris fellowships have been another important element in local Rotary success in meeting obligations to the Rotary Foundation. At such time as a donor's contributions total one thousand dollars, he too becomes, or may designate, a Paul Harris Fellow.

Such support has enabled the local Rotarians to obtain one undergraduate and one graduate scholarship for two young Marquette women: Karen McClellan, who left Yale for a year at Ludwig-Maximilians-Universitat in Munich (1979-80),[8] and Ann Richards, a Northern Michigan University graduate who chose to study in Valencia, Spain (1980-81).

World Youth Exchange

The Central States Rotary Youth Exchange Program, organized in 1972 in the American Midwest, became the nucleus for the World Youth Exchange for high school students which now extends to twenty-eight nations. At the urging of Busharat Ahmad and Allen Raymond, the Marquette Rotary Club began to participate in 1974, and since then Raymond, Lee Luff, Glenn Stevens, Ardeshir Payan, and John M. Maitland have served as the club's exchange officers. Luff was the outbound coordinator for District 622 (1979-81), and Ahmad has been the district's exchange chairman since 1980.

From 1972 to 1981 district sponsorship increased from four to twenty-one inbound and from three to twenty outbound students annually. During the past six years, the Marquette club alone has served a total of ten inbound and twelve outbound youths, and two more of the latter were selected to spend the year 1981-82 in Denmark and Brazil. Each of the foreign visitors has lived in Marquette with from one to four host families, almost all of them Rotarian.

Vicki Wilson, daughter of Rotarian William and Rotary Ann Betty Wilson, inaugurated the local movement when she left Marquette on August 14, 1975, for a year in Halmstad, Sweden. Eleven days later Eiji Matsuda arrived from Kyoto, Japan, to stay with the Wilsons for three months and with two other Rotary families for equivalent periods while enrolled at Marquette Senior High School.

Expunged from the club's records is the listing of its second inbound student, who arrived in the summer of 1977. From the beginning she ignored basic terms of her Rotary commitment and soon divorced herself from it and from Marquette High. With but four days' notice, Gayle Cameron of Croydon, New South Wales, Australia, replaced her in January, 1977.

In marked contrast to her predecessor, Miss Cameron became a great favorite with the Rotarians. In February she gave a "fine program" about her city and family, and two months later joined Raymond in a radio broadcast about the exchange program. During the summer she traveled coast-to-coast as one of two hundred young people from twenty-seven countries in the "Rotary Exchange USA Tour 1977," then went back to her studies for another semester at MSHS. At an International Night in September, an affair to which Ishpeming and Munising Rotarians also were invited, Miss Cameron was honored along with students from ten other nations, most of them enrolled at Northern.

Outbound as well as inbound students have related their travel experiences at meetings of the Marquette Rotary Club. In 1977 returnee Brian Turner told of his sojourn in Australia, and the next year two other of the city's young people, Jeanne Snitgen and David Prouty, reported on their impressions of Finland and Brazil.

In the spring of 1978 Julie Shapiro, an Ontonagon-White Pine Rotary Club exchange student from South Africa, gave a "fascinating slide show on Capetown." Two locally based foreign students, Peter Eriksson and Kirsi Ruokoski, appeared before the Marquette Rotarians the next fall. Eriksson informed the group that from sixty-five to eighty-five percent of the average Swedish family's income was going to taxes. Miss Ruokoski, who showed color slides of her native Finland, emphasized the beauty of its sixty-five thousand unpolluted lakes. Late in 1979 French-born Eric Schott's "candid comment about the lack of challenge to students in MSHS raised a few eyebrows."

Ahmad and Luff bore major responsibility for arranging a club sponsored District 622 Rotary Youth Exchange conference from October 19 to 21, 1979, at the local Holiday Inn. Ahmad, district vice-chairman of the RYE at the time, opened the late Friday afternoon session, past District Governor Terry Cowan performed the introductions, and a brief meeting of exchange officers followed. After a dinner for upwards of a dozen foreign students, the executive committee conducted its preliminary business. The next morning four workshops were held. Luff as district outbound coordinator chaired one of them; Mrs. Busharat (Adeeba) Ahmad, another for host parents; and Katherine Wright, a third one for parents of outbound students. Workshop reports, an address by District Governor Roger Seidl, and recreation occupied the conference members on Saturday afternoon.

The evening meeting was an expanded Marquette Rotary Ann International Night, at which four foreign students, one of them Eric Schott, projected slides and gave brief narratives about their homelands. Dancing followed. The conference concluded Sunday morning with presentations to inbound and outbound guests.

In January, 1980, Marquette exchange student Linda Lawrence reflected before the local Rotarians on her year in Sweden, during which she witnessed the Nobel Prize presentations in Stockholm. Shortly afterward Elias Goldstein, a young man who had come from Venezuela speaking no English, demonstrated his "remarkable progress" when discussing conditions in his country. During the academic year 1980-81 Marquette's Steve Taube commented on Sweden, and Hilda Lagrem from Norway, Herwig Sonderegger from Austria, and Naomi Kawata from Japan showed color slides of the spectacular scenery in their native lands. In recent months Bus-

FOREIGN EXCHANGE STUDENTS

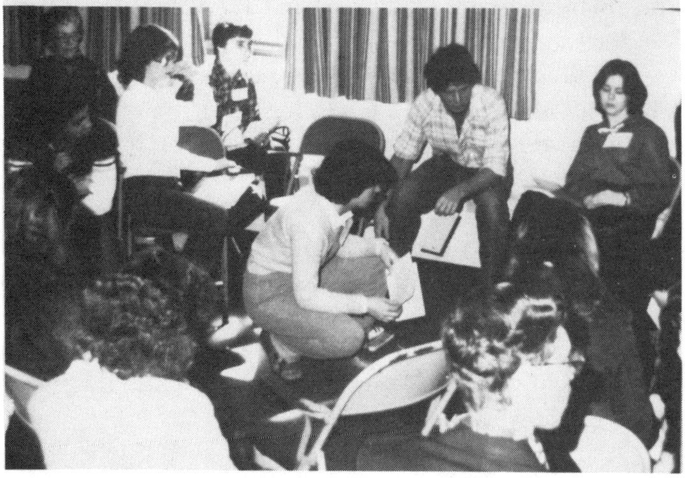

harat and Adeeba Ahmad have entertained foreign students from all over the district at their home and as their guests at luncheon meetings of the Marquette Rotary Club.

Group Study Exchanges and Sister Club Relationship with Yokaichi, Japan

The Rotary International Group Study Exchange Program, like that of the Rotary Youth Exchange, is conducted on the district level. Paired districts must, within a two-year period, send and entertain teams of twenty-five to thirty-five-year-old non-Rotarian men, broadly representative of business and the professions, on four- to six-week visits guided by a Rotarian from their district. The host district drafts a comprehensive study plan and assumes the cost of internal travel, lodging, and meals.

Following a visit in 1973 of four young men from India, Marquette Rotarian J. Willis Owen, chairman of the selection committee for District 622, dispatched one member of Rotary and four other delegates of required age to that country. One of the latter was Lloyd Sidwell of Marquette, who on December 31 gave the local club members a "Before" address and on March 11 and 24, 1974, presented a two-part "After" slide program on his experiences abroad.

An inbound group from Australia visited the district in August of 1975, and Robert Maust of Marquette left the following January with the paired outbound delegation. Upon his return Maust in April favored the local Rotarians with "a superb slide/talk exposition of the recently concluded six-week visit. . . ." He was accorded club membership immediately.

Toward the end of 1977 Ahmad, club president and later a Paul Harris Fellow, went to Pakistan with a personal gift of one thousand units (one hundred doses each) of polio vaccine which he nevertheless donated on behalf of the Marquette Rotarians. While there he also conducted an eye clinic. A short-lived sister club affiliation with the Karachi Central Rotary organization ended without a return visit by a Pakistani representative or delegation.

A sister city as well as a Rotary club relationship grew out of a 1977 trip by Michigan Governor and Rotarian William G. Milliken to Yokaichi, Japan, pursuant to the "People to People" program inaugurated by President Eisenhower many years before. When a delegation of Yokaichi citizens came to Marquette to evaluate a sister city relationship, Pryse and Louise Duerfeldt had Rotarian Susumu Fujii as their house guest from July 30 to August 6, 1978. At the regular Rotary meeting on the thirtieth, Mr. Fujii exchanged club flags with President Raymond, commenting that "We establish [through this meeting and visit] more friendly relations between our cities as sister cities." Subsequently, Duerfeldt became project director for a Marquette city and Rotary Club visit to Yokaichi.[9]

In the interim a group study exchange team of six men from District 139 (Finland) came to the Upper Peninsula in May of 1979. Busharat Ahmad served as coordinator of their activities within the Ishpeming-Marquette-Munising-Manistique area. The visiting delegation arrived in Marquette from Houghton on the morning of Friday, the twenty-fifth, attended an adjourned noon meeting of the local Rotary club held

DR. BUSHARAT AHMAD
IN PAKISTAN

in combination with those of the three neighboring communities mentioned, taped a thirty-minute interview at WLUC-TV, toured the Air Force base, then had dinner and spent the evening with their host families.

Before leaving for Escanaba and Iron Mountain the next Tuesday, the visitors traveled to Ishpeming, particularly to see Cleveland-Cliffs Iron Company mining and pelletizing facilities along with the National Ski Hall of Fame and Suicide Hill, attended religious services and inspected area churches, and spent their last full day in Marquette at Northern Michigan University, the Marquette County Historical Society, and Presque Isle, where they had a picnic.

An all-Rotary delegation consisting of Pryse Duerfeldt, Allen Raymond, Kenneth Hogg, City Commissioner William Wilson, and their Rotary Anns represented Marquette and the club during the long contemplated outbound mission to Yokaichi, where the sister club and sister city agreements were signed in August, 1979. The group's pictorial record of the trip testifies to the warmth and graciousness with which they were received by the citizens of a most beautiful Japanese city about the size of Marquette. At a regular meeting of their home club on February 11, 1980, the Duerfeldts, spokesmen for the travelers, narrated with the aid of two projectors one of the most artistically and technically impressive color slide programs ever presented to the local organization.

However, it was not only the joy of fellowship but the sadness of tragedy which brought to maturation the friendship emerging between the two widely separated, culturally dissimilar communities. On August 19, 1979, Pryse Duerfeldt had become so absorbed in photographing a corn harvester on a Japanese farm that he ignored the danger from its approaching blade until it sheared off both his feet above the ankles. Husband and wife immediately fashioned and applied tourniquets to his legs while awaiting further medical assistance.

Chairman of Northern's department of psychology and a specialist in mental and emotional problems of handicapped persons, Duerfeldt recalls suddenly becoming aware that his character and professional training and experience, all were being put to a nearly ultimate test. His pride and courage were to serve him magnificently during the weeks and months of convalescence which lay ahead. These included hospitalization at Nagoya, Japan, until September 10.

Accompanied by Usaburo Mochida, vice-mayor of Yokaichi, and Yoshio Nishioka, vice-treasurer of Shiga Prefecture, the Marquette delegation arrived home on September 12. Two days later eighty Rotarians and Rotary Anns welcomed the visitors at a dinner. Other guests included City Commissioners Glenda Robinson and William Pesola; Assistant City Manager (now Rotarian and Manager) David Svanda; Jack Van Dyke, Michigan chairman of the sister city program; and Mary Soper, Governor Milliken's Upper Peninsula representative, who transmitted a letter of greeting from the state's chief executive.

The Japanese emissaries received Marquette Rotary Club flags, certificates of honorary Upper Peninsula citizenship, and a collection of rocks indigenous to the region as additional tokens of appreciation for their solicitude and presence.[10] The

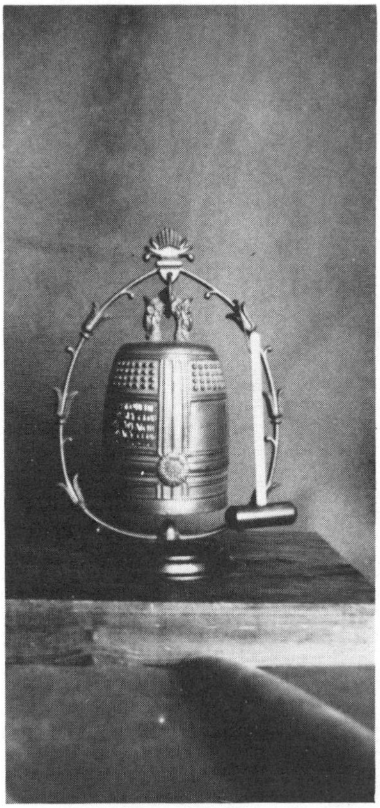

Bronze Bell: Yokaichi
Rotary Club Gift to
Marquette
Rotary Club

Marquette City Commissioner William Wilson and
Yokaichi Mayor Masajiro Yamada Signing Sister City
Agreement, August 13, 1979,
Witnessed by Allen Raymond, Betty Wilson,
and Louise and Pryse Duerfeldt

August 12, 1979, Sister Rotary Club Agreement
Signing: Yokaichi Rotary Club President Keijro Ishido
and Pryse Duerfeldt

Group Picture Taken After Signing of Sister Club Agreement

club later named Duerfeldt a Paul Harris Fellow, and he similarly honored his wife Louise.

Early in 1980 the announcement was made that Lee Luff would lead the District 622 group study exchange team to Finland during the spring. On March 24 he introduced the other members to the club. The visit, extending from May 6 to June 14, was made as scheduled.[11] Early in 1981 Luff and Rev. Thomas Wickstrom of Palmer gave slide talks about the trip.

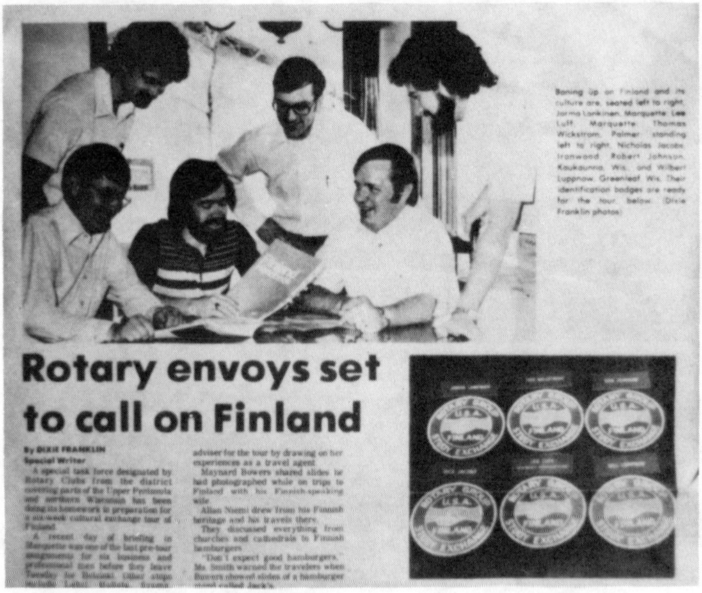

Rotary envoys set to call on Finland

By DIXIE FRANKLIN
Special Writer

Boning up on Finland and its culture are, seated left to right, Jorma Lankinen, Marquette; Lee Luff, Marquette; Thomas Wickstrom, Palmer; standing left to right, Nicholas Jacobs, Ironwood; Robert Johnson, Kaukauna, Wis., and Wilbert Luppnow, Greenleaf, Wis. Their identification badges are ready for the tour, below. (Dixie Franklin photos)

Continuing hostilities in the Middle East, particularly the ever present Arab-Israeli clashes, the Iranian revolution and hostage crisis, and the Russian invasion of Afghanistan, have furnished a somber background for the Marquette Rotary Club's efforts at international understanding. In two timely and much appreciated presentations during the early part of 1980, Ahmad and Payan shared their perceptions of the conflicts; at their second appearance they were joined by Mowafy. On November 3, Rotarians Mowafy and Frank Allen, together with NMU's Miodrag Georgevich assessed the chances for peace in that most unpredictable, dangerous part of the world. Col. Lionel Roberts, 410th Bomb Wing Commander at K.I. Sawyer AFB, through his narration and a film, *SAC—America's Global Shield*, on February 23, 1981, left the Rotarians with the reassurance that whatever the state of readiness in the other branches of service, the Air Force is prepared for all eventualities.

Other Interests

A sampling of the Marquette Rotary Club's 1980 weekly programs indicates some divergence between the dynamic concern for world affairs and a less obvious but persistent devotion to local matters. In his farewell talk as a member of the local group, Dr. Richard Potter summarized the latest developments within the jursidiction of the Marquette County Health Department. Speakers from outside Rotary dealt with such topics as the 1980 Census, the ways in which energy is used for residential purposes, and the work of the Alger-Marquette Community Action Board. Mrs. Phillip (Sally) May, chairperson of the finance committee of the Marquette County Board of Commissioners, gave a masterful analysis of the current budget and of problems in local government funding.

Coach Rick Comley and the seniors from Northern's runner-up NCAA championship hockey team, also two area men who served as officials for the Winter Olympics at Lake Placid, were featured at three luncheon meetings. In April, 1981, Comley and a slightly less successful squad which was eliminated in the semifinals of the national tournament returned with another review of their last encounters.

At a temporarily low point in club enthusiasm for the student exchange program, The ROTATOR editor noted in the issue of December 3, 1979, that only five Rotary Anns had attended a luncheon to explore ways of broadening the base of distaff interest. He observed further, "The lack of support by club members—less than a handful have invited either of the two exchange students to participate in any kind of activity, and host families have been extremely difficult to obtain—has raised the question of whether or not the Club wishes to continue the programs and, if so, at what level."

Recovery from this feeling, if not complete, has reached the point that the most recent club survey indicates a general pride in local accomplishments in the international realm. The success of almost any undertaking depends on the leadership and dedication of a relatively few persons. There is still in some quarters a nostalgia for the years when exchanges were unheard of and assistance to students was confined to loans to truly needy and responsible as well as able Marquette boys. An indeterminate number of Rotarians remain skeptical of outright grants to young people who are able enough, though not particulary impoverished.

But even the "silent" opposition appears to be diminishing before the pressure of world events and the talent and charm of foreign visitors. Until recently we Americans have assumed that we have had much to teach members of other nations. Now we are discovering that we have as much to learn from them.

Continuity

An overview of the local Rotary club's history suggests that changes in the composition and attitudes of the community are pretty well reflected in those of the organization. The rapid growth of Northern and of health related services accounts for the fact that NMU faculty and staff and medically trained men today comprise about one-fourth of the 125 club members. Although the group cannot claim the president of Northern, it has had four vice-presidents briefly on the roster at the same time, and Allan Niemi, recently retired as vice-president for student affairs, has been the first head of the club since James H. B. Kaye to come from that institution.

A stabilizing continuity has been maintained through "old family" father-son—and now grandson—relationships. More than a score of fathers and sons have belonged to the club. Daniel, Mason, and Douglas Pearce are grandsons of Ernest L. Pearce. Peter Frazier and James P. Grundstrom are other third generation members.

Despite losses, the average age of the Marquette Rotarians is about fifty, approximately the same as that of the original group in 1916, and length of affiliation averages probably ten to eleven years. Bill Owen's twenty-eight years of perfect attendance, all but seven of them with the local club, has helped to compensate for attrition, as have the influx and durability of new but mature members. As of November 23, 1981, 584 men were known to have been in active association with the Rotary Club of Marquette since its founding.

A most striking feature of the club is its lack of patriarchs. The members with longest Rotary tenure who regularly come to meetings—Linc Frazier, Jenner, Pat LaFreniere, Clark, Bennett, and Treloar—participate actively. Although he no longer covets the desserts of more delicate eaters, Bob Clark still composes limericks. Matt Bennett sits, as always, near an exit in order to respond quickly to medical emergencies.

With the exception of Walter H. Schultz, the real patricarchs—James J. Beckman (the earliest past president now living, with a record fifty-three years of continuous membership), Albert H. Burrows, Charles B. Hedgcock, and Nelson D. Rupp—either reside elsewhere or spend much of their time away from the city. Conway Peters, who joined the club in 1923, it will be recalled, died on June 15, 1980, in Albion, Michigan.

After his retirement from Northern Michigan University in 1966, Albert Burrows made Oskaloosa, Iowa, his base for teaching at William Penn College and for culmination of 150,000 miles of travel on six continents. In a letter written in 1980 at the age of eighty-four he stated, emphatically, his conviction that service clubs are "the cement of humanity," providing cities and towns with "an esprit de corps that elected officials cannot match."[12]

More than thirty-seven years ago Burrows wrote the longest piece, brief though it is, that an active member of the Marquette Rotary Club ever has had published in *The Rotarian*:

The Rotarian's Job

Rotary stands for service. Rotary serves the local community, the nation, and—the Fourth Object—the world. The job of the Rotarian is to exemplify the service goal. Fortunately in a smooth-functioning free-enterprise economy greater service to "others" generally brings greater profits to "self." However, when profits accrue through catering to base desires or through monopolistic manipulation, then the true Rotarian will realize that time and eternity and the immaterial, as well as the material, surround and affect everyone. He will realize that a man is not profited even though he gains great pecuniary reward when he sacrifices his ideals of service to the selfishness of self. Great material profits accompanied by great spiritual losses result in a net life value deficit. Rotarians are not perfected individuals. No one and no group reaches perfection. Rotarians have not practiced fully the implications of their ideal as expressed in their motto. And if they could practice their ideals perfectly, then simultaneously their ideals would become practical realizations and cease to be ideals. In this latter case they would need to establish a new and higher ideal or ethical growth would be completed and stagnation would be the only possible change. But the Rotary motto—Service above Self—contains a service-to-others ideal that constitutes an adequate and eternal challenge to every Rotarian.[13]

—December 1944

13
PERSPECTIVE AND CHALLENGE

It is often recalled that Paul Harris founded the first Rotary club because he was lonely. Less well remembered is the richness of his previous experience. Harris was raised by his paternal grandparents in the small town of Wallingford, Vermont. His autobiography, *My Road to Rotary*, is filled with nostalgic allusions to the loving-kindness of his aged guardians, whom he idolized, and to the friendly, trusting warmth of a community in which serious crime was almost unknown. Interspersed are occasional, uncharacteristically bitter references to the anxieties engendered by his parents, so improvident and self-indulgent that they could not take care of their children.

In Paul's hale and courageous grandparents the Puritan virtues of integrity, industry, and frugality, combined with great respect for formal education, were softened by unselfishness, simplicity, tolerance, and avoidance of controversy. In rural Vermont nature was both a harsh disciplinarian and a gentle culturist which rewarded honest toil with good health, good habits lightly borne, modest prosperity, and a serenity of spirit akin to complacency and smugness. Live and let live was the rule.

American schools in Harris's day stressed a pride in heritage, patriotism, and good citizenship to which he enthusiastically responded. Beyond the eighth grade they prepared students mostly for college. In 1900 only ninety-five thousand high school diplomas and few more than twenty-nine thousand college and university degrees were awarded in the entire nation. Obviously, education at advanced levels was a privilege not a right, and its fortunate beneficiaries were an elite. Prescribed courses in the humanities and sciences were basic to grooming for the professions and public office although Harvard, under the aegis of President Charles Eliot, already was revolutionizing education by permitting election among a wide variety of offerings.

Study at three universities culminated in a law degree for Harris. Then followed a five-year "internship" throughout the country in and out of the occupations of journalist, fruit picker, teacher, actor, ranch hand, hotel clerk, and salesman; also travel in the Caribbean, British Isles, and parts of continental Europe. By 1905 Harris at the age of thirty-seven was a seasoned lawyer with nine years of practice in Chicago. Hopeful and insatiably curious about human nature, he had given much thought to the principles of Rotary.

The National Matrix

There could have been no better time nor place—the heartland of the United States—for Harris to launch his enterprise. The greater part of the country was still agricultural, and most urban workers, like their rural counterparts, applied their muscles and skills directly to production of life's necessities. By later standards, laborsaving factory machines and household appliances were few. The railroads were a decade from their apogee; the automobile and airplane had just appeared. Washington, D.C., was geographically remote from most people, and state capitals more nearly resembled county seats than government loci for the equivalent of average-size nations that some have become.

The ebullient Theodore Roosevelt, personification of the country's youthfulness, optimism, and vitality, was in the White House. The population of the United States was little more than a third that at present, and, as always, America was the destination of "huddled masses yearning to breathe free." Possessed of an immense quantity of the earth's treasure and a multitude of entrepreneurs eager to exploit it, the nation was emerging rapidly as a world power.

There was a darker side. In 1900 life expectancy at birth was little more than forty-seven years (thirty-three for nonwhites), proof in itself of the persistent rigors of existence even in the United States. The poor, the sick, the friendless had neither the time nor the education to record their sufferings. That task was left to more literate folk—to journalist Jacob Riis in his *How the Other Half Lives* (1890), to sociologist Edward A. Ross in *Sin and Society* (1907), and to other writers, notably Lincoln Steffens, Ray Stannard Baker, Ida Tarbell, and Upton Sinclair, whom Roosevelt dubbed "muckrakers" for their dramatizations of the ills of an industrializing, urban society. Paul Harris was dismayed by the lack of ethics among Chicago businessmen.

But optimism prevailed even among the poverty-stricken. Idealized for their boldness, imagination, and ingenuity, men of affairs, however many were feared for their ruthlessness, commanded respect and admiration sufficient to contain labor unrest and to retard unionization. Most successful merchants and industrialists demonstrated such enthusiasm, pride, and competence as to persuade the public as well as themselves that their greatest satisfaction came from their accomplishments rather than their profits.

Black citizens long had wondered what real good the abolition of legal servitude had done them. Nevertheless, they too could find inspiration in Booker T. Washington's rise from slave to Presidential adviser by outdoing whites in toil, honesty, and thrift.

It was no accident that America's one indigenous philosophy has been pragmatism, conceived in the latter nineteenth century to free the individual to conduct his own search for truth in a dynamic, evolving society. Nor is it surprising that one of the four most widely read books at the time was Edward Bellamy's utopian romance,

Looking Backward 2000-1887 (1888), describing a genteel, frictionless, socialistic order whose material benefits everyone shared equitably. At the birth of Rotary, the United States, while exuding optimism especially in the upper reaches of society, was striving at all levels for freedom balanced by restraint—for a kind of moving equilibrium.

Paul Harris—Father of Rotary and Model Rotarian

Paul Harris's life spanned the period between the end of the Civil War and that of World War II. Preserving the boy in the man while going from unhurried, rural simplicity to the excitement and professional opportunities of a great metropolis, he established Rotary on the firm foundation of personal friendship, high ethical standards, mutual business advantage, and, two years later, service beyond the group. His ultimate goal was a "neighborly world" in which Rotarians would be "ambassadors of good-will to high and low, rich and poor, to all races, to the devotees of all religious faiths and to members of all political parties, purveyors of tolerance, forbearance, justice, kindliness. . . ."[1]

After two global conflicts had both frustrated its physical growth and afforded extraordinary opportunities for philanthropy, Rotary International was to receive its greatest tribute ever when it was invited to send consultants to the United Nations Conference on International Organization at San Francisco in April, 1945. At least forty-nine Rotarians attended as official delegates or advisers for thirty-three of the fifty nations represented.[2]

As founder and chief inspiration for a movement which after only forty years had attained such distinction, Paul Harris was fulfilled as few men are privileged to be. Except that he was childless, he seems to have achieved all he may have sought in life. In 1910 he married Jean Thomson, his "bonnie Scottish lassie." Not long after, he took her to "Comely Bank," their home on a wooded hill on the outskirts of Chicago, which they shared until his death in 1947. Despite Rotary's demands on his time, Harris never gave up his connection with his law firm.

Harris is remembered still as a moderately tall, spare man of quiet, easy grace and humor—modest to the point of shyness—but a perceptive, congenial companion and a fluent speaker and conversationalist nonetheless. Although in his later years he made several almost ceremonial tours which took him to countless clubs in many parts of the world, he carefully refrained from trying to influence the course of Rotary in any major way. His chief mission seems to have been to remind men of the things that unite them, not those which cause division. He was content to personify the ideals of Rotary as best he could and to watch it generate its own momentum in fellowship and service.

Harris was critical of the modern axioms that people's economic wants are insatiable and that a man's ability and worth to society can be measured by his wealth. Rotary's founder cited Spinoza, Charles Steinmetz, and Luther Burbank among others, as examples of first-rate men who saw money as a means to ends, not as an end

Paul Harris

Jean Harris

in itself. He noted that Albert Einstein refused to go to Princeton at what he considered a "preposterous" salary and insisted that it be much reduced.[3] One can imagine Harris's response to the current argument that high salaries and perquisites are indispensable in attracting top administrative talent.

Naturally sanguine though he was, Harris knew that change inheres in life and that, as he stated, "Prosperity leads to mental and physical indolence, and is the forerunner of destruction." He clearly recognized the dangers growing out of selfishness and personal ambition, and he viewed the "god of indulgence and pleasure" as "more perversive than the money-god."[4] He surely would have agreed with the Connecticut schoolboy's terse response to a history examination question: "The fall of Rome was due to carelessness."

A passage from Harris's autobiography is worth quoting in full:

> We Americans are hero worshippers; it would be well for us to choose our heroes wisely. Who can be blind to the fact that we worship at the shrine of productivity? What shall we do when all the wants have been satisified? Think up new wants and put them into production? Having geared ourselves to high productivity, perhaps there is no other way out at present. Men must have work and that means production. It's easy enough to scramble eggs but not easy to unscramble them.[5]

He added, however: "Productivity of course should not be discouraged; it is too full of possibilities;" among them the airplane's shrinking of the globe to make international understanding and good will inevitable.[6]

G. K. Chesterton once compared, unfavorably, "The Rotarian Age," as he called it, with that of Victoria. George Bernard Shaw, declining to address a convention of British and Irish Rotarians in Edinburgh, is said to have commented, "I can tell where Rotary is going without travelling to Edinburgh to find out. It is going to lunch: and that is as far as it will ever get in this country."[7]

The stereotype persists of Rotary—its many worldwide achievements notwithstanding—as a "knife and fork" organization which limits its membership to a complacent, conservative, moneyed elite, superficial in thought and judgment, shunning controversy, and salving conscience with "Band-Aid" treatment of profound social ills.

Like most stereotypes, this one contains a germ of truth. Nevertheless, critics overlook the obligation and record of Rotarians in exemplifying fellowship and service in all facets of their lives and in contributing to the general welfare in ways extending far beyond the confines of their organization. To cite an example from the Marquette experience—would George Shiras have established his cultural foundation had he not been inspired by his years of happy association with, and loyalty to, the local Rotary club? Perhaps not even he could have answered that question. But would anyone claim that he might have done still more for the community had he not been a Rotarian? And what about the individual as well as associational achievements of members of the many other international service groups patterned after Rotary?

Maxwell K. Reynolds, Jr., son of the distinguished Marquette Rotarian, has never joined Rotary nor any of the other local service clubs. Nevertheless, because of his many contributions to the community, few of them generally known, the local organization in 1980 named him, the first person outside it to be so honored, a Paul Harris Fellow. His son-in-law, Lee Luff, after completing his current term as club president, is scheduled to become Marquette's fourth district governor (1983-84).

It is true that Harris himself dwelt on pastel shades to the neglect of deeper hues in the color spectrum and that his fine analytical mind never was quite able to subdue a roseate cast to his emotions. However, he lived and died at the zenith of American power, when few people anticipated that within a decade after his demise the country would pass what some observers believe to have been its optimum population of 150,000,000, or that by the 1960s it might be overstraining its material and spiritual resources, both.

Then, Now, and Again

Seventy-seven years after the founding of Rotary, the problems and opportunities before the nation and the planet are vastly different from those which existed at its inception. It is one thing for an essentially healthy, growing economy to suffer from a relatively short breakdown in the distribution of an abundance of goods as well as services, as happened in the United States in the 1930s. It is quite another for a still exploding world population to press unremittingly upon precious, irreplaceable resources which are becoming exhausted or increasingly expensive to extract.

Today the time-honored assumption that material production is automatically creating a promised land of universal prosperity, brotherhood, and peace is being challenged as never before. The immense technological superstructure of the industrialized nations has succeeded marvelously in pouring forth a torrent of commodities and in bringing people and nations together physically through rapid transportation and almost instant communication.

Nevertheless, the cost in social fragmentation and confusion has been great. The extent of what critics during the Great Depression denounced as maldistribution of wealth in the United States, not to mention the rest of the world, may defy precise statistical measurement,[8] but there is no mistaking its stark, tragic reality. The misgivings expressed in Marquette by Grove Patterson in 1930 and by William J. Norton in 1941 have as much validity today as when they were uttered. They are underscored by the now inescapable fact that technological unemployment, which for sixty years or more has been dismissed as at worst a temporary condition sure to be alleviated by new opportunities in an expanding economy, confronts all of the industrialized West as a brutal, possibly permanent, phenomenon.

There can be little doubt that mankind is at its most perilous moment in history. Among futurists, the most optimistic see the world as a cocoon from which man only now is starting to emerge on his way to conquering the cosmos. The most pessimistic perceive Earth as a tiny planet covered by a thin, intricately woven tapesty of organisms among which man is spreading like cancer, determined to destroy himself and all other life, probably between the years 1984 and 2000. People who seek salvation in a permanent balance of terror can take heart from the unanimity of opinion voiced by an international group of medical experts, Soviets included, that an all-out thermonuclear war will make impossible any medical aid to survivors.[9]

At the moment, the most sanguine forecasters are hardly less extreme in their views than prophets of doom are in theirs. Herman Kahn, a long-run optimist, welcomes the mature post-industrial society[10] of the future, when automation and computerization are fully developed. He expects that, after a brief critical period, science and technology will solve the problems of energy and material shortages and set mankind on a course toward greater productivity than ever before. He is confident of the time when multi- or transnational corporations will be of such dimension as to employ up to a million workers each worldwide.[11]

Geochemist Harrison Brown was criticized as too gloomy in his pioneer work, *Challenge of Man's Future* (1954), in which he called for an "understanding of the relationships between man, his natural environment, and his technology" and for a "victory of wisdom and knowledge over stupidity and dogma." Brown published a sequel, *The Human Future Revisited*, in 1978. In this he expressed grave concern that industrial civilization may have become too inflexible and fragile to survive "discontinuities in the flow of energy, minerals, and food," along with "systems failures, terrorism, and wars."[12]

Anticipating much the same result, the late E. F. Schumacher, for twenty years economic adviser to Britain's National Coal Board, sought the preservation of democracy, the enrichment of human existence, and achievement of greater resilience in industry through imaginative conception and skillful application of "appropriate" or "intermediate" technology.

In his *Small Is Beautiful* (1973), Schumacher concluded, largely, it appears, from statistics contained in the famous report, *The Limits to Growth* (1972), prepared at the Massachusetts Institute of Technology for the Club of Rome, that "the 5.6 per cent of the world population which live in the United States require something of the order of forty per cent of the world's primary resources to keep going." He added that America's industrial system "could be called efficient only if it obtained strikingly successful results in terms of human happiness, well-being, culture, peace, and harmony."[13] He doubted that it did.

Addressing the Economic Club of Detroit in October, 1980, David Rockefeller looked forward to increased production resulting from plant modernization and further automation in the United States, but warned of a consequent "two-tier society, with satisfying and well-rewarded work for some, while the rest are left to grapple for unskilled jobs." He also cautioned that generational divisions may occur as fewer workers are called upon to support growing numbers of retirees. He noted in addition the problems of minority groups, legal and illegal immigrants, and unemployed youths.[14]

There is much controversy about whether a return to the political and economic philosophy and domestic policies of the 1920s will succeed in restraining inflation, solving energy and materials shortages, protecting the environment, reducing crime, and creating meaningful, satisfying employment for additional millions of workers in the private sector of the economy, all at the same time. If construction and factory modernization do produce a boom, what will be the long-range effects? And will an open-ended arms buildup stimulate or depress the economy and keep or destroy world peace?

Clarence B. Randall long ago eloquently stated his conviction that freedom "is indivisible and sole. There are no 'freedoms': there is simply freedom, and it runs as the breadth of life through every phase of the American tradition." He perceived, too, that where there is freedom from external control, there must be self-control: "Free enterprise is not a hunting license."[15]

If the neo-conservatism now in ascendancy is to succeed, it will have to be accompanied by a recognition that where there is great freedom, there also must be acceptance of great responsibility, whether in political, economic, religious, or academic enterprise.

The Spirit and Potential of Rotary

Sooner or later the world will realize, though perhaps too late, that it no longer can afford the age-old polarization between people, whether rich or poor, who seek satisfaction mainly in wealth and power and those who strive, like Paul Harris and his grandparents, for understanding, mutual friendship, and ability and opportunity to serve. Light does not emanate from darkness contending against darkness, nor freedom from either individuals or armies locked in combat for the distribution of spoils. Throughout history saints and sages have reiterated that true peace depends not upon appeasement or force, but, through reason or revelation, upon common vision and perceptions grounded in equity.

In the industrial nations there is no greater practical need than for a conscious, deliberate turning from excessive complexity and indiscriminate production toward simple living and a far deeper appreciation of humanity and of the only planet most of us will ever visit. Success in making this transition will require a trust which goes beyond legality to empathy; an artistry conducive to morality; technology appropriate to conservation, not waste; and the will to do what must be done.

Bringing the immense technological apparatus of the industrialized countries back under control will tax the patience, courage, and skill of a bomb squad. Fred Astaire spoke to a larger audience than he knew when he advised a young dance partner, "Don't be nervous, but don't make any mistakes."

Although reason is essential to solutions of today's problems, still more important is good will. Reduced concentrations of wealth and power will be achieved, not by class conflict or other threats to those who hold them, nor by dwelling too much on the self-defeating results of avarice, but by creation of an atmosphere which allows the immeasurably greater satisfactions of sharing, so graphically demonstrated in Rotary, to flourish.

The tragic failure of the many estimable opponents of American Negro servitude was their inability to portray themselves as genuinely happier, freer people than the slaveholders they were trying to persuade to give it up. The positive approach of Rotary has a much greater potential for eradicating tyranny in all its forms.

For three hundred years American institutions of higher learning perceived as their paramount task the education of students for good citizenship and for leadership in the professions and in civic affairs. They strove to accomplish this through balanced programs leading to breadth of knowledge in the humanities, social studies, and sciences.

After World War II, however, burdened by having to prepare hordes of young people for entrance into the labor market even while holding them back from it, the nation's colleges and universities fell victim to vocationalism and overspecialization. Despite his eloquence and his sensitivity to what was happening, Harvard President James B. Conant during the 1940s and 1950s was much less successful in restoring coherence to school curricula than Charles Eliot, however unwittingly, had been in fragmenting them a half century before.

If only by default, Rotary and other service clubs may prove to be as admirably equipped as any lay organizations for cultural leadership, in the United States at least, in the critical decades ahead. Whatever its shortcomings—surely sins of omission rather than of commission—Rotary has demonstrated in organization and function the validity and effectiveness of true Jeffersonian democracy.

Rotary's thousands of clubs, linked in voluntary association for fellowship and service, are limited by little else than member classification and attendance requirements. The weekly club meetings; rotation in office; quick and easy communication throughout the non-Communist world via publications such as *The Rotarian* and *Revista Rotaria*; and access to ample funds, directly through the Rotary Foundation and indirectly through the philanthropy of individual members, make almost boundless its opportunities to benefit all mankind.

As a past president of Rotary International once said: "Rotary is indeed at work in the world, in a world which is too dangerous for anything but truth and too small for anything but fellowship." The Axis powers knew what they were doing when during the 1930s and 1940s they forced the disbanding, temporarily, of 484 clubs with 16,700 members.[16]

Tooling Up

During the Marquette Rotary Club's sixty-five-year history, the population of the city nearly doubled, to 23,336 in 1980, while that of the county proceeded at a slower pace to 74,115. By today's standards these units still are small, but, as has been noted, trends observable in the more populous portions of the country have become evident here.[17]

Considering its geographical remoteness especially, the local Rotary organization during the past two years has experienced a surge of vitality which, if representative on a very small scale of what is being felt by affiliates generally, promises a major impact on world affairs. The Marquette Rotarians now are corresponding and exchanging gifts and ideas with counterparts in many regions of the world as well as in the United States, while the youth and group exchange programs flourish as never before.

On December 1, 1980, Rotarian Stig Ryhagen of Forshaga, Sweden, a retired steel executive and father of 1963-64 exchange student Åke Ryhagen, exuded Rotary warmth when speaking about his long association with clubs at home. Visiting Marquette for the first time, the elder Ryhagen by his presence alone testified to the opportunities for lasting friendship through Rotary's international contacts.

An event of special significance to Marquette in cementing bonds of cordiality with its sister city in Japan occurred when a nineteen-member delegation from Yokaichi spent part or all of the week of August 10 to 17, 1980, in the area. At noon on Sunday, the tenth, Mayor Masajiro Yamada and sixteen others of the group arrived at the county airport, where they were greeted by Marquette Mayor Glenda Robinson; Pryse Duerfeldt, coordinator for the visit; the Marquette Ambassadors; and by other citizens before dispersing to the homes of sixteen host families, six of them Rotarian.

The schedule for the Japanese was a busy one. On Sunday evening they witnessed a Frisbee tournament at the Cliffs Ridge Ski Area, whose manager, Colonel Weesen, presented them with gifts for their new museum in Yokaichi. The next evening, they attended a regular meeting of the Marquette City Commision. Here the first hour was given to an official welcome and an exchange of gifts. Those from Japan included a handcrafted representation of Mount Fuji and an exquisite porcelain doll. The commission reciprocated with dolomite clocks and pen sets, and the city with a watercolor.

During the rest of the week, the visitors attended the Upper Peninsula State Fair in Escanaba; heard a concert featuring instrumental jazz and classical music and a children's choir; witnessed a speed (ice) skating and a Marquette Figure Skating Club exhibition; toured the Northern Michigan University campus; and inspected the Marquette County Historical Society library and museum, the Peter White Library, and the John Burt House. The two Girl Scouts in the group were taken to the Scout camp in Gwinn.

Tuesday night the Marquette Rotarians and Rotary Anns, the Japanese delegation, and guests both Japanese and American "whooped it up Western style at the Holiday Inn" in contrasting cowboy and kimono garb. Congressman Robert Davis came with the gift of an American flag which had flown over the nation's capitol. Entertainment included a square dancing demonstration and vocal numbers by the Marquette Choral Society. On other occasions the Japanese dined at the Old Marquette Inn and at the Northwoods Supper Club, where Rotarian Ronald Klumb acquainted them with a bison buffet. With members of the city commision, they were received at the home of Commissioner Robert Ling.

Vice-Governor Naoyoshi Maekawa of Shiga Prefecture, Michigan's "Sister State," in which Yokaichi is located, arrived in Marquette with a liaison officer on Wednesday for a two-day stay. Following inspection of city facilities and a tour of the flight line at the Sawyer Air Force Base, the two men joined their colleagues at a reception at the Matthew Bennetts', where Vice-Governor Maekawa and Michigan Governor William G. Milliken met and exchanged gifts.

A picnic on Friday was held in spite of threatening weather, and the visitors were given rides in boats and antique cars. Rotarian Frank Oatley drove Mayor Yamada around Presque Isle in a 1931 Model A. Ford. The *Mining Journal*, which concluded week-long coverage with two full pages of photographs, reported that sixteen delegates appeared tired when they left for home on Sunday, August 17. Another, a young woman, stayed on to become a student at Northern Michigan University.

Several 1980 summer and fall Marquette Rotary Club programs dealt with Upper Peninsula economic development, election issues, and personal and community welfare. On September 22 Robert E. Hunter, a retired industrialist previously connected with the General Motors Corporation and with the Ford and Weatherhead companies, which he had served as a vice-president and president respectively, addressed the Rotarians on "Cleveland—A Text Book Case."[18]

Hunter, who maintains residences in both Cleveland, Ohio, and Marquette County, described the "aging" of northern cities caused by outmoded capital equipment; by loss of population, industry, and tax revenue; and by addiction to federal aid. Having headed an Operations Improvement Task Force which studied Cleveland's management problems, Hunter was able to analyze in great detail the many difficulties of that city and to relate them to those of Marquette.

Hunter first listed nine important advantages enjoyed by Marquette: the absence of a race problem; presence of a city manager form of government; population growth; an expanding tax base; no short term notes; separate accounting for utilities; require-

RETURN VISIT BY
YOKAICHI DELEGATION
TO MARQUETTE
August, 1980

Yokaichi Club President Hiromu Deme, Shiga Prefecture Vice-Governor Naoyoshi Maekawa, Marquette Club President Burt Parolini

"Cowboys and Kimonos" Theme of Rotary Dinner Welcoming Sister City Delegation, August 13, 1980

Duerfeldt Embracing Maekawa (left) and Toshimitsu Imai, Shiga Liaison Officer

ment of a five-year capital outlay budget plan; a treasury surplus; and, "as far as is generally known," no "heavy buildup of deferred maintenance or capital expenditures."

Then he cautioned:

> In spite of all these pluses, Marquette could in 25 years, without working too hard at it, have a host of the same problems Cleveland faces today. You don't have a Kucinich[19] about whom you learned through national media. Yet as an outsider following the local media, [I have noted that] one of your commissioners ran a pretty close second during the last year. Many more of these and you will really have problems. You are in a very critical period.

The speaker predicted that Marquette's population and tax bases will not grow much in the near future, but he viewed with concern the emergence of pressure groups such as the parents of junior hockey players, prospective patrons of the new marina, and utility customers, all desiring low charges or rates in spite of high investment and operating costs at less than capacity usage. Hunter concluded, "If these [problems] are not faced up to, you start a downward course which can only vary in magnitude of the potential problems to that of Cleveland and other aging cities."

When, at the first meeting of the club in 1981, Waba Treloar gave his annual assessment of world conditions, he dwelt with sober eloquence on the same issue as Gregor Ziemer had in 1948: whether, as still the most powerful nation in the free world, the United States can and will provide the leadership required of it.

Two weeks later, on January 19, 1981, President Burt Parolini asked the Rotarians to devote the entire session to an examination of the club's strengths, weaknesses, and opportunities for improvement. The responses were too varied to permit a brief summary, and none was distinguished for novelty. However, the president later appointed three special committees on 1) fund raising, 2) Rotary fellowship enrichment, and 3) welcoming new members.

Parolini himself favors the establishment of a general or charitable trust consisting of a specified amount of money to be obtained within a definite number of years. This will allow routine funding of contributions for community services while dues and receipts from meals not eaten, amounting in all to about five thousand dollars annually, can be earmarked for club and district administrative expense.

In Summary

An early 1981 newspaper column of memorabilia contained this paragraph:

> Hardly anybody understood better how to handle the expense of things than Dr. Joseph Peck, who said: "It costs a lot less, if you learn early that all is vanity, and that most folks spend money they haven't got on things they don't need to impress people they don't like." List Dr. Peck among those once numerous old-timers who made it a rule never to buy anything on time except a house.[20]

If everyone in the nation suddenly became converted to Peck's rule, chaos would follow, surely. But the reference is valuable for the perspective it gives on how far we Americans have wandered from the restraint prevalent at the time of Rotary's founding. Paul Harris and his grandparents found happiness in nourishing food, adequate shelter, warm clothing, congenial family and friends, and employment which gave meaning to their lives and fulfilled their desires for self-respect and service to others.

In a world in which so many have so little and so few so much, is it not a challenge to Rotarians to remain humble before truth, to try to teach and lead by example, to delight in simple pleasures, and to value even the most meager talents among the least privileged members of the human community?

During the summer of 1980 the Council on Environmental Quality and the Department of State published in three volumes the much heralded, controversial *Global 2000 Report to the President: Entering the Twenty-First Century*. Seeking to reassure the public despite the essentially gloomy findings of the study, its compilers concluded:

> . . . the problems of preserving the carrying capacity of the earth and sustaining the possibility of a decent life for the human beings that inhabit it are enormous and close upon us. Yet there is reason for hope. It must be emphasized that the Global 2000 Study's projections are based on the assumption that national policies regarding population stabilization, resource conservation, and environmental protection will remain essentially unchanged through the end of the century. But in fact, policies are beginning to change. . . .[21]

Inspired, perhaps, by President Ronald Reagan's appeals for a revival of voluntarism to take up the slack created by diminished government appropriations for social welfare programs, free-lance writer Francis Barton, in the December, 1981, issue of *The Rotarian*, not only capsulized the findings of *Global 2000*, but summoned Rotarians everywhere to action. He did this by evoking the words and authority of Michael Wright, sometime assistant director of the President's Task Force on Global Resources and Environment:

> My work takes me to most of the major airports in the world and to many minor ones. In all these busy places, I have seen the Rotary insignia, with days and hours of club meetings posted. As much as any organization, Rotary International will determine if "The Global 2000 Report" contains predictions of what is going to happen, or of what could have happened."[22]

Almost thirty years ago Matt Bennett remarked informally after a noon meeting of the Rotary Club of Marquette, "We don't so much need more knowledge as the ability to use what we have."

Regular Luncheon Meeting, June 1, 1981

ADDENDUM

In the spring of 1982 a seven-minute motion picture film titled *Week End Frolic of the Marquette Rotary Club at the Peter White Camp May 13, 1916* (see pages 9 and 10 supra) was discovered in the basement of the Delft Theater. It soon was acquired by Jack Deo of the Superior View Studio, Marquette, who kindly projected it for the author.

Despite deterioration, the clip clearly identifies each of the sixteen Rotary guests by name as he is greeted with handshakes by Alfred O. and Morgan W. Jopling, father and son, at the entrance to the camp lodge. Discernible, also, are James H. B. Kaye, subjected to mock heckling as he addresses the group; portions of croquet and baseball games; a three-canoe race; and most or all of the men riding in a large horse-drawn wagon.

Taken together, the film, a seven-page typescript appended to the club minutes, and a dozen photographs still extant make this first outing the most thoroughly recorded social event in the organization's history.

APPENDIX

A–*Roster of the Rotary Club of Marquette*
B–*Service Through Other Agencies*

APPENDIX A

Roster of the Rotary Club of Marquette

PRESIDENTS

Frank J. Jennison	1916-17
Arch B. Eldredge	17-18
James H. B. Kaye	18-19
John R. Van Evera	19-20
Edward A. Macdonald	20-21
Ernest L. Pearce	21-22
Harlow A. Clark	22-23
William S. Wright	23-24
Ralph R. Eldredge	24-25
August Syverson	25-26
Arthur F. Jacques	26-27
Albert E. Miller	27-28
Charles A. Boyd (resigned)	28-29
L. Roy Walker (completed Boyd term)	
Willard M. Whitman	29-30
Frank B. Spear, Jr.	30-31
Christian E. Urbahns	31-32
James T. Roach	32-33
Simon R. Anderson	33-34
J. Cloyd Bowman	34-35
James J. Beckman	35-36
Charles F. Retallic	36-37
L. Burton Hadley	37-38
Glenn E. Seifert	38-39
L. N. Jones	39-40
John D. Morrison	40-41
Charles P. Drury	41-42
Philip B. Spear, Jr.	42-43
Emery E. Jacques	43-44
W. J. Weber	44-45
C. Morgan Beckman	45-46
Earl H. Closser	46-47
Edlore J. LaFreniere	47-48
Bernard L. York	1948-49
Edward L. Pearce	49-50
James L. Wilson	50-51
Leonard C. Smith	51-52
Robert H. Clark	52-53
Wilbert H. Treloar	53-54
Richard J. Barry	54-55
Bernhardt J. Pederson	55-56
Roy W. Fletcher, Jr.	56-57
Don M. Pearce	57-58
Lesley J. Cory	58-59
Elmer K. Carlson	59-60
Robert B. Brebner	60-61
Robert M. Ling	61-62
Ray A. Nelson	62-63
Frederick C. Sabin	63-64
L. Wallace Bruce	64-65
Robert J. Pearce	65-66
Edward J. Stratton	66-67
George C. Franzen	67-68
Wesley E. Perron	68-69
Paul J. LaFreniere	69-70
Arthur L. Hiebel	70-71
Colonel E. Weesen	71-72
Morgan J. Gingrass	72-73
Lincoln B. Frazier	73-74
Victor G. Holliday, Jr.	74-75
Patrick T. Kelly	75-76
Ronald L. Garberson	76-77
Busharat Ahmad	77-78
Allen D. Raymond III	78-79
Allan L. Niemi	79-80
Burt E. Parolini, Jr.	80-81
Lee R. Luff	81-82

DISTRICT GOVERNORS

James H. B. Kaye (15) 1920-21	Harlow A. Clark (10) 1926-27	Earl H. Closser (622) 1973-74

OFFICERS AND BOARD OF DIRECTORS
1916-1917

Frank J. Jennison	President
Ernest L. Pearce	Vice-President
Peter W. Phelps	Secretary
Alfred F. Maynard	Treasurer
Arthur F. Jacques	Sergeant at Arms

Board: Jennison, Phelps, Arch B. Eldredge, Austin Farrell, Henry R. Harris, Alton T. Roberts, George J. Webster

CHARTER MEMBERS

George N. Conklin (1850-1945)
Proprietor, Jeweler
Thomas M. Cunningham (1869-1945)
Physician
Arch B. Eldredge (1853-1918)
Lawyer
Austin Farrell (1858-1925)
Manager, Pioneer Iron Co.
Pig Iron
Joseph C. Gannon (1876-1965)
Manager, Gannon Grocery Co.
Grocer, Wholesale
Henry R. Harris (1861-1939)
General Manager, L. S. & I. and M., M. & S. E. Railways
Transportation, Railroad Executive
Arthur F. Jacques (1874-1945)
Manager, James Pickands & Co.
Coal, Retail
Frank J. Jennison (1861-1935)
Cashier, Marquette National Bank
Banker
Morgan W. Jopling (1883-1942)
Chairman, Peter White Land Co.
Real Estate, Land Company
John D. Mangum (1859-1918)
Secretary, Marquette Commercial Club
Publicity Agent
Alfred F. Maynard (1857-1938)
Vice-President, St. Luke's Hospital
Hospital
Ernest L. Pearce (1885-1964)
General Manager, Lake Shore Engine Works
Machinery, Miscellaneous
Peter W. Phelps (1865-1943)
Proprietor, Peter White & Co.
Insurance, General
Alton T. Roberts (1881-1957)
Proprietor, Emblagaard Dairy
Creamery and Dairy
Theodore Schneider (1881-1937)
President, Schneider & Brown Lumber Co.
Lumber
James E. Sherman (1849-1931)
Manager, John M. Longyear Co.
Mining Lands
Edward O. Stafford (1858-1956)
Proprietor, Stafford Drug Co.
Druggist, Retail
George J. Webster (1870-1934)
General Manager, Charcoal Iron Co. of America
Chemicals

1979-1980	OFFICERS	1980-1981
Allan L. Niemi	President	Burt E. Parolini, Jr.
Thomas L. Gagnon	Vice-President	Pryse H. Duerfeldt
Burt E. Parolini, Jr.	Vice-President	Lee R. Luff
Stewart A. Kingsbury	Secretary	Stewart A. Kingsbury
Lloyd E. Fairbanks	Treasurer	Lloyd E. Fairbanks

DIRECTORS
1979-1981

Raymond S. Camilli, Pryse H. Duerfeldt, Leonard S. Elder, Barrington G. Ellis, Michael F. Fassbender, Thomas L. Gagnon, Robert B. Glenn, David O. Higley, Irvin W. Horton, Stewart A. Kingsbury, Edward N. Locke, Lee R. Luff, Boris Martysz, Daniel S. Mazzuchi, William A. Mudge, Jr., Daniel M. Pearce, Emil H. Vajda, John Weting, Allen D. Raymond III, ex officio (1979-80); Allan L. Niemi, ex officio (1980-81)

ACTIVE MEMBERS
1916-1982

Grouped within years of first affiliation
(terminal dates not given)

1966-1982

Russell W. Adams
Busharat Ahmad
Frank Allen
David L. Allie

Henry J. Barsch
Calvin Barton
Jack Batchelor
Kenneth F. Beck
Wilbert A. Berg
Joseph P. Bickler
Robert L. Bouschor
Robert G. Boynton
Larry E. Braak
Chester Briggs
Lawrence C. Brooks

Raymond S. Camilli
Francis L. Cardoni
Dale W. Carnell
Donald H. Carros
Thomas P. Casselman
J. Eugene Chambers
Lou W. Chappell
Donald G. Chinnery
Arnold M. Cohodas
Larry A. Cohodas
Victor Cooney
Paul E. Cowley
J. Michael Coyne

Nicholas G. Dellis
Theodore E. Doane
Pryse H. Duerfeldt

James C. Elder
Leonard S. Elder
Stanley W. Elder
Barrington G. Ellis
Donald R. Elzinga
Martin G. Eskelinen

Lloyd E. Fairbanks
Michael F. Fassbender
Louis Ferrari
Keith M. Forsberg
Peter W. Frazier
John E. Frey

Thomas L. Gagnon
Ronald L. Garberson
Keith H. Gardella
Paul C. Gerrish
James C. Ghidorazi
Donald J. Giesen
Robert P. Gilstrap
Mark E. Glendon
Robert B. Glenn
Gary J. Gorsalitz
Gary R. Govanus
Ronald D. Gramenz
Norman L. Gruber, Jr.
James P. Grundstrom

Eugene A. Halker
Gerald J. Harrington
George A. Hazeres
Douglas G. Heath
William K. Hetrick
Arthur L. Hiebel
David O. Higley
Victor G. Holliday, Jr.
Donald E. Hooper
Dan P. Hornbogen, Jr.
Irvin W. Horton
Alfred M. Hunt

William F. Iacoe

Ralph W. Janka
Randall S. Johnson

Gordon A. Johnstone
Jack R. Jones, Jr.

Ralph S. Kaziateck
Patrick T. Kelly
Keith C. Kepler
Keith Killoran
Stewart A. Kingsbury
Ronald E. Klumb
Paul J. Koebele
Adam A. Komosa
Edward J. Kraft
Helmut Kreitz
Jon N. Kukuk

Robert B. Lamb
Tim Larson
Edward N. Locke
George E. Lott, Jr.
Patrick J. Lowney
Don L. Lucas
Less R. Luff
William R. Lyons

Keith McCleod
David H. McClintock
Thomas R. McNabb
John M. Maitland
William J. Malandrone
Willard L. Martin
Boris Martysz
Robert N. Maust
Daniel S. Mazzuchi
Roy T. Minkin
Mark C. Moore
Robert E. Moore
August R. Moratti
V. Harvey Mortensen
Mohey A. Mowafy
Thomas J. Mudge
William A. Mudge, Jr.
Richard A. Munro
Bernard J. Myler

Michael J. Nagelkirk
Robert C. Neldberg
Allan L. Niemi
D. Neil Nystrom

Frank B. Oatley

John B. O'Day
Daniel E. Olsen
Wayne E. Olsen
William E. Olsen
David D. Olson

Burt E. Parolini, Jr.
Joseph L. Paulson
Ardeshir M. Payan
Daniel M. Pearce
Douglas G. Pearce
Mason M. Pearce
Wallace G. Pearson
Keith G. Pederson
William E. Pesola
Frederick J. Peterson
Steven C. Pelto
George P. Petry
Christ J. Pfohl
David Piehl
Richard J. Potter
Gregory Ptacin

Allen D. Raymond III
William I. Rein
Ronald W. Richards
Eugene Rowland
Dan Rupp
E. Eugene Russell
Randy O. Ryan
David A. Rykhus

Kenneth R. Saari
John St. Germain
James Schneider
E. Peter Schumer
James R. Sesslar
H. Erik Shaar
Lyle F. Shaw
Patrick D. Slugg
James D. Smeberg
Eric M. Smith
Kenneth C. Smith
Milton D. Soderberg
Michael C. Spafford
Lloyd Steinhoff
Glenn R. Stevens
John R. Stevenson
Clarence B. Stortz
Samuel F. Stout

Robert C. Stow
Matthew J. Surrell
David A. Svanda
Terry Szczepanski

Lawrence A. Tavernini
Donald R. Taylor
John C. Taylor
Glenn S. Thomas
Gary C. Tigges
James L. Tourtillott

Paul R. Uimari

Emil H. Vajda
Thomas J. Vicary

Anton B. Wadel
Irving M. Wagner
Robert T. Wagner
David R. Wall
Colonel E. Weesen
Alvin P. Wendt
William Wentzel
John Weting
Thomas A. Wickstrom
Carroll H. Williams
William F. Wilson
Lee S. Wolff
Harry Wood

Rico N. Zenti

1951-1965

A. L. Amolsch
William C. Anderson
Carl Arbogast
Rex A. C. Atwood

Patrick L. Bennett
Marshall W. Berg
S. Peter Berg
T. Boyd Bolitho
John Borgen
Henry J. Bothwell
Robert B. Brebner
Robert L. Brocklehurst

L. Wallace Bruce
Raymond J. Buchkoe
Fred J. Bye

Paul M. Cargo
Elmer K. Carlson
Emery Chartier
James W. Clark
Richard J. Closner
Donal T. Conley
Lesley J. Cory
John S. Crawford

Anthony B. De Lape

Leo F. Erkkila
Willard C. Evert

John L. Farley
F. L. Ferzacca
William Flanigan
A. J. Fleury
Anthony H. Forbes
George C. Franzen
P. O. Fure

Morgan J. Gingrass
Thomas Griffith
Gerald E. Grundstrom

Edgar L. Harden
Martin Harney
Charles W. Hayward
Gilbert J. Heard
Roy E. Heath
Clyde W. Hecox
Paul J. Hettle
Louis T. Hildebrand
George E. Hill
Kenneth S. Hogg
Vern O. Holgate
Edward S. Holman
George A. Houghton, Jr.
Elston R. Huffman
Paul D. Hunter

Wilson Irey

Robert H. Jean
George W. Johnson
Gerald L. Johnson
Warren E. Johnson

John Kolhek
John C. Kuivinen

Paul J. LaFreniere
John W. Leadbetter
Leonard A. Lindquist
Robert M. Ling
Richard A. Lutey

Robert C. McCarthy
Nolan B. McKevitt
Jack D. McKichan
Daniel McLean
George Mancuso
Carl A. Martin
John F. Martin
Norman L. Matthews
Thomas Moore
Robley H. Morrison
Dayton H. Mudd
Richard H. Myers

Ray A. Nelson
Charles W. Nicholas
Walford E. Nystrom

Richard F. O'Dell
Allan F. Olson
J. Willis Owen

Albert W. Payne
Don M. Pearce
Bernhardt J. Pederson
Wesley E. Perron
Everett Peterson
J. Herbert Peterson

Kenneth J. Roberts

Frederick C. Sabin
Arvid A. Savola
Lawrence Schuster
Robert Scott
James J. Scullion
Charles T. Smedman
Norbert W. Smith
Richard P. Sonderegger
John R. Stephenson
Robert W. Stephenson
Edward J. Stratton
Daniel Sturt
Edward A. Swanson

Donald W. Teisberg
Harold C. Ternus
William A. Todd
James L. Tomlin

Leo Van Conant
Leslie L. Van Dine
Almon V. Vedder
Jack B. Veiht

Robert P. Ward
Lawrence W. Westphal
George M. Wilson, Jr.
Donald J. Wirth
K. Charles Wright
William E. Wright

Zigmund A. Zasada
Jack E. Zeigler
Donald G. Zettle

1931-1950

H. S. Ablewhite
James R. Acocks
Max P. Allen
Henry C. Anderson

Richard J. Barry
C. Morgan Beckman
Charles E. Begole
Hugh Bennett
Matthew C. Bennett
Arthur A. Benson
Ralph E. Benson
M. C. Bergstrand
Robert Berry
James Cloyd Bowman
Leo W. Bruce
Leonard W. Brumm
James C. Bullock
Albert H. Burrows
Gerald F. Bush
Edward F. Byerly

Arthur G. Callahan
D. K. Campbell
Fred J. Campbell
W. Paul Chamberlain
A. Dougal Chisholm, Jr.
Robert H. Clark

Maurice Clarke
Earl H. Closser
James A. Clulo
Roy Clumpner
S. Howard Connors
T. P. Cook
William S. Cooley
Marvin L. Coon
M. C. Cooperstock
R. T. Cushing

Eugene G. Day
John N. Deglman
Phil De Graff
Arthur C. De Vries
Joseph C. Dewey
William Doell
G. F. Dressel

Eugene R. Elzinga
Lee C. Ewell

Roy W. Fletcher, Jr.
A. Emerson Fleury
William J. Fountain
Lincoln B. Frazier
Clayton P. Frei

Leo F. Gannon
Stephen L. Garber
John Gerling
John Graf
L. P. Graffunder
Nelson D. Griswold

L. Burton Hadley
Lynn H. Halverson
Alex P. Hamby
Richard C. Hammerschmidt
Ralph T. Hanna
Robert R. Harrison
Charles B. Hedgcock
R. C. Heynen
Joe M. Hill
Victor G. Holliday
William C. Hoppes
Lane Horrigan
Russell E. Horwood
S. Victor Hytinen

Ward R. Jacobson
Emery E. Jacques
R. Wesley Jenner
F. J. Johnson
Martin M. Johnston
L. N. Jones

E. M. Kaake
Thomas Kelly
Forest J. Kepler
J. H. Kline
Benjamin E. Knauss

Edlore J. LaFreniere
Warren T. Lambert
Joseph O. Leonard
S. Lojocano
Arnold J. Lutey

Camden McVey
Donald E. Mellin
Franz Menze
Bernard T. Micklow
C. V. Money
Claude L. Mosher

N. G. Narotzky
Douglas Nash
Oscar Niemi
Max W. Nunemaker

Samuel F. Oakey
Carl A. Olson
E. T. Olson
Herman E. Olson
Harold C. Overholt

Edward L. Pearce
Robert J. Pearce
Webster H. Pearce
S. Morris Pell
Harry G. Pellow
Thor W. Person
Robert T. Peters
F. J. Phillips
James R. Pollock
R. B. Porter

John G. Rank
Ed E. Rasmussen
Alfred A. Reiter
Arthur F. Runkel
Carroll C. Rushton
Frank J. Russell, Jr.

Henry St. Onge
Howard Sanregret
Herman C. Schmidt
William H. Schneider
Ed Scholtz
Walter H. Schultz
John B. Schuyler
Glenn E. Seifert
Robert S. Shahbaz
Frank Shaw
George Smedman
Leonard C. Smith
Sidney Smith
Bennett Sonaltone
Philip B. Spear, Jr.

Henry A. Tape
Sverre Thorvaldson
Munro L. Tibbitts
Frank Tonella
Wilbert H. Treloar
Lionel C. Trepanier

T. Ray Uhlinger

Frederick C. Vosburg

Orville R. Walker
Burt L. Watt
John R. White
Ed L. Wilmers
James L. Wilson
Harold E. Wright
James W. Wright

Bernard L. York
Frank Young
Roy O. Yungbluth

Walter M. Zillgitt

1916-1930

George M. Altmann
Simon R. Anderson
Alfred E. Archambeau

K. Sidney Baker

James J. Beckman
Arthur K. Bennett
Edward S. Bice
George E. Bishop
Charles A. Boyd
Raymond W. Boyer
Herbert J. Bryce
Henry A. Buchholtz
Samuel H. Buck
Frederick P. Burrall

Theodore B. Catlin
Samuel A. Chamberlain
John F. Chambers
D. Fred Charlton
Lew Allen Chase
Fred I. Chichester
Harlow A. Clark
George B. Cumming

Clyde T. DeHaas
Eugene DeHaas
J. Rex DeHaas
N. Grant DeHaas
Arthur E. Delf
Englebert A. Derleth
Norman J. Dobson
John A. Doelle
Charles P. Drury
Clifton F. Drury
Martin I. Dunnebacke

Allan M. Edyvean
Ralph R. Eldredge

Horace F. Ferry
Louis J. Flanigan
Martin J. Flanigan
Emery E. Freeman

Hugh S. Gallup

Thomas A. Gowling

David M. Hackney
Robert L. Harris
Charles Havill
Frank Heath
Dan P. Hornbogen
Edward J. Hudson
Anthony L. Huetter
Frederick W. Hyde

Harvard Jean
Ray Johns
William J. Johnston
Elmer W. Jones
Alfred O. Jopling
James E. Jopling

James H. B. Kaye
Ralph Kendricks

John Lammi
Harry D. Lee
John M. Longyear, Jr.
Rudy Loucks
C. E. Lytle

Edward A. Macdonald
Courtney S. McIntyre
John McNamara
Elmer R. McPhee
Roscoe C. Main
Albert E. Miller
John D. Morrison
John M. Munson

Earle M. Parker
Carroll Paul
Albert J. Pearce
H. H. Pellow
Herbert E. Perkins

Conway Peters
Daniel W. Powell

Charles F. Retallic
Maxwell K. Reynolds
James T. Roach
Carl E. Rogers
Olin A. Rogers
George W. Rowell
Nelson D. Rupp
James Russell
Eber F. Rydholm

Henry A. St. John
Fred J. Schultheis
M. E. Scott
George Shiras, 3rd
Frank B. Spear, Jr.
Philip B. Spear
August Syverson

Percy G. Teeple

Christian E. Urbahns

John R. Van Evera

Neil Waldo
L. Roy Walker
Edward C. Watson
Gurn S. Webb
W. J. Weber
James G. Wells
John West
Willard M. Whitman
Simon A. Williams
William S. Wright

Roscoe C. Young

Raymond H. Zerbel

HONORARY MEMBERS 1916-1982

Arthur K. Bennett
James Cloyd Bowman
Raymond W. Boyer
Henry A. Buchholtz
Samuel H. Buck
Harlow A. Clark
George N. Conklin
Joseph C. Gannon
Edgar L. Harden
Henry R. Harris
Robert L. Harris
Russell E. Horwood
Frank J. Jennison
Elmer W. Jones
Alfred O. Jopling
James H. B. Kaye
Harlan J. Larson
John M. Longyear
John M. Maitland
Alfred F. Maynard
Richard F. O'Dell
Earle M. Parker
Peter White Phelps
Maxwell K. Reynolds
James E. Sherman
George Shiras, 3rd
Peter C. Sianis
Frank B. Spear, Jr.
Edward O. Stafford
John W. Stone
Edward J. Stratton
Clifford A. Swanson
Henry A. Tape
Percy G. Teeple
Christian E. Urbahns
Willard M. Whitman
Ed L. Wilmers

PAUL HARRIS FELLOWS OF THE ROTARY FOUNDATION

Wilbert H. Treloar	1976	Pryse H. Duerfeldt	1980
Edlore J. LaFreniere	1977	Maxwell K. Reynolds, Jr.	1980
Busharat Ahmad	1979	Adeeba Ahmad	1981
Paul J. LaFreniere	1979	Dan Rupp	1981
Louise G. Duerfeldt	1980	Joan Reynolds Luff	1982
Lincoln B. Frazier	1982		

APPENDIX B

Service Through Other Agencies

Not always coterminous with Rotary membership

MAYORS		*CITY COMMISSIONERS*	
Chosen annually by the voters until 1914:			
John M. Longyear	1890-91		
James E. Sherman	1897		
John D. Mangum	1901		
James Russell	1902		
Elected for five-year terms until 1951:			
Harlow A. Clark	1919-24	Ernest L. Pearce	1914-26
Edward J. Hudson	29-34	James E. Sherman	14-23
Arthur F. Jacques	34-39	Gurn S. Webb	21-26
James J. Beckman	44-49	Edward J. Hudson	23-29
		Ralph R. Eldredge	29-33
		Simon R. Anderson	33-43
		William H. Schneider	43-50
		Leo W. Bruce	45-50
		Allan F. Olson	48
		Leonard W. Brumm	48-50

Charter amendment in 1949 caused all terms to expire on December 31, 1950.

CITY COMMISSIONERS AND MAYORS

Commissioners elected for two-year terms.
Mayors (terms in parentheses) chosen annually by and from the commissioners.

Leonard W. Brumm (1952-53; 1954-55)	1950-55
Bernard L. York (1951-52; 1953-54)	51-54
Lynn H. Halverson	52-57
Richard C. Hammerschmidt (1956-57)	54-60
James W. Clark (1957-58)	55-58
Elmer K. Carlson (1961-62)	60-66
Robert E. Moore (1966-67)	65-67
Patrick J. Lowney (1970-71)	1968-71
Paul J. LaFreniere (1971-73)	68-73
William J. Malandrone (1973-75)	71-75
Richard J. Closner	71-72
Robert C. Stow	74-76
Frederick J. Peterson	76-77
William F. Wilson	77-79
Robert M. Ling (1980-—)	78-—
William E. Pesola	79-81

CITY MANAGERS

James R. Pollock 1946-49	James A. Clulo 1949-55	Thomas Moore 1962-65	Thomas R. McNabb 1965-80

David A. Svanda
1980-—

MARQUETTE AREA CHAMBER OF COMMERCE
Established 1930

PRESIDENTS

Philip B. Spear	1930	Franz Menze	1958
Edward J. Hudson	31	Patrick L. Bennett	60
August Syverson	37	John F. Martin	61
August Syverson	38	Robley J. Morrison	62
Philip B. Spear, Jr.	39	Robert M. Ling	64
Philip B. Spear, Jr.	40	Bernard J. Myler	68
Lincoln B. Frazier	42	James J. Scullion	69
R. Wesley Jenner	43	Irving M. Wagner	71
C. Morgan Beckman	46	D. Neil Nystrom	74
Gerald F. Bush	47	Robert L. Bouschor	75
Harold C. Overholt	48	David L. Allie	76
Carl A. Olson	49	Daniel S. Mazzuchi	77
Leonard C. Smith	53	Lloyd E. Fairbanks	78
Robert H. Clark	55	Thomas L. Gagnon	79
Don M. Pearce	57		

EXECUTIVE VICE-PRESIDENTS (OFFICE DIRECTORS)

Ben E. Knauss	1950-62	Allan F. Olson (interim)	1969
Robert J. Pearce (interim)	65	Allen D. Raymond III	77-80
		Lee R. Luff	80-—

MARQUETTE AMBASSADORS CLUB
Established 1963

Busharat Ahmad
Patrick L. Bennett
*Robert B. Brebner
L. Wallace Bruce
J. Eugene Chambers
Lou W. Chappell
Leonard S. Elder
Lloyd E. Fairbanks
John L. Farley
P. O. Fure
Thomas L. Gagnon
James P. Grundstrom
*Clyde W. Hecox
Arthur L. Hiebel
Ronald E. Klumb
*Robert M. Ling
Patrick J. Lowney
Lee R. Luff
Richard A. Lutey
Daniel S. Mazzuchi
Robert E. Moore
*Richard H. Myers
Bernard J. Myler
*Ray A. Nelson

MARQUETTE AMBASSADORS CLUB (CONT.)

D. Neil Nystrom
Herman E. Olson
Daniel M. Pearce
Robert J. Pearce
Chris J. Pfohl
James J. Scullion
John R. Stephenson
Robert C. Stow
David A. Svanda
*James L. Tomlin
Jack E. Ziegler

*Charter members

HONORARY MEMBERS

Edgar L. Harden
Lincoln B. Frazier
R. Wesley Jenner
Bernard J. Myler

ST. LUKE'S HOSPITAL BOARD OF TRUSTEES

John W. Stone	1897-1909
John M. Longyear	97- 03
Albert E. Miller	97- 39
Daniel W. Powell	1903- 17
Morgan W. Jopling	09- 19
Alfred F. Maynard	11- 21
Peter W. Phelps	11- 41
Frank J. Jennison	12- 15
Henry R. Harris	15- 29, 31- 39
Alton T. Roberts	17
Philip B. Spear	17- 23
Simon A. Williams	17- 25
Edward A. Macdonald	21- 27
Edward S. Bice	23- 61
Harlow A. Clark	23- 56
Roscoe C. Young	25- 40
Maxwell K. Reynolds	27- 52
Nelson D. Griswold	37- 39
John D. Morrison	39- 68
Eugene G. Day	39- 50
Lincoln B. Frazier	39- 73
C. Morgan Beckman	45- 49
James J. Beckman	50- 69
James H. Kline	52- 68
Don M. Pearce	61- 72
Allan F. Olson	64- 73
Richard A. Lutey	67- 73
L. Wallace Bruce	67- 73
Clyde W. Hecox	69- 73

ST. MARY'S HOSPITAL ADVISORY BOARD OF TRUSTEES

Emery E. Jacques	1954-56
Victor G. Holliday	54-59
Ray A. Nelson	57-63
Jack E. Zeigler	58-64
John D. Morrison	61-63
Leo W. Bruce	61-64
Lesley J. Cory	61-67
Clyde W. Hecox	63-69
Paul J. LaFreniere	65-72
R. Wesley Jenner	65-73
Bernard J. Myler	66-73
Russell W. Adams	69-72
Robert E. Moore	72-73

MARQUETTE GENERAL HOSPITAL BOARD OF TRUSTEES

(St. Luke's and St. Mary's Hospitals merged in 1973.)

Lincoln B. Frazier	1973-77
Clyde W. Hecox	73-—
Allan F. Olson	73
R. Wesley Jenner	73-78
Bernard J. Myler	73-76
Richard A. Lutey	73-—
L. Wallace Bruce	73-—
Robert E. Moore	73-—
Robert C. Neldberg	77-—
K. Charles Wright, M.D.	77-—

BAY CLIFF HEALTH CAMP
Established 1933

BOARD OF DIRECTORS and MARQUETTE COUNTY COMMITTEE MEMBERS

Roy W. Fletcher, Jr., Vice-Chairman, 1958-74
Ernest L. Pearce, Treasurer, 1934-57

Harlow A. Clark	1934-48	Bernard L. York	1957-61
Ernest L. Pearce	34-59	R. Wesley Jenner	58-67
Maxwell K. Reynolds	48-52	J. H. Kline	58-68
Roy W. Fletcher, Jr.	53-—	Frank J. Russell, Jr.	58-—
Gerald E. Grundstrom	53-54,	M. C. Cooperstock, M.D.	61-62
	65-—	Edward L. Pearce	53-66
William C. Anderson	55-71	Henry J. Bothwell	63-—
Robert B. Brebner	55-—	Norman L. Matthews, M.D.	63-—
Edgar L. Harden	56-66	Herman E. Olson	63-69
Robert H. Clark	57-64,	Richard A. Lutey	77-—
	70-—	Lloyd E. Fairbanks	80-—

Medical Directors: M. C. Cooperstock, M.D., 1934-51
Norman L. Matthews, M.D., 1951-76

MARQUETTE COUNTY CHAPTER OF THE AMERICAN RED CROSS
Established 1917

(listings based on incomplete records)

CHAPTER CHAIRMEN

Peter W. Phelps	1917-19
Edward A. Macdonald	19-22
Ernest L. Pearce	23-25,
	41-42,
	46-47
Philip B. Spear, Jr.	47-50

DRIVE CHAIRMEN

John D. Morrison	1924
Emery E. Jacques	41
Robert H. Clark	45
Max P. Allen	47?
William E. Wright	51

Edward S. Bice was treasurer for almost thirty-three years—from the founding of the chapter to November, 1949.

Robert J. Pearce, W. J. Weber, A. D. Chisholm, Matthew C. Bennett, Eugene R. Elzinga, and George E. Hill are among the Rotarians who have been active in the organization.

Mrs. Philip B. (Mary) Spear in the early days served as executive secretary.

UNITED WAY (MARQUETTE COMMUNITY CHEST) OF MARQUETTE COUNTY
Established 1925

DRIVE CHAIRMEN

Alton T. Roberts	1925	Louis Hildebrand	1953
Ralph R. Eldredge	26	Elmer K. Carlson	57
August Syverson	27	R. Wesley Jenner	58
Albert E. Miller	28	Louis Hildebrand	59
Clayton P. Frei	34	Robert E. Moore	60
L. Burton Hadley	36	Robert C. McCarthy	61
Richard C. Hammerschmidt	37	Ben E. Knauss	65
Carroll C. Rushton	38	Robert J. Pearce	67
Lincoln B. Frazier	40	Robert C. Neldberg }	69
George E. Bishop	42	George P. Petry }	
Munro L. Tibbitts	44	cochairmen	
Albert H. Burrows	45	Irving M. Wagner	73
Arthur C. De Vries	46	E. Eugene Russell	75
Leonard C. Smith	50	Robert B. Glenn	78
Louis Hildebrand	52	Thomas L. Gagnon	81

COUNCIL PRESIDENTS
(based on incomplete records)

Harlow A. Clark	1929-31,	Arthur C. De Vries	1947-52
	34-35	Munro L. Tibbitts	52-53
Lincoln B. Frazier	41-42	Kenneth S. Hogg	67-68
Albert H. Burrows	45-47		

CHILD & FAMILY SERVICES OF THE UPPER PENINSULA

In 1919 Harlow A. Clark and Frank A. Bell of Negaunee, with the assistance of Dr. Charles P. Drury and Edward Bice, organized an Upper Peninsula branch of the Michigan Children's Home Society (renamed Michigan Children's Aid Society in 1921). Clark and Bice were president and secretary-treasurer, respectively, from 1921 to 1948. Bice was a board member for a total of thirty-eight years. Local Rotarians who later served as presidents were Munro L. Tibbitts, 1948-60, and Robert H. Clark, 1960-63.

Meanwhile, a Marquette Family Welfare Agency was established in 1929, renamed Family Service Society in 1946, and incorporated in 1954. Among its presidents were Rotarians Ernest L. Pearce, 1929-30, and Albert H. Burrows, 1946-55, along with Rotary Anns Mrs. Frank B. (Rachel) Spear, Jr., 1932-37, and Mrs. Lincoln B. (Anne) Frazier, 1955-66.

In 1966 the two groups merged to form the Michigan Children's Aid and Family Service Society of the U.P. It became the present Child & Family Services of the Upper Peninsula in 1972. Rotary and Rotary Ann presidents of the consolidated organization have been John D. Morrison, 1967-68; Lesley J. Cory, 1968-71 and 1972-73; Clyde W. Hecox, 1975-77; Mrs. Frazier, 1977-79; and P.O. Fure, 1979-—.

HIAWATHALAND COUNCIL OF THE BOY SCOUTS OF AMERICA

Organized in 1912 as the Hiawatha Area Council embracing Marquette and Alger Counties two years after Scouting came to the city of Marquette

PARTIAL LIST OF MARQUETTE ROTARIANS WHO AS ADULTS HAVE BEEN ASSOCIATED WITH SCOUTING IN THIS VICINITY

Max P. Allen
Simon R. Anderson
Arthur K. Bennett
Robert B. Brebner
Leonard W. Brumm
Samuel H. Buck
Gerald F. Bush
Thomas P. Casselman
Harlow A. Clark
Arthur C. De Vries
Charles P. Drury
Ralph R. Eldredge
Barrington G. Ellis
Lloyd E. Fairbanks
Peter W. Frazier
Edgar L. Harden
Charles B. Hedgcock
Irvin W. Horton
S. Victor Hytinen
R. Wesley Jenner
Benjamin E. Knauss
Edlore J. LaFreniere
Robert M. Ling
V. Harvey Mortensen
William A. Mudge, Jr.
Ray A. Nelson
Herman E. Olson
J. Willis Owen
Burt E. Parolini, Jr.
Edward L. Pearce
Ernest L. Pearce
Maxwell K. Reynolds
James T. Roach
Arvid A. Savola
Glenn E. Seifert
Eric M. Smith
Frank B. Spear, Jr.
Philip B. Spear, Jr.
Sverre Thorvaldson
Christian E. Urbahns
Robert T. Wagner
L. Roy Walker
W. J. Weber
Willard M. Whitman
K. Charles Wright

Eldredge appears to have been the first scoutmaster of Troop 307. Mortensen is the current scout executive. Ishpeming Rotarian Burton H. Boyum, who has served several terms as council president, in recent years has been the mainstay of Scouting in this region.

PENINSULA WATERS COUNCIL OF THE GIRL SCOUTS OF AMERICA

Mrs. Frank B. (Rachel) Spear, Jr., Mrs. Harlow A. (Nellie) Clark, and Mrs. Olin A. Rogers, all Rotary Anns, were three of the four women who founded the organization. The first two, assisted initially by Charles P. Drury and Willard M. Whitman, remained steadfast supporters for many years. Unfortunately, the council records and newspaper accounts are too meager to make possible further mention of Rotary or Rotary Ann involvement.

UPPER PENINSULA CHILD GUIDANCE CLINIC 1944-1967

A local advisory committee which included Carroll C. Rushton (chairman), Henry A. Tape, Ernest L. Pearce, Charles P. Drury, Willard M. Whitman, Harlow A. Clark, and Maxwell K. Reynolds, also Mrs. Frank B. (Rachel) Spear, was broadened into a local advisory council and then into the Upper Peninsula Child Guidance Clinic Board. Although the sequence and some of the dates are conjectural, Marquette Rotarians who served as board presidents were Rushton, 1944-47; Don M. Pearce, 1947-50; William C. Anderson, 1950-53; James J. Beckman, 1953-56; and Richard F. O'Dell, 1962-65.

ALGER-MARQUETTE COMMUNITY MENTAL HEALTH CENTER
Established 1967

An Upper Peninsula Adult Mental Health Clinic, paralleling the U.P. Child Guidance Clinic, was established in October, 1960. Wilbert A. Berg was board president of this organization, 1961-67, when the Alger-Marquette Mental Health Compact (which at first included Delta County) was formed. At that point the Child Guidance and Adult Mental Health agencies in the central Upper Peninsula merged into what today constitutes the Alger-Marquette Community Mental Health Center. Dr. David R. Wall was medical director of the adult and community units, 1961-73. Dr. K. Charles Wright has been active as a committee and board member in the mental health movement for the past quarter century.

MARQUETTE BOARD OF EDUCATION

Edward S. Bice	1909-27
Henry A. St. John	14-43
Alton T. Roberts	19-22
Frank B. Spear, Jr.	27-44
Nelson D. Rupp	33-39
Edlore J. LaFreniere	39-51
Herman E. Olson	1944-68
Marion L. Sonderegger (Rotary Ann)	61-72
Jayne Hiebel (Rotary Ann)	72-—
Keith M. Forsberg	74-—

NORTHERN MICHIGAN UNIVERSITY BOARD OF CONTROL

Lincoln B. Frazier	1964-65
John L. Farley	65-75
Frederick C. Sabin	1967-—
G. Katherine Wright (Rotary Ann)	73-—

PETER WHITE PUBLIC LIBRARY BOARD OF TRUSTEES

Arthur E. Delf
John W. Stone
Daniel W. Powell
Arthur F. Jacques
Mary N. Spear (Rotary Ann)
Helen L. Paul (Rotary Ann)
Harlow A. Clark
Clyde T. DeHaas
Robert H. Clark
Robley H. Morrison
George E. Hill
Raymond J. Buchkoe
Kay T. Elzinga (Rotary Ann)

MARQUETTE COUNTY HISTORICAL SOCIETY PRESIDENTS

John M. Longyear	1918-22
Harlow A. Clark	39-46
Robert H. Clark	54-57
Richard F. O'Dell	57-60
Richard P. Sonderegger	1960-66
Wesley E. Perron	72-75
Wilbert H. Treloar	79-—

SHIRAS INSTITUTE BOARD OF TRUSTEES

Peter W. Phelps	1937-43
Frank B. Spear, Jr.	37-45
Ralph R. Eldredge	37-58
Herman E. Olson	43-—
Frank J. Russell, Jr.	1945-—
Philip B. Spear, Jr.	45-62
Allan F. Olson	64-—

NOTES

CHAPTER 2

[1]The quotation is from the *New York Times*, January 25, 1916, p. 2. For the figures on war costs see ibid., January 1, 1916, p. 8.

[2]Ibid., December 19, 1915, p. 7.

[3]Ibid., January 25, 1916, p. 5.

[4]Theodore Roosevelt to Ethel Roosevelt Derby, June 1, 1913, *The Letters of Theodore Roosevelt*, ed. Elting E. Morison et al. (8 vols.; Cambridge: Harvard University Press, 1951-54), VIII: 1450-51 (1450).

[5]In addition to the materials contained in a folder marked "Correspondence and Documents, 1915-1921" in the records of the Rotary Club of Marquette, Marquette County Historical Society, Marquette, Michigan, see typescripts of addresses by Ernest L. Pearce, "The Organization of Our Club," and Ralph R. Eldredge, "The History of the Marquette Rotary Club," delivered on January 18, 1926, at the organization's tenth anniversary banquet.

[6]Allen D. Albert to Frank J. Jennison, November 9, 1915.

[7]A nine-page typed copy of Governor W. J. Zimmers' address to the club is filed in "Correspondence and Documents, 1915-1921." It is undated and unsigned.

[8]*Daily Mining Journal* (Marquette, Mich.), January 26, 1916, p. 8 (hereafter cited as *DMJ* or *MJ*); *Mining Journal* (weekly), January 29, 1916, p. 8. The editorial is on page 4.

[9]Pearce, "The Organization of Our Club."

[10]*DMJ*, May 29, 1942, pp. 1, 3; John Munro Longyear, *Landlooker in the Upper Peninsula of Michigan* [ed. Helen Longyear Paul] (Marquette: Marquette County Historical Society, 1960): *Dictionary of American Biography*, s.v. "Longyear, John Munroc [*sic*]."

[11]Kenyon Boyer, "Early Days of the Marquette Chamber of Commerce," typescript of radio talk in "Historical Highlights" (24 vols., 426 nos.; Marquette, 1954-63), XV, No. 281 (April 10, 1960), 3; Boyer, "Marquette Chamber of Commerce & Previous Business Associations," ibid., XXIII, No. 422 (November 10, 1963), 4; *DMJ*, September 25, 1913, p. 10.

[12]Allan W. Cunningham to the author, February 18, 1980, and enclosed xerox of obituary, no place or date.

[13]*DMJ*, March 25, 1942, pp. 1, 2. George Shiras, 3rd, *Justice George Shiras Jr.*, edited and completed by Winfield Shiras (Pittsburgh: University of Pittsburgh, 1953), contains a biographical sketch of George Shiras, 3rd, in the "Editor's Preface," pp. xi-xx, and references to him throughout the text.

[14]Charles P. Drury, "Report of Health Officer," Marquette Commission Government, *Reports of the City of Marquette, for the Year Ended December 31, 1918* (Marquette, Mich., 1919), pp. 80-86 (82); *DMJ*, October 16, 1918, p. 10; October 22, p. 8.

[15]Drury, "Report of Health Officer," *Reports . . . 1919* (Marquette, Mich., 1920), pp. 85-94 (87); *DMJ*, November 8, 1918, p. 8; November 11, p. 8; December 20, p. 10; January 13, 1919, p. 8; January 14, p. 10.

[16]Drury, "Report of Health Officer," *Reports . . . 1919*, p. 86; *DMJ*, November 4, 1918, p. 8; December 6, p. 8; December 7, p. 10; February 25, 1919, p. 8; April 12, p. 4; April 15, p. 10.

[17]Drury, "Report of Health Officer," *Reports . . . 1918*, p. 80; ibid., *1919*, pp. 85-86; ibid., *1920* (Marquette, Mich., 1921), pp. 105-12 (105-106).

[18]For a complete account see Alton T. Roberts, "When Foch Came to America," *The American Legion Monthly*, 7 (August 1929), 20-23, 67-69.

CHAPTER 3

[1]U.S. Census of 1930, *Mines and Quarries, 1929*, p. 144.

[2]*DMJ*, July 5, 1921, p. 8.

[3]*DMJ*, July 2, 1921, p. 3.

[4]*DMJ*, August 29, 1921, p. 2.

[5]*DMJ*, April 27, 1920, p. 2.

[6]*DMJ*, July 30, 1920, p. 8; September 17, 1921, p. 8; September 20, p. 8; September 21, p. 10; September 26, p. 2; November 21, p. 2; December 2, p. 2; December 27, p. 10; December 29, p. 5; *MJ* (Centennial Edition), May 10, 1949 [Sports Section], pp. 5, 7; notes of R. Wesley Jenner, April 9, 1981.

[7]*MJ*, May 10, 1949 [Sports Section], p. 7.

[8]*DMJ*, September 15, 1925, pp. 2, 10.

[9]Boyer, "Early Golf Clubs," in "Historical Highlights," VIII, No. 41 (July 24, 1955), 1-4. Horatio Seymour, Jr., and his family lived in Marquette from 1882 to 1903. A civil engineer, he was resident manager of the Michigan Land & Iron Company, Ltd. He was a *nephew* of Horatio Seymour, governor of New York and Democratic candidate for President in 1868.

CHAPTER 4

[1]*DMJ*, May 20, 1922, pp. 5, 8; May 22, p. 8.

[2]Chase was the author of two books and numerous articles. He was president of the Michigan Academy of Science, Arts and Letters in 1926-27 and was a member of the Michigan Historical Commission from 1930 until 1942.

[3]*DMJ*, June 2, 1924, p. 2.

[4]*DMJ*, July 21, 1928, p. 4; July 23, p. 5.

[5]*DMJ*, July 23, 1928, p. 5.

[6]*DMJ*, May 20, 1930, p. 2; June 11, 1931, passim; June 12, pp. 1, 12.

[7]*DMJ*, May 17, 1928, pp. 1, 4-6; May 18, pp. 1, 7.

[8]*DMJ*, September 11, 1928, p. 2; September 12, pp. 3, 11.

[9]One entry was considerably ahead of its time: "Ralph Snow was the guest of Arthur Delf. Mr. Snow at present is an attorney in Cleveland. Formerly he was the man that married Phil Spear." (May 21, 1933).

[10]Randall practiced law in Ishpeming from 1915 to 1925 except while in military service, 1917-19. As president of the Inland Steel Company, he spoke for the entire steel industry in protesting government seizure of the nation's mills during a long strike in 1952. He was a prolific writer of books and articles.

[11]*DMJ*, November 30, 1926, p. 2.

[12]*DMJ*, February 22, 1927, p. 3.

[13]*DMJ*, December 31, 1929, p. 6; January 3, 1930, p. 2; Union National Bank (Marquette), *Union National Messenger*, I, No. 8 (January 1930).

CHAPTER 5

[1]*DMJ*, May 19, 1930, pp. 1, 10; May 20, pp. 1, 10.

[2]*DMJ*, May 19, 1930, pp. 1, 6, 7; May 20, pp. 1, 7, 10.

[3]*DMJ*, May 20, 1930, pp. 1, 14.

[4]*DMJ*, May 21, 1930, p. 2.

[5]*DMJ*, October 4, 1933, p. 3, October 6, p. 2; October 7, pp. 2, 5; October 9, p. 3.

[6]Information from John A. Vargo, executive director of the Bay Cliff Health Camp.

[7]*DMJ*, August 1, 1933, p. 2.
[8]"And I Went To That Luncheon Club Meeting," *DMJ*, March 4, 1936, p. 7.
[9]*DMJ*, May 14, 1941, p. 7.
[10]*DMJ*, December 14, 1939, p. 2.
[11]*DMJ*, September 22, 1937, p. 2.
[12]*Simple Workable Respirator* [n.p., n.d.]; M. K. Reynolds, "Marquette Creates Iron Lungs for an Emergency," *Hygeia*, 18 (December 1940), 1077-80, 1100-02. Lincoln Frazier headed the engineering staff.
[13]*DMJ*, June 20, 1941, pp. 3, 12.

CHAPTER 6

[1]L. W. Brumm, Robert H. Clark, Lincoln B. Frazier, Joe Hill, Daniel P. Hornbogen, Warren T. Lambert, Harold C. Overholt, Glenn E. Seifert, and Philip B. Spear, Jr.
[2]*DMJ*, July 8, 1943, p. 2.
[3]Kellan again served as pianist from January, 1946, until April, 1948, when, on an interim basis, Hamby replaced him. Rotarian Harold E. Wright of Northern's music department was the accompanist for most of the academic year of 1948-49. De Vries remained as song leader until his resignation from the club in June, 1951.
[4]For years at a time, the one-page ROTATORS have had the member and officer listings on the reverse side. Separate annual directories also have been published. In the earliest days and since 1976, these have consisted of a sheet or page for each member in small, loose-leaf binders. Photographs are included today.
[5]On June 2, 1919, President John R. Van Evera read an "Inaugural Message to New Members," but the agenda was so crowded that the induction could not have taken much time.
[6]*MJ*, June 15, 1949, p. 5; July 6, 1955, p. 4.
[7]*MJ*, May 16, 1947, pp. 2, 8.

CHAPTER 7

[1]*MJ*, June 18, 1947, p. 4; June 19, p. 2; June 20, p. 2.
[2]*DMJ*, June 27, 1945, p. 6.
[3]*MJ*, June 14, 1948, p. 7; June 15, p. 4.
[4]*MJ*, June 14, 1948, pp. 1-3. The newspaper placed total attendance at 650, a figure considerably higher than that indicated by the club's records.
[5]Ibid., p. 8.
[6]Ibid., p. 1.
[7]Ibid., p. 7.
[8]*MJ*, June 15, 1948, p. 4.
[9]Liephart later was national head of the Young Republicans.
[10]James Cloyd Bowman, "These Are Four-Square Boys," *The Rotarian*, 73 (December 1948), 26-28.
[11]Letter to the author, December 30, 1979. On July 29 and August 12, 1968, Roberts, son of Forest and Esther Roberts, gave the Rotarians slide talks about his life during several weeks among Indians of the Upper Amazon near the Brazil-Peru border.
[12]Letter to the author, January 21, 1980.
[13]Telephone conversation with the author, January 21, 1980.
[14]Among other proposals were the planting of trees, shrubs, and flower gardens; elimination of litter and rubbish; face-lifting of commercial buildings; underground conduits for all power and telephone lines; and improvement of the city's water supply "by stopping industrial contamination at its source."
[15]Kenyon Boyer was a member of the *Mining Journal* staff who fast was becoming the leading authority of Marquette's history. By the time of his death in 1963, he had served for many years as managing director of the Marquette County Historical Society. Scripts for his radio talks on "Historical Highlights" of the area have been aired frequently in recent years.

[16]*MJ*, July 1, 1949, pp. 1-2, 14; July 2 and 5, passim.
[17]George N. Skrubb for the Marquette Planning Board, *Marquette, Michigan/City Plan* [Marquette, 1951].

CHAPTER 8

[1]*MJ*, December 3, 1953, p. 5.
[2]*MJ*, May 22, 1956, pp. 2, 5.
[3]Marquette Rotarian John Morrison served on the Reconstruction Finance Corporation board which supervised the White Pine Copper Company loan and its use. Notes of R. Wesley Jenner, April 9, 1981.
[4]*MJ*, March 28, 1961, p. 2.
[5]*MJ*, September 28, 1954, p. 4.
[6]*MJ*, April 14, 1959, p. 5.

CHAPTER 9

[1]Note from Allan Olson to the author, May 23, 1980.
[2]The nine brothers and six of their sons on March 19, 1966, played a regulation hockey game against the Pekin (Illinois) Stars in a March of Dimes benefit. Score: Olsons 14, Stars 5.

For distinguished military service in World War II, Allan Olson received the Silver Star, Bronze Star with Oak Leaf Cluster, and, the Croix de Guerre with Silver Gilt Star and citation from General Charles de Gaulle. During much of the fifties and sixties Olson was general manager while Wesley Jenner was president of the Cliffs Dow Chemical Company. Olson was the charter president of the Upper Peninsula chapter of the American Chemical Society. Information from Olson and from a Lakeview Arena display case.
[3]*MJ*, March 20, 1961, p. 10; March 23, 1964, p. 14.
[4]*MJ*, May 14, 1952, p. 2.
[5]Hedgcock suffered a severe illness after his retirement in 1956. A dozen or more years later, during one of his infrequent visits to the Rotary Club, he was complimented on how well he looked. He tapped his chest and murmured somberly, "Bum ticker—borrowed time, borrowed time." Today (1981), at ninety-five, he lives with a daughter in New Jersey.
[6]Note from Allan Olson to the author, May 23, 1980.
[7]*MJ*, May 23, 1962, p. 12.
[8]*MJ*, October 9, 1962, p. 2; February 8, 1963, p. 3.
[9]*MJ*, January 26, 1963, p. 3; January 29, 1963, p. 2.
[10]*MJ*, January 26, 1963, p. 2.
[11]*MJ*, January 29, 1963, p. 2; February 1, 1963, p. 2; February 4, 1963, p. 4; February 6, 1963, p. 20.
[12]*MJ*, January 30, 1963, p. 2.
[13]*MJ*, February 1, 1963, p. 2; February 5, 1963, p. 3.
[14]Telephone conversation with Roy Heath, February 15, 1980.
[15]*MJ*, February 8, 1963, p. 3; February 12, p. 3.
[16]Ernest L. Pearce, Introduction to "The Big Year" (photograph album), Pearce Papers, Marquette County Historical Society; *MJ*, February 23, 1963, p. 4.
[17]Pearce, Introduction to "The Big Year."
[18]The fourth brother, David, has been president of the Rotary Club of Traverse City, Michigan.
[19]For a full account see *MJ*, January 18, 1966, p. 2.
[20]Prepared with the assistance of Pearce; past Presidents E. J. LaFreniere, Robert Clark, and Ray Nelson; also George Franzen, Thomas Griffith, and Edward Stratton.

CHAPTER 10

[1]*MJ*, January 19, 1963, p. 2; David H. McClintock to the author, August 9, 1980. After returning to Marquette, McClintock was Northern Michigan University's coordinator of cap-

ital outlay and campus development until 1977. He also served on the Marquette planning board for more than twelve years, two of them as chairman, until 1981.

[2]*MJ*, May 12, 1967, p. 5; May 13, 1967, p. 5; May 15, 1967, p. 7.

[3]*MJ*, February 8, 1969, p. 3; March 7, 1967, p. 2.

[4]*MJ*, April 30, 1977, p. A-20; May 3, 1977, p. 15.

[5]*MJ*, April 29, 1977, p. 6.

[6]*MJ*, April 30, 1977, p. A-20.

[7]Letterhead (1980) of Child & Family Services of the Upper Peninsula.

[8]*MJ*, January 7, 1967, p. 6; April 12, 1974, p. 2; December 14, 1967, pp. 4-5; March 11, 1976, p. 3.

CHAPTER 11

[1]*MJ*, October 3, 1975, p. 7A; October 4, pp. 3A, 5A.

[2]*MJ*, December 2, 1975, pp. 1A, 3A.

CHAPTER 12

[1]*MJ*, July 17, 1973, p. 4.

[2]*MJ*, May 20, 1974, p. 2.

[3]*MJ*, April 12, 1976, pp. 1, 2, 17.

[4]Robert B. Glenn, "The State of Things," *Michigan Academician*, X (Winter 1978), 245-47.

[5]James P. Walsh, *The First Rotarian: The Life and Times of Paul Percy Harris, Founder of Rotary* (Shoreham by Sea, West Sussex, Gr. Br.; Redwood Burn Limited, Trowbridge & Esher for Scan Books, 1979), pp. 303-304; *Adventure in Service* (Evanston, Ill., and Zurich: Rotary International, 1949), pp. 107-109. The goal was reached on May 9, 1951.

[6]*Historical Review of Rotary* (Evanston, Ill.: Rotary International, n.d.), p. 31; *The Rotarian*, 136 (March 1980), 45.

[7]*Historical Review of Rotary*, pp. 20-21; *The Rotarian*, 138 (February 1981), 43.

[8]A copy of Miss McClellan's final written report is in the club's files.

[9]*MJ*, August 1, 1978, p. 2A; *U.P. Sunday Times*, August 6, 1978, p. 2A.

[10]*MJ*, August 20, 1979, p. 1A; September 13, pp. 1-2A.

[11]Dixie Franklin, "Rotary envoys set to call on Finland," *MJ Upbeat*, May 4, 1980, p. 16.

[12]Letter to the author, March 21, 1980.

[13]65 (December 1944), 53. Quoted by permission of *The Rotarian*.

CHAPTER 13

[1]Paul P. Harris, *This Rotarian Age* (Chicago: Rotary International, 1935), p. 257. Quoted by permission of Rotary International.

[2]Walsh, *The First Rotarian*, p. 272.

[3]Harris, *This Rotarian Age*, pp. 148-50.

[4]Harris, *This Rotarian Age*, p. 149. Quoted by permission of Rotary International.

[5]Paul P. Harris, *My Road to Rotary* (Chicago: A. Kroch and Son, 1948), p. 277. Quoted by permission of Rotary International.

[6]Harris, *My Road to Rotary*, p. 277.

[7]Harris, *This Rotarian Age*, p. 1; Walsh, *The First Rotarian*, pp. 23, 150.

[8]Ann Chittenden, "Mystery of Income Distribution: Economists Want Clearer Data," *New York Times*, November 6, 1976, p. 29.

[9]*Time*, January 12, 1981, p. 22; *Detroit Free Press*, March 17, 1981, p. 7A.

[10]Daniel Bell, a Harvard sociologist, coined the term "post-industrial society" in an unpublished paper written in 1962 and elaborated upon in his *The Coming of Post-Industrial Society* (New York: Basic Books, 1973). The concept embraces changes in "five dimensions,

or components": economic sector, occupational distribution, axial principle, future orientation, and decision-making. (p. 14.)

[11]Herman Kahn, *World Economic Development, 1979 and Beyond* (New York: Morrow Quill Paperbacks, 1979), p. 233.

[12]Harrison Brown, *The Challenge of Man's Future* (New York: Viking Press, 1954), pp. xi-xii, 266-67, and his *The Human Future Revisited: The World Predicament and Possible Solutions* (New York: W. W. Norton, 1978). p. 273.

[13]E. F. Schumacher, *Small Is Beautiful: Economics as if People Mattered* (New York: Harper & Row, 1973), pp. 110-13; Donella H. Meadows et al., *The Limits to Growth* (New York: Universe Books, 1972), pp. 56-59. Richard J. Barnet, "A Reporter at Large: The World's Resources, I—The Lean Years," *The New Yorker* (March 17, 1980), 45-81, estimates, like Schumacher, that the United States in the past thirty-five years has "bent, burned, or melted" about forty percent of the planet's nonrenewable resources utilized by all nations. (p. 45.)

[14]Barry Rohan, "Rockefeller sees dangerous split," *Detroit Free Press*, October 7, 1980, p. 30.

[15]Clarence B. Randall, *A Creed for Free Enterprise* (Boston: Little, Brown, 1952), pp. 20, 25.

[16]*Adventure in Service*, pp. 6, 102.

[17]For example, on March 20, 1981, the city had a worker head count of 315 (compared to an average of 224 for 1961) or an estimated full-time-equivalent number of 220 employees, exclusive of seventy-eight for the board of light and power, whose workers were included in the 1961 tally. Information from the city manager's office; Lyle W. Smith, personnel director; Ronald Heaviland, head of the parks and recreation department; and Thomas McNabb, former city manager.

[18]A copy is in the club's files.

[19]Dennis J. Kucinich was mayor of Cleveland, 1977-79.

[20]L. M. Boyd, "Peck's Rule," *Detroit Free Press*, January 28, 1981, p. 7D.

[21]Gerald O. Barney, Study Director (3 vols.; Washington: Government Printing Office, 1980), I:3.

[22]" 'Global 2000': A comprehensive report looks to earth's future," *The Rotarian*, 139 (December 1981), 32-33. Quoted by permission of *The Rotarian*.

BIBLIOGRAPHY

Because of the author's obviously heavy reliance upon the records of the Rotary Club of Marquette and the ease with which any interested scholar can examine them, information pertaining to the organization which is not attributed specifically to other sources is drawn from its files or from the Marquette *Mining Journal* and for the most part has not been cited in footnotes.

These holdings are in the Marquette County Historical Society and in the Longyear Building almost opposite on North Front Street in Marquette.

The club's records are virtually complete for the period before 1967 and are adequate for the time since. They include the minutes of the regular weekly meetings and of the board of directors; club bulletins, particularly The ROTATOR, which in recent years has supplanted the weekly minutes; financial and other reports; correspondence (that in the folder labeled "Correspondence and Documents, 1915-1921" is valuable for the facts of genesis); rosters and directories; scattered membership cards; printed pamphlets and programs; photographs, flags, and banners; and typescripts of early histories; P. W. Phelps, "A Brief History of Marquette Rotary Club," December 1, 1916; Ernest L. Pearce, "The Organization of Our Club," and Ralph R. Eldredge, "The History of the Marquette Rotary Club," both dated January 18, 1926; J. Cloyd Bowman, "Twentieth Anniversary Banquet," February 21, 1936; Ernest L. Pearce, untitled history of the club, [May 10, 1941], and "Induction of New Members," December 13, 1943.

The Marquette County Historical Society is also the repository of several boxes of Ernest L. Pearce Papers containing letters, memoranda, newspaper clippings, scrapbooks, and photographs. Much of this material pertains to Rotary.

Indispensable to students of general Marquette history is the Kenyon Boyer compilation of "Historical Highlights," consisting of typescripts of 426 talks given weekly over local radio station WDMJ from 1954 to 1963. In twenty-four slim volumes, these are preserved in the John M. Longyear Research Library of the MCHS.

PUBLISHED MATERIAL

Adventure in Service. Evanston, Ill., and Zurich: Rotary International, 1949.

Barnet, Richard J. "A Reporter at Large: The World's Resources, I—The Lean Years," *The New Yorker* (March 17, 1980), 45-81.

Barton, Francis. " 'Global 2000': A comprehensive report looks to earth's future," *The Rotarian*, 139 (December 1981), 32-33.

Bell, Daniel. *The Coming of Post-Industrial Society*. New York: Basic Books, 1973.
Bowman, James Cloyd. "These Are Four-Square Boys," *The Rotarian*, 73 (December 1948), 26-28.
Brown, Harrison. *The Challenge of Man's Future*. New York: Viking Press, 1954.
———. *The Human Future Revisited: The World Predicament and Possible Solutions*. New York: W. W. Norton, 1978.
Burrows, Albert H. "The Rotarian's Job," *The Rotarian*, 65 (December 1944), 53.
Chittenden, Ann. "Mystery of Income Distribution: Economists Want Clearer Data," *New York Times*, November 6, 1976, p. 29.
Conant, James Bryant. *The American High School Today*. New York: McGraw-Hill Book Co., 1959.
Council on Physical Therapy of the American Medical Association, *Simple Workable Respirator*. [n.p., n.d.].
Detroit Free Press. 1980-1981.
Dictionary of American Biography, s.v. "Longyear, John Munroe [*sic*]."
Drury, Charles P. "Report of Health Officer," Marquette Commission Government, *Reports of the City of Marquette . . . 1918, 1919*, and *1920*. Marquette, Mich., 1919-1921.
Franklin, Dixie. "Rotary envoys set to call on Finland," *MJ Upbeat*, May 4, 1980, p. 16.
Glenn, Robert B. "The State of Things," *Michigan Academician*, X (Winter 1978), 245-47.
The Global 2000 Report to the President: Entering the Twenty-First Century, Vol. 1; Vol. 2, *Technical Report*; Vol. 3, *The Government's Global Model*, Gerald O. Barney, Study Director. Washington: Government Printing Office, 1980.
Harris, Paul P. *My Road to Rotary*. Chicago: A. Kroch and Son, 1948.
———. *This Rotarian Age*. Chicago: Rotary International, 1935.
Harvard University. Committee on the Objectives of a General Education in a Free Society. *General Education in a Free Society*. Cambridge: Harvard University Press, 1952.
Historical Review of Rotary. Evanston, Ill.: Rotary International, [n.d.].
Kahn, Herman. *World Economic Development, 1979 and Beyond*. New York: Morrow Quill Paperbacks, 1979.
Longyear, John Munro. *Landlooker in the Upper Peninsula of Michigan*. [Ed. by Helen Longyear Paul] Marquette: Marquette County Historical Society, 1960.
Marquette Commission Government. *Reports of the City of Marquette . . . 1918, 1919*, and *1920*. Marquette, 1919-1921.
Marquette, Michigan, Charter [of 1951]. Marquette, 1951.
Meadows, Donella H., et al. *The Limits to Growth*. New York: Universe Books, 1972.
Mining Journal (Marquette, Mich.). 1916-1981. Titled *Daily Mining Journal* before 1946. The *U.P. Sunday Times* and the *Mining Journal Upbeat* have been added features in recent years.
Morison, Samuel Eliot. *Three Centuries of Harvard, 1636-1936*. Cambridge: Harvard University Press, 1936.
———, and Commager, Henry Steele. *The Growth of the American Republic*. 2 vols. 5th ed., rev. and enl.; New York: Oxford University Press, 1962.
New York Times. 1915-1916, 1976.
Randall, Clarence B. *A Creed for Free Enterprise*. Boston: Little, Brown, 1952.
Reynolds, M. K. "Marquette Creates Iron Lungs for an Emergency," *Hygeia*, 18 (December 1940), 1077-80, 1100-02.
Roberts, Alton T. "When Foch Came to America," *The American Legion Monthly*, 7 (August 1929), 20-23, 67-69.
Roosevelt, Theodore. *The Letters of Theodore Roosevelt*. Ed. by Elting E. Morison et al. 8 vols. Cambridge: Harvard University Press, 1951-54.
The Rotarian.
Schumacher, E. F. *Small Is Beautiful: Economics as if People Mattered*. New York: Harper & Row, 1973.
Shiras, George, 3rd. *An American Plan for the Promotion and Maintenance of International*

Peace; Summary and Revision of an Address Before the Rotary Club of Marquette, Michigan, August 10, 1924 . . . Supplementary Statement—January 10, 1926. [n.p., n.d.].

———. *Hunting Wild Life With Camera and Flashlight*. 2 vols. 2nd ed.; Washington, D.C.: National Geographic Society, 1936.

———. *Justice George Shiras Jr*. Ed. and completed by Winfield Shiras. Pittsburgh: University of Pittsburgh, 1953.

Skrubb, George N., for the Marquette Planning Board. *Marquette, Michigan/City Plan*. [Marquette, 1951].

Union National Bank (Marquette). *Union National Messenger*. Vol. I, No. 8, January 1930.

U.S. Census, 1920-1980; also *Mines and Quarries, 1929*.

Walsh, James P. *The First Rotarian: The Life and Times of Paul Percy Harris, Founder of Rotary*. Shoreham by Sea, West Sussex, Gr. Br.: Redwood Burn Ltd., Trowbridge & Esher for Scan Books, 1979.

ACKNOWLEDGMENTS AND PICTURE CREDITS

The sheer number of names following indicates the generous assistance I have received in writing this book. Although I cannot detail the ways in which most people have contributed, I wish at the outset to express my warm appreciation to the 1981-82 President of Rotary International, Stanley E. McCaffrey, for his Foreword and to the National Director Loret Ruppe of the Peace Corps for her letter, which is reproduced on the back of the jacket. Over many years staff members of Rotary International in Evanston, Ill., have been unfailingly prompt, efficient, and courteous in supplying information, permissions to quote, and photographs: Sidney B. North, Michael R. Fishbach, Kirk Morledge, Gordon D. Moyer, and, most recently, Ms. Judy Lee, Ms. Patricia Perrine, and Nelson W. Price.

Equally welcome has been the assistance of these persons and institutions, most of them in the Marquette area, but some scattered from New Hampshire to California and north into Canada:

Rotarians and Rotary Anns Who Are or Have Been Affiliated With the Rotary Club of Marquette: Busharat and Adeeba Ahmad, James J. Beckman, Matthew C. Bennett, Wilbert A. Berg, Henry J. Bothwell, L. Wallace Bruce, Albert H. Burrows, Robert H. and Lottie Clark, Theodore Doane, Pryse H. and Louise Duerfeldt, Leonard S. Elder, Lloyd E. and Mary Ann Fairbanks, Roy W. Fletcher, Jr., George C. Franzen, Lincoln B. and Anne Frazier, Ronald L. Garberson, Thomas Griffith, Roy E. Heath, Jayne Hiebel, R. Wesley Jenner, Stewart A. Kingsbury, E. J. LaFreniere, Edward N. Locke, Lee R. Luff, David H. McClintock, Nolan B. McKevitt, Thomas R. McNabb, John M. Maitland, Norman L. Matthews, V. Harvey Mortensen, William A. Mudge, Jr., Robert C. Neldberg, Ray A. Nelson, Allan L. Niemi, Allan F. Olson, Burt E. Parolini, Jr., Robert J. Pearce (deceased), Wesley E. Perron, Frederick J. Peterson, Gregory Ptacin, Allen D. Raymond III, Frederick C. Sabin, James D. Smeberg, Richard P. and Marion Sonderegger, David A. Svanda, Edward J. Stratton (dec.), Donald R. Taylor, W. H. Treloar, David R. Wall, John Weting, Carroll H. Williams, and Donald G. Zettle.

Personnel of the Marquette Area Chamber of Commerce, Peter White Public Library, Northern Michigan University Library, and Marquette County Historical Society (hereafter designated MCHS). All have been invariably kind. At the MCHS the current director, Frank Paull, Jr.; Mrs. Esther Bystrom (dec.), former director; Mrs.

Joan Weesen, Mrs. Shirley Peano, Ms. Kaye Hiebel, Mrs. Susan Nostrand, and Mrs. Roberta Zorza from the beginning of my study have been most gracious in granting access to Marquette Rotary Club and other materials, in checking facts, and in locating and permitting the reproduction of illustrations. The Rotary Club of Sault Ste. Marie, Michigan, provided an early Marquette club banner. *Other Persons*: Robert M. Bordeau, Mrs. Jeannette S. Bowden, Mrs. Sandra Busch, Mrs. Shirley Caceras, James L. Carter, Mrs. Karen Deel, Miss Olive Fox, Ms. Dixie Franklin, Roy E. Froling, Mrs. Militza Georgevich, Gordon D. Gill, Miss Frances Grawn, Robert A. Hanson, Ronald Heaviland, Harold N. Herlich, Jr., Mrs. Millicent Jensen, Alan R. Kropp, Mrs. Mabel Leskee, John E. McDonald (dec.), Ellwood A. Mattson, Miss Elba M. Morse (dec.), John J. O'Neil (dec.), Mrs. Burt E. Parolini, Sr., Mrs. Edna Paulson, Maxwell K. (Jr.) and Phyllis Reynolds, C. Fred Rydholm, Harold E. St. Arnauld, Wiljo A. Sarkela, Kenneth C. Schellhase, Henry A. Skewis, Alan Smetana, James R. Smith, Lyle W. Smith, James F. Sodergren, Mrs. Robin Stephens, Paul N. Suomi, Rollin K. Thoren, Mrs. Mary Lou Tillison, Mrs. Claudia Tollefson, Mrs. Susan Tuch, John A. Vargo, William Vercauteren, and William G. Wedlake of the Marquette area; Mrs. Oscar B. Bjorge, Portland, Ore.; Mrs. Beatrice Boynton, Vancouver, B. C.; Allan W. Cunningham, El Cajon, Calif.; Mrs. Julie Fallowfield of McIntosh and Otis, New York City; Mrs. Olive Hanson, Zephyrhills, Fla.; Carl Hendershot, Ms. Mary B. McManman, and Steven Toth, Bay City, Mich.; Arthur C. Hentrich, Ottawa, Ill.; Bob L. Huston, Hollywood, Calif.; Ms. Connie Lamm, American Legion Library, Indianapolis, Ind.; Eugene M. Kepler, Clearwater, Fla.; P. J. McMahon, New Orleans, La.; Allyn Roberts, Madison, Wis.; Forest A. Roberts, Sarasota, Fla.; Kenneth G. Summersett, Newberry, Mich.; and Norman Thomas, Cincinnati, Ohio.

I am particularly indebted to Pryse Duerfeldt, Wesley Jenner, John Maitland, Burt Parolini, and Wesley Perron, who have read the entire manuscript, and to Busharat Ahmad, Robert Clark, Lincoln Frazier, E. J. LaFreniere, and Lee Luff, who have read major portions of it, for their encouragement and many helpful suggestions. Responsibility for statements of fact and interpretation remain mine.

Throughout the past three years Pryse Duerfeldt, sensitive to words and talented in photography, and Burt Parolini, possessed of an extraordinarily practical imagination and effectiveness, have been pillars of support—at literally all hours of the day and night.

Ralph Waldo Emerson once wrote: "My chief want in life is someone who shall make me do what I can." My own need may be the same, but I am most grateful for a Rotary Ann who, instead of applying pressure, has done all that one person can possibly do for another in removing obstacles to accomplishment. Thank you, Louise.

The publishers wish to acknowledge the following for their courtesy in supplying and permitting the reproduction of illustrations. Particularly in the case of out-of-town institutional sources, the name of the person directly rendering the service is given in parentheses; where known and appropriate, the photographer is identified.

Busharat Ahmad, 145, 148 (bottom left), 178, 179, 181
American Legion Library (Connie Lamm), Indianapolis, Ind., 15
Bay Cliff Health Camp (John Vargo), 48 (top)
Henry Bothwell, 140
Brown Brothers (Meredith M. Collins), Sterling, Pa., 38
Photos by Tom Buchkoe, 24 (above), 139 (bottom), 198 (bottom right)
Robert Clark, Frontispiece (bottom center), 81—photo by Beauchamp's Studio
Dartmouth College Library (Barbara Krieger) and Evelyn Stefansson Nef, 58
Arthur De Vries, 90 (bottom)
Photos by Louise Duerfeldt, 183 (top left), 198 (bottom left)
Photos by Pryse Duerfeldt, front end sheets (top right), 134, 148 (center left, bottom right), 201
Leonard (Sam) Elder, 148 (center right)
Lincoln Frazier, 48 (center, bottom), 49 (center, bottom), 56 (above), back end sheets (top: left, center, right)
Glenbow Archives (Georgeen Klassen), Glenbow-Alberta Institute, Calgary, Alta., 44
Hiawathaland Council (Harvey Mortensen), Boy Scouts of America, 144
Robert Jean, 97 (below)
Photos by Lemon's Studio, Frontispiece (bottom right), 119 (below)
Photo by Virginia Long, 55
David McClintock (U.S. Navy photo by Edward Steichen), 131
Marquette Commission Government. *Reports of the City of Marquette . . . 1920* [p. 8], 17 (top)
Marquette County Historical Society, front end sheets (top left and bottom), Frontispiece (top, center right), 6, 7, 10, 11, 17, (center, bottom), 18, 20, 22—aerial photo by "Ernie," 24—exterior photo by Tom Buchkoe, 35, 40, 47, 48 (center, bottom), 49 (top), 56 (below), 94, 97 (above), 100, 104, 119 (above), 125, 126, 127, 139 (center), 154, back end sheets (bottom—photo by Ike Wood)
Marquette General Hospital (Claudia Tollefson), 32, 139 (top, bottom—photo of Marquette General by Tom Buchkoe)
Marquette Public Schools (Millicent Jensen), 114
Michigan Manual . . . 1945-46, 130
Mining Journal, Frontispiece (center left, bottom right—Closser photo by Lemon's Studio), 67 (right—U.S. Navy photo), 86, 101
Mining Journal Upbeat, May 4, 1980 (p. 16), 184
Photos by William Mudge, Jr., 143, 148 (top: left, right)
National Archives, drawing by Joseph Cummings Chase (obtained by Donald Taylor), 37
Ray Nelson, 90 (top, center), 91
Northern Michigan University, Frontispiece (bottom left), 116, 117, 137 (below)
Photo by Louise O'Dell, 142
Photo by Allan F. Olson, 111
Radio Station KVOD (Ed Koepke), Denver, 71 (left)
Rotary International, Foreword (Nelson W. Price); 12, 19, 191 (Judy Lee, Patricia Perrine)
Frederick Sabin, 167 (below)
George N. Skrubb. *Marquette, Michigan/City Plan* (p. 11), 80
Alan Smetana, 137 (above)
Photos by Joseph R. Sullivan, 71 (right), 118
Toledo Blade (obtained by Gregory Ptacin), 43 (right)
Toledo-Lucas County Public Library, Toledo, Ohio, masthead and headlines from photographic copy provided by, 43 (left)
Photos by Masatoshi Tomita, Shiga Prefectural Press, Japan, 198 (top, center)
U.S. Air Force photo (obtained by Donald Taylor), 67 (left)
Colonel Weesen, 141, 169, 170
Charles Wright, 167 (above)
Harold Wright, 166 (right)

Yokaichi Rotary Club, Japan (photos by Atumi Hibino), 183 (top right, center, bottom)
Donald Zettle, 166 (left)
Gregor Ziemer, Rancho Palos Verdes, Calif., 76

Photo finishing by Pryse Duerfeldt and Tom Buchkoe

Duerfeldt designed MRC banner currently in use

Paper courtesy of Mead Corporation

INDEX OF PERSONAL NAMES

INDEX OF SUBJECTS

Lincoln B. Frasier (at far right with friend to his left) was one of a party which made a three-week, 37,000-mile air journey commemorating the fortieth anniversary of the 1928 Richard E. Byrd expedition to Antarctica.. Frazier presented Marquette Rotary Club banners to the officers' club at Thule, Greenland (center), and to naval personnel at McMurdo station, Antarctica (left), prior to final flights in November, 1968, over the North and South Poles.